A HISTORY OF GUJARAT

A
HISTORY OF GUJARAT
FROM THE EARLIEST PERIOD TOTHE PRESENT TIME

BY

EDALJI DOSABHAI,

Retired Deputy Collector,
Ahmadabad.

GYAN

Published by

Gyan Publishing House
5, Ansari Road
Daryaganj, New Delhi-110002
Phone: 011-47034999, 9811692060
E-mail: books@gyanbooks.com

Distribution Network
gyanbooks.com
India, USA, Canada, UK, Australia, France

ISBN : 978-81-212-3517-4 (PB)
First Published, 1894

2nd Impression 2020

Printed at: Gyan Press, Delhi.

A
History of Gujarat
Author: Edalji Dosabhai

A

HISTORY OF GUJARÁT

FROM THE EARLIEST PERIOD TO THE PRESENT TIME

BY

EDALJI DOSÁBHAI,
Retired Deputy Collector,
Ahmadábád.

PRINTED AT

The United Printing and General Agency Company's Press

by Ranchodlál Gungárám :

AHMADABAD.

1894.

TO

G. BOILEAU REID, ESQUIRE,

INDIAN CIVIL SERVICE,

COMMISSIONER OF THE NORTHERN DIVISION

OF THE BOMBAY PRESIDENCY,

THIS HISTORY

OF A PROVINCE

WITH THE ADMINISTRATION OF WHICH HE HAS BEEN

SO LONG AND HONOURABLY ASSOCIATED

IS RESPECTFULLY DEDICATED,

AS A TOKEN

OF SINCERE GRATITUDE AND ESTEEM,

BY

THE AUTHOR.

PREFACE.

The want of a connected History of the province of Gujarát having been greatly felt so far back as the year 1850, the Gujarát Vernacular Society, then only recently started under the fostering care of the lamented Mr. A. K. Forbes, advertised that a prize would be awarded for such a history written in the vernacular. The present writer was at that time one of the senior pupils in the Government English School, and depending mainly on Bird's Translation of the Mirát-i-Ahmadi and Grant Duff's History of the Maráthás, he set himself to compile a brief compendium of the History of Gujarát. The book was approved of by the Society, and the prize was duly awarded. Mr. Forbes, in his report of the Society for 1850, wrote as follows:—

> " While on this subject, I may add that I have in my possession a compilation by Edalji Dosábhai, written in very good Gujaráti, and giving a useful summary of the History of the province. This may be published immediately, and may be a very good school-book ".

Doctor Seaward, in the report of the following year, stated:—

> " The second publication is the History of Gujarát by Edalji Dosábhai. It is essentially a school-book and a very useful one too, and is now used in all the Vernacular schools of the city. Two hundred copies were published, of which very few remain ". * * *

The author having soon afterwards obtained service under Government, he could not command the leisure necessary for revising and republishing the work. Portions of it, however, were admitted into several of the earlier educational text books, and Mr. Bájibhai Amichand, the proprietor of one of the vernacular presses at Ahmadábád, published a third edition on his own responsibility.

On his retirement from Government service, the compiler became desirous of re-issuing the book. Since its first publication, however, in 1850, a vast amount of additional information has become available from the Rás Málá, a storehouse of Gujaráti folk-lore, and from the researches of Dr. Bühler and other eminent scholars. The author also thought it desirable to continue the History to the present time, placing under contribution for this purpose several of the volumes of the Bombay Gazetteer and the official Administration Reports. In the hope that such a connected History from the earliest to the latest times may prove useful not only to students in Gujarát itself but to all who take an interest in the country, the author, acting on the advice of several of his friends, undertook to compile the work in English. He was greatly encouraged in his endeavours by the Rev. George P. Taylor, B. D., of the Irish Presbyterian Mission, author of the Student's Gujaráti Grammar. With a view to ensure correct English idiom and general accuracy, this gentleman very kindly undertook to revise the manuscript, and he further supplied several books on loan from his valuable library. Indeed it is owing largely to his cordial assistance and encouragement that the work has now been brought to completion, and the author takes the present opportunity of expressing his grateful acknowledgments to his kind and esteemed friend. He is also under deep obligation to Mr. E. Giles, M. A., Educational Inspector, N. D., for his kindness in going through the whole of the manuscript and for many useful suggestions and corrections. His warm interest in the work has greatly encouraged the author to proceed with its publication.

The information contained in this History has been gathered mainly from the undermentioned sources :—

1. Mr. A. K. Forbes's Rás Málá.
2. Mr. Bird's Translation of the Mirát-i-Ahmadi.
3. Sir E. C. Bayley's Local Muhammadan Dynasties of Gujarát.
4. Lieut. Col. J. W. Watson's History of Gujarát.
5. Grant Duff's History of the Maráthás.
6. Volumes 2, 3, 4, 5, 6, 7 and 8 of the Bombay Gazetteer.
7. Administration Reports.

Several other trustworthy works by eminent scholars such as Sir William Hunter's Indian Empire, Lieut. Col. Tod's Rájasthán, Mr. Dutt's Ancient India, Mr. Eliot's Rulers of Barodá, and Elphinstone's History of Gujarát have also been of much use.

In the spelling of proper names the Hunterian system has been followed in the main.

For the sake of ready reference, in addition to the usual index a detailed chronological summary has been given in the Table of Contents.

In conclusion the author begs to state that in the hope of making the book as useful as possible, he has spared no pains to obtain full and accurate information; and he will feel himself amply rewarded, should his work meet with the approbation of the reading public and especially of scholars interested in the annals of Gujarát.

CHRONOLOGICAL TABLE OF CONTENTS.

PART I. HINDU PERIOD.

Chapter VII.

Chapter VIII.

PART II. MUHAMMADAN PERIOD.

Chapter I.

Chapter II.

DATE.	SUBJECT.	PAGE.
1410	Despatch of troops under prince Ahmad against Ásá Bhil	64
1410	The prince compels Muzaffar Sháh to drink poison	64
	CHAPTER III.	
1410	Accession of Sultán Ahmad	65
1411	Suppression of rebellions	65
1412	Founding of the city of Ahmadábád ...	66
1413	Sultán Ahmad's march against Sorath, and the taking of the lower fort of Junághad.	71
1414	Imposition of tributes on several chiefs of Sorath	71
1415	Despatch of an army to destroy the Hindu temples at Siddhpur.	71
1416	Invasion of Gujarát by the king of Málwá; his repulse.	71
1416	Destruction of Nándod.	71
1417	Invasion of Málwá by Sultán Ahmad ...	72
1418	Sultán Ahmad's march on Chámpáner; its chief forced to pay tribute	72
1419	Capture of Sán-Kherá Bahádarpur. ...	72
1420	Imposition of tribute on Gohilwár. ...	73
1422	Escape of the chief Sárangji, who assumes the title of Ráwal	73
1421	Ahmad-sháh's further expedition on Málwá.	73
1426	Founding of Ahmadnagar.	75
1427	Death of the Idar chief Punjá	75
1429	Mahim taken by the King of Ahmadnagar (Deccan), and retaken by Sultán Ahmad	76
1429	Imposition of tribute on Bundi and Kotá ...	76

CHAPTER IV.

CHAPTER V.

CHAPTER VI.

Chapter II.

Chapter VIII.

Chapter IX.

Date.	Subject.	Page.

Chapter X.

PART IV.

Chapter I.

Date.	Subject.	Page.

Chapter II.

Chapter III.

Chapter IV.

CHAPTER X.

Events in Gujarát and Kachh.

CHAPTER XI.

Baroda affairs.

Chapter XX.

Civil administration.

APPENDICES.

HISTORY OF GUJARÁT,

PART I.

EARLY HISTORY,

HINDU PERIOD.

CHAPTER I.

KRISHNA, king of Dwárká. The Pa'ndavs at Vairát-nagar. Asoka the Great. Kanishka extends his conquests as far as Gujarát. His vassals become independent under the title of the Kshatrapas. The rule of the Gupta, the Valabhi, and the Chávadá dynasties.

FROM 1400 B. C. to 942 A. D.

VERY little is known of the early period of the history of Gujarát under its ancient Hindu Rulers. The author of the Mirát-i-Ahmadi, compiled in or about A. H. 1175 (A. D. 1761) by the then Bádsháhi Diwán Ali-Muhammad-Khán, in his opening chapter, states that the country of Gujarát was once governed by Rajputs and Kolis, and that the Rájá of Kanauj, as the paramount power in Hindustán, used to receive tribute from several chiefs, themselves independent each of the others. Evidently Ali-Muhammad-Khán had not obtained information for the period anterior to Vanráj's time, and his history, therefore, commences only with the reign of that king. Regarding the origin of Vanráj, he states that Sávatsingh, one of the slaves of the Kanauj Rájá, was put to death on a criminal charge, and his house being given up to plunder, Sávatsingh's wife fled towards Gujarát, where she shortly afterwards gave birth to a son. This infant it was who subsequently became the founder of the city of Anhilvár Pátan.

Later researches, however, and notably those by Mr. A. Kinloch Forbes, author of the Rásmálá, and Colonel James Tod, the historian of Rájasthán, have shown that the kingdom of Gujarát existed long before the time of the Chávadá dynasty, and also that Vanráj, so far from being of low origin, was, in reality, of royal parentage. The earliest mention of a principality in Gujarát, that has yet been traced is in the Mahábhárata, from which it appears that Krishna, now worshipped as an incarnation of Vishnu, who was an ally of the Pándavs, established a principality in Gujarát about 1300 or 1400 B. C. This principality appears to have been Okhámandal, which Krishna subjugated after a hard struggle with the Kálás (the ancestors of the present Vághers), and established his capital at Dwárká. It further appears that the Pándvs, in their wanderings (1400 B. C.), found Vairát-nagar governed by Queen Sadishva of the Bhil race, whose brother Kichak was slain by Bhim for an attempt on Draupadi, wife of the five Pándavs. The modern town of Dholká, situated twenty-two miles south-west of Ahmadábád, is supposed to stand on the site of this ancient Vairát-nagar,* but this is doubted by some. After this period no further information regarding Gujarát is obtainable, until we reach the third century before Christ, when Asoka† the Great, king of Magadha (Bihár), who ruled from B. C. 263 to 222, caused his famous edicts to be inscribed on the rock at Girnár. From this it appears that Souráshtra, or at least the greater portion of that peninsula, was under the rule of that king, and was probably governed through Satraps or Deputies, and their head quarter was, it is believed, at Junághad. We then find that in the first century after

* Vide Bombay Gazetteer Vol. IV, page 337.

† This king belonged to the Maurya dynasty, vide Bombay Gazetteer Vol; VIII, page 272.

Christ, the great conqueror Kanishka,* who ruled from Kábul and Yarkand as far as Agrá, extended his conquests to Gujarát. A race of rulers known as the Kshatrapas, held sway in Gujarát, as the vassals of Kanishka, but these appear to have become independent during the time of that king's successors. They are supposed to have conquered Kachh, which remained a portion of the Gujarát principality in the time of the Valabhis also. Broach † and Cambay ‡ (Khambháyat) appear to have formed portions of their dominion. The Kshatrapas are known as powerful monarchs. Probably they worshipped both the Sun and the Fire. On their coins,§ the monarch is depicted wearing the Macedonian helmet, while the reverse shews a fire altar and representation of the sun and moon. They appear to have been overthrown by Gautamputra, the Andhra king of the Deccan, about A. D. 330, who, it is probable, held possession of Sauráshtra for about a century. But the Guptas of Kanauj, who ruled between the Gangá and the Jamná, were about that

* Colonel James Tod, late Political Agent, Western Rájputáná, in his annals of Rájasthán, Vol. I page 233, calls the invader by the name of Kanek-Sen, a descendant of the famous Rájá Rám of Ayodhyá, and adds that he wrested dominion from a prince of the "Prammara" (probably Parmár) race, and founded Wadnagar (A. D. 144). For the years and coins of Kanishka's reign, see pages 213 to 221 of Indian Antiquary Vol. X.

† Broach is a very ancient town, and belonged to the Maurya Kings, and afterwards to the Dádás, of whose time several coins and inscriptions have been found. Its original name is Bhrigukachha, or Bhrigukshetra, *i. e.*, the field of Bhrigu Rishi its founder.

‡ Cambay is also an ancient town. Its original name was Skambha-Tirth and also Trámbávati. For further details see Bombay Gazetteer Volume VI, page 213, also Asiatic Researches Volume IX, pages 117-244, and Sir H. Elliot's History of India, Vol. V, page 143.

§ The Rev. Mr. Taylor of the Irish Presbyterian Church had recently the good fortune to procure in the Ahmadábád Bazár a coin corresponding exactly with the description here given.

time rising into power, and king Chandragupta II. sent an army under the command of his son Kumár-pál to Sauráshtra, which he conquered in or about 432, and placing a vice-regent, named Chakrapál, at Vámansthali (the modern Vanthli) to rule in his behalf he returned to Kanauj. There is an inscription of the time of Kumárpál's successor Skandhagupta on the rock at Junághad, which shews that the Sudarśana lake at the foot of Girnár, which had burst its embankment seven years previously in consequence of excessive rain, was repaired in the 137th year of the Gupta era, that is in A. D. 456. Chakrapál also erected the temple of Vishnu on the top of the Jayanta hill the next year. It thus appears that the Guptas ruled supreme in Sauráshtra about that time. Skandhagupta seems to have been the last of the more powerful of the Gupta Kings. In his time his Senápati (Commander-in-Chief) Bhatárk, of the Ghelot race, came with a large army to Sauráshtra, and made his rule firm in that province. After Skandha's death in or about A. D. 468, and during the decline of the Guptas (who were finally overthrown by the foreign Huns), Bhatárk assumed the title of King of Sauráshtra, and founded the city of Valabhipur (about A. D. 479) which soon was made the capital, a lieutenant being left at Vámansthali. Traces of the ancient city are yet to be seen near the little town of Valá*, situated about eighteen miles to the north-west of Bhávnagar. Of the existence and importance of this Valabhipur there can be no manner of doubt. Its name frequently occurs in old manuscripts, and is mentioned in an inscription†

* Chief town of a 3rd Class State of that name under the present Káthiáwár Political Agency. The present Chief is a Bhaiád of the Thakor of Bhávnagar.

† See Indian Antiquary Vols. XI, page 305, XIV. pages 75 and 339, and XV. page 335.

on an ancient ruined temple in the territory of the Ráná of Udaipur, as well as in several other inscriptions and copper plates. Hiuen-Tsiang, the celebrated Chinese Buddhist priest, who travelled in India between A. D. 629 and 645, describes Valabhipur as a flourishing opulent city, possessing more than a hundred Buddhist monasteries. There were about a hundred families each possessing a fortune of upwards of a crore of rupees. The king's name has been given by this traveller, as Dhrou-Bhatta, son-in-law of Siláditya, the king of Kanauj. There is also an era called the Valabhi era, which dates from A. D. 318 (Vikram Samvat* 375). It is the same as the Gupta era, which the Valabhis appear to have adopted out of deference to their former rulers.

Not much is known of the doings of the Valabhipur kings. As regards their number and names the genealogical table given in Appendix B from the Káthiáwár Gazetteer, is based upon the information collected by the eminent scholar, Dr. Georg Bühler.

The destruction of Valabhipur has been popularly attributed to the wrath of a sage named Dhundlimal, who begged in vain for alms from the inhabitants, but this story† is so utterly improbable, that no detailed account of it seems necessary. Having regard to the natural features of the country round about Valá, and to the tradition that the rocks of Chamárdi were once washed by the waters of the ocean, the conjecture that a serious inundation may have been the cause of the destruction of Valabhipur is not improbable. All

* This era is popularly supposed to have been founded to commemorate the victory of the famous King Vikramáditya over the Scythians, but there is great controversy regarding the matter and the point does not appear to have been yet settled.

† See page 14 of the Râs Málá.

authors, however, agree in affirming that the city was sacked and overthrown by foreign invaders. The Rás Málá states that in the time of the last Siláditya, a Márwádi named Káku left his native town Páli, and settled in Valabhipur, where, though originally he had been so poor that he was known by the appellation of "Rank" (poverty-sticken), he in time amassed vast wealth. One day the king's daughter observed, in the tresses of "Rank's" daughter, a rich gold comb, studded with valuable jewels, but on her expressing a desire to possess herself of the same, Rank would not consent to part with the precious ornament at any price. Thereupon the king caused it to be wrested from him by force, but this act of injustice led to the ruin of Siláditya, for the Márwádi merchant resolved on vengeance, and heedless of all consequences to his country, waited on a foreign emperor, and, offering an immense sum for the assistance his troops could render, while also holding out hopes of rich plunder, induced him to advance against Valabhipur.

Under this promise the emperor invaded India with a large army, and defeated and killed Siláditya, after which the capital Valabhipur was pillaged and destroyed. The exact year of this invasion, and the name of the king who effected the destruction, nowhere appear. The Hon. Mountstuart Elphinstone conjectures that the emperor may have been Nausherwán the Just, but that king ruled in Persia from A. D. 531 to 579, when Valabhipur appears to have been enjoying peace under its own kings. Hence, though it is true that this king carried his arms into India, still he could not have been the destroyer of Valabhipur. Mr. Elphinstone indeed gives A. D. 524 as the year of the destruction of Valabhipur, but that year must be incorrect, inasmuch as the account of Hiuen-Tsiang shows Valabhipur to have been in a flourishing condition at the time of his visit in or about A. D. 640. There is, therefore, every reason to believe that the foreigners who overthrew Valabhipur were some early Arab invaders, who returned as rapidly as they came. After the fall of Valabhipur the inhabitants appear to have dispersed to different localities, and to have founded other towns, among which were Báli, Sundari, Nandol in Marwar, and Panchásar.

It was at the last mentioned place that the fortunes of the kingdom of Gujarát revived under the Chávadá dynasty, but whether these Chávadás were in any way connected with the Siláditya family has not been ascertained. The last king of the new dynasty was Jaysheker, during whose reign, in or about 696 A. D., an eloquent but fanatical bard, named Shankar, fulfilling the Gujaráti saying નાદાન દોસ્ત દુશ્મનની ગરજ સારે, (a foolish friend may prove an enemy), brought ruin upon his king and country. It happened that this bard, in the course of his begging-excursions abroad, entered the presence of Rájá Bhuwar of Kalyán in the Deccan.* The king being in open Darbár, surrounded by his courtiers and nobles, Shankar sang some verses in the monarch's praise. The king was pleased with the composition, and, when presenting the bard with the usual robe of honour, enquired of him, as to his name and home. In proud reply Shankar spoke in terms of unmeasured eulogy of his own country, Gujarát, with its capital Panchásar, and extolled so highly the valour of its sovereign, Jaysheker, and of his general Surpál, that jealousy was at once kindled in the breast of Rájá Bhuwar. He determined on speedily subduing Gujarát, and soon an army under the command of his chief general, named Mir, was marching towards Panchásar. It halted when only six miles from the capital,

* According to Dr. Bühler Kalyán was situated near Kanauj.

where, however, it was surprised and completely routed by Surpál and the Gujarát troops. Mir, having lost several of his officers, retreated in great confusion towards Kalyán. When still eight days distant from that city, Rájá Bhuwar joined the army with large reinforcements, and inspiring his soldiers with fresh courage, placed himself at their head. A second advance was made against Panchásar. After closely besieging the city for some fifty-two days, during which Surpál bravely repulsed several attacks, Bhuwar Rájá sought to corrupt that general from his allegiance to Jaysheker. But the brave Rajput scornfully rejected all such overtures, declaring that he was as inseparable from his king, as is water from the milk with which it has been mixed.

After this the siege was still continued, and Jayasheker found his troops were being seriously reduced in number. Anxious to preserve his dynasty, he besought Surpál, whose sister he had married, to convey her to some place of security. To this Surpál and the Ráni consented with great reluctance, and the two managed to escape from the besieged city, after which they took their course towards a forest. Rájá Bhuwar now offered to leave Jayasheker in undisputed possession of his territory on condition of his tendering his submission in the usual form, holding grass in his mouth, and bowing to the conquerer's feet, his hands being for the time tied behind him. Jayasheker, however, replied that he would prefer death in the battle-field to such humiliation, and a fierce fight ensued, in which Jaysheker fell, sword in hand. King Bhuwar to mark his esteem of the valour of his adversary, performed in person the funeral rites, observing that Jaysheker was an honour to those who had given him birth.

Gujarát thus passed under the dominion of the Kalyán King, who, after receiving the submission of the chiefs of

Kachh and Sorath, and spending a short time at Panchásar, returned to his capital, leaving a governor to administer the affairs of the newly acquired province.

Surpál, having, in the meantime, left his sister in the forests, was himself returning without delay to Jaysheker's assistance, when he heard of the latter's defeat and death. His first impulse was to rush on the enemy's camp, and thus share in the fate of the king, but on reflexion he resolved rather to avenge his master, and, if possible, regain the country on behalf of the infant prince whose birth his sister was expecting. Accordingly he withdrew to the forests and mountains of Girnár, whence, with a few chosen followers, he issued out from time to time to molest the deputy of Rájá Bhuwar.

The Ráni Rupsundari, after her brother's departure, met in the forest a kind-hearted Bhil woman, who, recognizing at once that she was a lady of high rank, gave her shelter, and promised to procure her food and necessaries. In her humble abode, at the full moon of Vaishákh, Samvat 752 (A. D. 696) a son, destined to be the future king of Gujarát, was born to the Ráni. Six years she patiently spent with her infant in the forest, after which period, however, a Jain Monk named Shilgun Suri, while on his way through the jungle, saw the prince sleeping in a cradle that was suspended from the branches of a tree, and, being struck with the child's noble appearance, made enquiries of the mother. Learning from her who she was, the pious monk took both the mother and child with him to his monastery, treating them with every token of respect. The child now received the name of Van-Ráj (forest king) by reason of his birth in the jungle. The next few years were spent in the monk's retreat at or near Rádhanpur,*

* Now belonging to Nawáb Bismillá Khán of the celebrated Bábi family.

until, at length, the time came when the boy could safely join his maternal uncle Surpál in the fastnesses of Girnár. Here he accompanied his uncle in many of his daring exploits, and bore himself in all so well, that Surpál grew confident of speedily realizing his long cherished hopes. When Van-Ráj was only fourteen years of age, his uncle died, and the youth had henceforth to rely solely upon his own ability and resources for the recovery of his father's throne. He first nominated those who had been of service to him during his misfortune to high honours, which were, however, for a long time merely nominal. But at length an opportunity occurred favourable to the establishment of an independent kingdom. Rájá Bhuwar had assigned the revenues of Gujarát to his daughter, and one day, as her officers who had come to collect the tribute were returning to Kalyán with a vast amount of treasure and many swift Káthiáwádi horses, Van-Ráj attacked the party, and, killing their chief, became possessed of immense booty. This enabled Van-Ráj to carry into effect his long contemplated plans, and in Samvat 802 (A. D. 746) he founded the once famous city of Anhilwár, in which he was formally enthroned on the 7th of Máha Vad. Hither his mother Rupsundari and the spiritual preceptor Shilgun Suri, who had so long protected her, were safely brought, and the image that they worshipped was installed in a temple under the name of Panchásar Párasnáth. The power of the Solanki dynasty of Bhuwar Rájá was, in process of time, destroyed throughout the province, and Anhilwár remained the capital of Gujarát until the year 1412 A. D., when Sultán Ahmad founded the city of Ahmadábád on the bank of the Sábarmati river. Anhilwár is said to owe its name to the fact that when Van-Ráj was in search of a site for the city, Anhil, a shepherd, consented to make known a suitable spot on the express condition that the city, when built, should be named after himself. The king, true to his promise, gave it the name of Anhilwár. In course of time, however, as the population and prosperity of the place increased, and it became more definitely *the city* of the province, it came to be frequently called Pátan (the city) and often the two names were combined in the compound form of Anhilwár Pátan.

The reign of Van-Ráj lasted sixty years, and at his death in A. D. 806, he left the kingdom, which he had re-established by his own valour, in a prosperous condition.

His successor to the sovereignty was his son Yog-Ráj, who, like his father, possessed military talents. He is also said to have been conspicuous for literary ability. During his reign of thirty-five years, he largely increased the extent and resources of his kingdom.

Very little has been recorded in connexion with the remaining five kings of the Chávadá dynasty. Their reigns, however, appear to have been prosperous, their dominion was extended in various directions, and, according to the accounts of Arabian travellors, the capital Anhilwár Pátan continued to be a centre of increasing commerce.

Sámant Singh, the last of the Chávadá dynasty, had no male issue, but he had given his sister in marriage to a chief of that same Solanki race to which belonged the Rájá Bhuwar who had effected the ruin of Van-Ráj's father and the destruction of the Panchásar kingdom. A son of this sister, named Mul-Ráj, was adopted by Sámant Singh, who one day, in a drunken bout, abdicated in his nephew's favour. Though he revoked his abdication after returning to a sober state, the nephew, nevertheless, laid claim to the Sovereignty, and, collecting some troops, overpowered and slew the king. Mul-Ráj forthwith usurped the throne, and to guard against possible rebellions, caused all the kinsmen of his mother (who had died when giving him birth) to be put to death. Thus the kingdom of Gujarát passed from under the sway of the Chávadás, and came under the dominion of the Solankis.

The Table in Appendix C gives the dates of the reign of each king of the Chávadá dynasty.

Before concluding this chapter, it is desirable to notice briefly the arrival during this period, and subsequent settlement in Gujarát, of the Pársis, a people now so widely known for their enterprise, especially in commercial matters. It would be foreign to the purpose of this work to narrate the circumstances that led to their losing their empire, one of the earliest and most illustrious in ancient history. Suffice it here to mention that in A. D. 641 their independence was finally overthrown by the rising power of the Arabs. In consequence of the fierce religious persecution that ensued, during which many of the Iránians accepted the Muhammadan faith, the greater portion of those who still clung to their own religion felt they could preserve it only by quitting their beloved native land. India had long been known to them. Their religious as well as political connexion with it had commenced in very ancient times. The expedition of Darius, son of Hystaspes (B. C. 521) is well known, and the Panjáb appears to have been a dependency of Persia from that year till B. C. 350. King Behrám surnamed Gor is known to have paid a visit to India in the fifth century A. D., to gain allies in his struggles with the Scythian tribes of White Huns and to have formed a matrimonial connexion with the house of a Hindu Prince.* Nausherwán the Just and his grandson Khushro Parvez were connected by treaties with several Hindu Kings. Khushro Parvez's son Shiroveyh is, indeed,

* See Dutt's ancient India Vol. III Page 61.

credited with having exiled his seventeen brothers to India when he mounted the throne of Persia, and from them are said to have descended certain royal families and races.* Under these circumstances, the persecuted Persians naturally turned their eyes towards India, the people of which country, being well acquainted with their former greatness, might be expected to grant them an asylum. They accordingly embarked in several ships, and landed at Diu near the gulf of Cambay, in or about A. D. 697. At this place they stayed for nineteen years, when, for reasons not now known, they left that island, and after a perilous voyage, arrived at Sanján, which, though now included in the Thána District, is naturally a portion of Gujarát. Sanján was, at that period, under the rule of a king named Jáde Ráná who, after becoming acquainted with the circumstances that led to their seeking a refuge in his kingdom, and after informing himself of the principles† of their religion, gave them permission to settle in his dominion on certain conditions. The chief of these conditions were that the Pársis should cease to bear weapons, that they should adopt the language of the country in preference to their mother tongue, that at their marriages they should perform certain additional

---

* For further details, see Asiatic Researches Vol: IX, pages 117-244. See also pages 325 and 377 of part 2 of Colonel Alexander Walker's Report regarding suppression of Female Infanticide, in which Persia is stated to have been the original residence of the Jádejá Rájputs, and the word Jám to have been derived from the Persian monarch Jamshed the fourth in descent from Kayomurz (supposed to be the first of the present race of mankind and the first monarch of Persia. See historical account of that country by J. B. Fraser, second edition page 102). See also note C on fire worship in upper India in Sir H. Elliot's History of India volume 5.

† The sixteen shlokas or stanzas in which these principles were formulated are contained in the appendix to Dr. Burgess' Notes of his visit to Gujarát and in Mr. Dosábhái Frámji Karáká's history of the Pársis.

ceremonies in accordance with prevalent Hindu customs, and that their women, though allowed to retain the Sadrá (shirt) and Kusti (sacred thread), emblems of the Zoroastrian religion, should adopt the dress of Hindu females. The Pársis accepted these conditions, and settled at Sanján (A. D. 716) * whence, in time, they sent out several colonies, amongst others to Navsári, Cambay, Broach, Surat, Variáv and Ankleshvar. It should be mentioned that about four centuries later, one of the Ráná's successors abrogated the prohibition to bear arms. At that time Alá-ud-din Khilji's army, under the command of Alaf-Khán, when invading Gujarát and the Deccan, had approached Sanján, whereupon the Pársis, in grateful remembrance of the shelter given by the Ráná's ancestor, responded to his request for military assistance. A body of fourteen hundred Zoroastrians came to his aid, and repulsed Alaf-Khán. Both the Pársi commander Ardeshir and the Ráná were, however, killed in a subsequent attack on Alaf-Khán's return with fresh re-inforcements, and, on the latter taking the town of Sanján, the Pársis were compelled to remove elsewhere.

* Samvat 772, Shráwan Shud 9th, corresponding to Yazd-e-Zardi year 85, month Tir, day Bahman, is the date of this settlement as given by Dastur Aspandiár Kámdin, high priest of the Pársis at Broach, in a pamphlet written by him in A. D. 1826, and quoted in Mr. Dosábhái Framji's History of the Pársis, vol. 1, page 30.

Chapter II.

THE SOLANKI DYNASTY.

The reign of Mulráj, Chámund,
Valabhsen and Durlabhsen.

From 942 to 1022 A. D.

Mul-Ráj the first king of the above named dynasty commenced his reign in A. D. 942. His energies had soon to be employed in protecting his kingdom from two powerful enemies, who, owing to the destruction of the Chávadá dynasty were tempted to invade Gujarát almost simultaneously. These were :—

1. The Rájá of Nágor or Sambhar (the present Ajmer) from the North.
2. The Rájá of Telingáná from the South.

Mul-Ráj established himself in the strong fortress of Kanth Kot on the frontier of Kachh, and, seeing that it would not be possible to cope with both the powerful enemies at one and the same time with success, he induced the Ajmer chief by large presents to retire to his own country. Mul-Ráj then attacked the army from Telingáná, and put it to flight with the loss of its general.

Freed thus from fear of foreign invasion, Mul-Ráj turned his attention to the capital, where he caused several temples to be built. At this period, also, he commenced the erection of the famous temple of Rudra-Mál at Shristhal (the present Siddhpur), a town held in great sanctity by the Hindus.

While Mul-Ráj was reigning at Anhilwár, the King in the peninsula of Sorath was one Grah Ripu, described as a demon in the ancient Hindu works. Grah Ripu was very powerful, and his stronghold of Vámansthali (the modern Vanthali), near Girnár, was considered impregnable. He was also most tyrannical and oppressed his subjects and the pilgrims that resorted to Somnáth-Mahádev. Tradition says that one day the Mahádev appeared to Mul-Ráj in a dream, and directed him to destroy Grah Ripu and his demons. Mul-Ráj, accordingly, after consulting his ministers, determined to carry out the wishes of the Mahádev, who had promised him victory. He summoned his allies, and marched against Sorath at the head of a large army among the acclamations of his subjects, who, as is usual on such occasions, thronged in great numbers to witness the military procession.

Grah Ripu, hearing of the approach of Mul-Ráj, also assembled his army, and called his friend Lákhá, the Rájá of Kachh, and also the Sindhu Rájá, to his aid. A sanguinary battle ensued, in which the Gujarát army was victorious, and Grah Ripu's army took to flight. Grah Ripu was himself struck down by the hand of Mul-Ráj, and taken prisoner. His ally Lákhá then proposed negotiations, but Mul-Ráj refusing to listen, Lákhá assailed him with great fury, and fell in the contest, pierced by Mul-Ráj's spear (A. D. 956). Thus complete victory crowned the expedition of the Gujarát king, who made his obeisance to the idol of Somnáth, and eventually returned to his capital with his army, bringing as plunder a vast amount of treasure and a number of elephants taken from the enemy.

Mul-Ráj, during his glorious reign of 56 years, extended the limits of the kingdom of Gujarát very considerably. By Lákhá's death he gained possession of Kachh, in addition to Sorath of which he became the lord by the fall of Grah Ripu. Several kings, to propitiate his favour, used to send him presents of gold, jewels and other valuable articles. On one occasion an ambassador from Láth* brought from his Rájá the

* Sir William Hunter includes in the Láth country, the Collectorates of Surat, Broach, Kaira and parts of Baroda. The grants published in the Indian Antiquary Vol. XII, pages 196 to 205 and Vol. XIV, pages 196 to 203, support this view.

present of an elephant, which having been pronounced by the astrologers as of bad omen, the king not only contemptuously turned away the ambassador and refused the present, but, when a favourable opportunity presented itself, even attacked the Láth country. During this expedition he was accompanied by his son Chámund, who, leading the van of the Gujarát army, killed the prince of Láth in battle. Thus Láth also was annexed to the Gujarát kingdom.

Towards the end of his reign Mul-Ráj suffered deep remorse for having unjustifiably killed his mother's kinsmen. In order to expiate his crimes he made frequent fasts, took vows, went on pilgrimages, and gave large presents to Bráhmans. At length he resolved to abdicate the throne, and take up his abode in the holy town of Siddhpur, then known by the name of Shristhal. Here he invited learned Brahmans* to settle with their families, and prostrating himself before them offered them his kingdom. The wise men, however, refused the gift, saying they would not be able to maintain possession of the kingdom. Mul-Ráj, therefore, alienated Siddhpur, Sihor and several villages for the endowment of the temples and support of the Brahmans. (A. D. 997). He also granted Valá to certain Bráhmans, but left its government in the hands of its chieftain. The latter is said to have been a descendant of Ebhal Valá, who flourished in or about 295 A. D., and concerning whom the

---

* The following is a list of the families which emigrated to Siddhpur under Mul-Ráj's patronage :—

105 from Prayág(Allábábád).
100 from Chyawun Ashram.
200 from Kapyá Kubja.
404 from Kuru Kshetra.
100 from Gangá-Dwár.
100 from Naemesha Aranya.
100 from Benares.

Vide Forbes Rásmálá, page 48.

following verse, given in the Káthiáwár Gazetteer, is still at times sung :—

> " At Wadhwán resides Ebhal who can withstand the onset of 200,000 men ;
> He defeated the Iránis with his spear,
> Of which the Sun is witness ".

Mul-Ráj also added much to the importance of Cambay by settling there a colony of the newly arrived Bráhmans and granting them a piece of land, about twenty square miles in extent, near the place where the Mahi enters the ocean, which the Bráhmans selected as the most holy place near the temple of Kumáriká. This grant appears to have been accompanied by the transfer of Cambay to its present site. Before this the city is supposed to have stood three miles inland. The temple of Kumáriká is said to have been situated on the ground at present occupied by the English Factory building.

After making these and other magnificent gifts, Mul-Ráj abdicated his throne in favour of his eldest son Chámund, and in his beautiful palace Ramiáshrum, (the house of delights) at Siddhpur, spent the remainder of his days in religious devotion.

Rájá Chámund's reign lasted only for twelve years and four months, but it was one of peace and prosperity. Some historians, however, place in his reign the invasion of Gujarát by Mahmud of Ghazni and the sack of the famous temple of Somnáth, but this cannot be correct, for, according to the best authorities, the invasion in question took place in A. H. 460, A. D. 1024, and thus sixteen years subsequent to the close of Chámund's reign. In 1025, Bhim–Dev was king of Anhilwár and if his grand-father Chámund was then alive, though in retirement, the mistake might readily be made of ascribing Mahmud's invasion to the period of Chámund's reign instead of merely to his life-time.

In A. D. 1009, Chámund Rájá abdicated, as his father had done before him, in favour of his eldest son Valabh, and proceeded to Benares on pilgrimage. On his way thither the Rájá of Málwá insulted him by taking from him his umbrella and other royal insignia. On his return Chámund informed his son of the insult done to him, so Valabh marched with an army to Málwá to punish the offender. On the road, however, he succumbed to an attack of small-pox. The army, therefore, returned in great grief to Gujarát, and Chámund then seated his second son Durlabhsen on the throne, himself returning as a penitent to Sukal Tirth* on the bank of the Narbadá, where he passed the remainder of his days.

Durlabh reigned for about eight years. He built several temples and the Durlabh-Sarovar (tank) at Anhilwár. His younger brother was Nág-Ráj, and the wives of both these brothers were daughters of the king of Márwár. Durlabh had no male issue, but Nág's wife gave birth to a son (Bhim-Dev), destined to become famous in the annals of Gujarát. When this nephew grew up to manhood, Durlabh resigned the kingdom into his hands, and both he and his brother Nág-Ráj retired as penitents, leaving to Bhim-Dev the burden as well as the splendour of a vast dominion. (A. D. 1022).

---

* This place is about ten miles above the town of Broach and a great fair is annually held there on the day of the full moon of the month of Kártik(November)at which about twenty five thousand pilgrims assemble.

CHAPTER III.

BHIM-DEV I. Mahmud of Ghazni's invasion of Gujarát.

FROM 1022 to 1072 A. D.

Soon after the accession of Bhim-Dev a great calamity befell the kingdom of Anhilwár. Mahmud, king of Ghazni in Afghánistán, whose name has already been mentioned, had, while Gujarát was enjoying peace under its Hindu rulers, made no less than fifteen expeditions against other parts of India, and had conquered Láhor, Mirat, Delhi and other cities in the North.

In A. H. 416, A. D. 1024, Mahmud made his sixteenth expedition with a view to destroy the famous temple of Somnáth, and thus strike a heavy blow at idolatry. In September of that year he left Ghazni by way of Multán, took Ajmer, and, leaving the mountain of Abu in the rear, arrived by forced marches at Anhilwár. Bhim-Dev probably not being fully prepared to meet him fled, and Anhilwár fell into the hands of the invader. Mahmud then made his preparations for marching on Somnáth, and in the month of January 1025 A. D., reached that place.

Here, notwithstanding the suddenness and rapidity of Mahmud's approach, the Hindus collected in large numbers, and made a bold stand in defence of their religion. On the first day of the attack by the Muhammadan troops the battlements were cleared by Mahmud's archers, and the Hindus, dispirited by the fierceness of the onset, had nearly lost the day. Instead of remaining firm at the ramparts they crowded into the precincts of the temple, and prostrating themselves with tears in their eyes before the idol implored its aid. The Muhammadans immediately seized the opportunity thus offered by the temporary desertion, and, having applied their scaling ladders to the strong walls, mounted them with shouts of "Allahu Akbar" (God is most great). The Rajputs, however, rallied in defence, and fought with such vigour that by evening the Muhammadans, unable to retain the footing they had gained, had to retire.

The next day the attack was renewed, but the assailants, as soon as they scaled the walls, were hurled down by the besieged.

The third day the princes who had arrived to the rescue of the garrison, hoping to divert Mahmud from the attack, presented themselves in order of battle. Mahmud, leaving a force to prevent the garrison sallying out, himself advanced to meet them. The contest was maintained with great fury on both sides, and the arrival of Bhim-Dev with reinforcements discouraged the Muhamadan troops very much. Mahmud, perceiving this, himself strove to cheer his soldiers, and soon thereafter made such a vigorous attack, that the ranks of the Hindus broke, and five thousand of them lay dead on the battle-field. The garrison, seeing this, abandoned the defence, and fled by a gate towards the sea. The Muhammadans were thus masters of the district including the neighbouring town of Pátan Somnáth.

Mahmud now entered the celebrated temple. It was a superb building of hewn stone. Its spacious roof was supported by pillars carved and set with precious stones. So numerous and brilliant were the jewels, that a single lamp is said to have sufficed to light the sanctuary in which the idol was enshrined. The image itself stood nine feet high above the floor of the temple, and reached six feet deep below. It was daily bathed in water brought all the way from the Ganges by water-carriers stationed at different places. Mahmud gave orders to destroy the shrine and to break the idol in pieces. He proposed to bury some of the fragments under the threshold of the mosque of Ghazni, and others at the entrace to his own residence in that city, in order that they might be trodden under foot by the believers. While the work of demolition was proceeding, the devotees offered Mahmud an enormous ransom if he would desist from further mutilation; but the only reply received from him was that he would rather be known as the destroyer than as the seller of idols. So the work of destruction continued, and, ultimately, in addition to the precious stones above mentioned, a large amount of treasure is said to have been found concealed in the vaults.

Having made the requisite arrangements at Somnáth, Mahmud marched on the fort of Gandábá,* situated about 68 miles from Anhilwár to which Bhim-Dev had fled. On arrival he found it to be a fortification surrounded by deep water on all sides. Two divers were brought to him, who informed Mahmud that there was a ford, but that if the tide came in as they were crossing all would perish. Mahmud, therefore, after humbly invoking the aid of the Almighty, set out at an hour when the tide was low, and, advancing through the water with his cavalry, safely landed them below the fortification walls. Seeing this, Bhim-Dev took to flight, and the fort fell an easy prey to the invader, who here also obtained enormous booty.

Mahmud, thus victorious, returned to Anhilwár, and, being much pleased with the open, extensive country, its rich soil, and good climate, expressed a desire to stay in Gujarát for some years. His nobles, however, dissuaded him from this intention, representing that Gujarát was too distant from his own country, which was inhabited by a hardier race of people.

* Supposed to be the present waste site of Ghandvi on the Káthiáwár Coast.

Hence after lingering only a few months in the Province the Sultán determined to return to Ghazni, taking with him the treasure and jewels obtained from Somnáth.*

Before leaving Gujarát, the Sultán considered it politic to place it in charge of some one chosen from among the people of the country, who would be under pledge to govern it for Mahmud as his deputy and send him the annual tribute. The nobles informed him that of the old dynasty there were two men known as Dábisálims,† one of whom was ruling in a distant part of the country, and the other wandering abroad as an anchoret. Although the nobles praised the lay Dábisálim very much for his honesty, and said they were confident he would send the annual tribute faithfully, Mahamud's choice fell on the ascetic priest. This latter had promised to send the king each year a sum equal to the revenue of Kábul and Khorásán together. The anchoret found no difficulty in persuading Mahmud that if the other Dábisálim continued free he would, after the Sultán's departure, do every thing in his power to usurp the throne. Mahmud accordingly marched against him, arrested him and took him off to Ghazni. A few years after this, when the

* The sandal-wood gates of the temple of Somnáth, taken by Muhamad to Ghazni as a trophy of his victory and fixed to the doors of his mosque in that city, were recovered by the English troops during the Kábul war in A.D. 1842,and in that year were brought back to India. The identity of the gates is, however, doubted by Sir William Hunter, who considers them a modern forgery. The gates were deposited at Agrá.

† It is not clear who these Dábisálims were, save that they were holy personages of royal extraction. They had however long since lost their patrimonial territories, which had been usurped by the Solankis.

See Asiatic Researches, Volume IX. pp. 180—185.

Sir H. Eliot calls them Devá Silá or the meditative kings. See Muhammadan Historians, Vol. IV, p. 183.

It is not improbable that the word Dábisálim may have some connexion with the Dábhis, a branch of the Rajputs.

anchoret had become firmly seated on his throne, he succeeded by means of presents to the Sultán and his ministers, in inducing the former to surrender the still imprisoned Dábisálim to him. The reigning Dábisálim had, it is said, caused a dungeon to be made under his throne for the expected prisoner, but Providence had willed otherwise, and the proverb "Whoso diggeth a pit shall fall therein" was literally fulfilled in this case.

It was customary, says the Mirát-i-Ahmadi, for the king, when about to receive a prisoner of mark, to advance one stage to meet him, and make him run before his horse, carrying a pitcher of water on his head as far as the precincts of the palace. According to this custom Dábisálim, the anchoret, marched out one stage from his capital. There was, however, some delay in the prisoner's arrival, so the Dábisálim passed the hours in hunting. After a time, being tired, he gave his followers the order to halt, and fell asleep himself under a tree, having previously covered his face with a red handkerchief. There were many vultures in the neighbourhood, and one of these, mistaking the red cloth for a piece of flesh, descended and carried it away in its talons. In the act of seizing it, however, the bird's claws pierced the eyes of the sleeping prince, who was thus permanently blinded. A great tumult forthwith arose in the army, and meanwhile, the other Dábisálim arrived. The king's attendants, perceiving that their master was now incapacitated for ruling the kingdom, at once determined to transfer their allegiance to Dábisálim the prisoner, and accordingly they all made their obeisance to him. They further constrained the blinded Dábisálim to submit, and placing the pitcher, which had been brought for the Ghazni prisoner, on his head compelled him to run before them to the palace. Here he was put into the very dungeon he had himself given orders to build for another.

We must now revert to Muhamad Ghazni after he left

Anhilwár. His return march was not at all so prosperous or so speedy as had been his advance. The route by which he proposed to go back was occupied by Bhim-Dev, who in the meantime had managed to collect a force, and by Visal-Dev, the Rájá of Ajmer. His army was, by this time, much reduced owing to losses incurred both by the attack on Somnáth and by the change of climate. Mahmud therefore did not consider it politic to risk, in his weakened condition, another battle. Accordingly he determined to return by a new route through the deserts of Sindh. In this march the army suffered great distress from want of water and provisions. Many of the soldiers died raving mad from the intolerable heat of the desert and from thirst. In a sadly shattered state Mahmud at last reached Multán with the remnant of his army, and thence proceeded to Ghazni (1026–27 A. D.). His death occurred in A. D. 1030. After this owing to dissensions among his descendants and to many other causes, Gujarát, in common with the rest of India, enjoyed an immunity from foreign invasion for the long period of 160 years.

After the return of Mahmud to Ghazni, Bhim-Dev regained possession of his kingdom. It is not clear, however, in what year and by what means he did so. He certainly had assumed royal power before 1032 A. D., for an inscription, dated that year, tells of the temple of Yugádináth at Delwárá having been built by Vimal-Shá, Bhim's vice-regent, so that thirteen years subsequent to Mahmud's death, when the kings of Delhi, Ajmer, and other sovereigns, taking advantage of the weakness of Mahmud's successors, attacked and retook Hánsi, Tháneshwar, Láhor, and other cities, Bhim-Dev had already obtained full sway over Anhilwár, and accordingly he did not join the Hindu confederacy. This brought down upon him the displeasure of the confederates, and the Rájá Visál-Dev of Ajmer accordingly marched on Gujarát.

Visal-Dev's advance on Gujarát brought into conflict the armies of Gujarát and Ajmer. The result being adverse to the former, Visal-Dev expressed his willingness to withdraw on condition of being allowed to build a town at the place of his victory. This proposal was assented to, and he retired after laying the foundation of the town of Visalnagar on the spot where the two armies had engaged in battle. Bhim-Dev then marched against Sindh, and subdued that province.

His contemporary at Málwá was the celebrated Rájá Bhoj. There were altercations between these kings, in which Bhim-Dev appears on the whole to have obtained a decided advantage. It was during his reign that Vimal-Shá, whom Bhim-Dev had sent as his deputy to Abu, built on that mount, in A. D. 1032, the superb marble shrine already mentioned as dedicated to Yugádináth. Vimal-Shá also erected the temples at Khambhália on the hill of Arásur near the shrine of Mátá Bhaváni. Bhim-Dev's queen Udáyámati built a very hand-some váv (a well approached by flights of steps) at Anhilwár itself, which is still known as the Ráni's Váv.

After an eventful reign of over fifty years, Bhim-Dev, following the example of his predecessors, determined to abdicate his throne in favour of his eldest son Kshem-Ráj ; but on this prince's refusal to be separated from his father, a younger brother, Karan, was installed on the throne in A. D. 1072. Both Bhim-Dev and Kshem-Ráj then went into retirement, and spent the remainder of their days in religious meditation.

Chapter IV.

The reigns of Karan Rájá and Sidh-Ráj Jay-Singh.

From 1072 to 1143 A. D.

During Karan Rájá's reign there was no foreign war. He was thus able to devote himself to the consolidation of his kingdom and to the subjugation of that part of his country which is called the "Mewás".* This was inhabited by wild tribes, and was difficult of access owing to its dense forests. He defeated and slew the chief of the Bhils named Ashá at Ashával, and built a temple in honour of the goddess Kochrav. He also founded the city of Karnávati.† Karan-Rájá next caused to be constructed a large reservoir, called Karan-Ságar, at a village not many miles from Anhilwár, and in order to bring water into this tank he is said to have directed towards it the course of the river Rupeyn, which originally flowed in the direction of the Ran. He also built several other useful public works.

When Karan-Rájá died in A. D. 1094, his son Siddh-Ráj was a mere child, and accordingly it was arranged that his mother Mainal Devi, the daughter of the king of Chandrapur in the Deccan, should govern in his name with the assistance of her ministers. Mainal Devi was a very wise and able queen, and she, like her husband before her, devoted her attention to

---

* Mewás embraces the villages to the North of the Mahi, situated near its ravines. They were once the terror of the country. They are ruled by minor chiefs, who pay tribute to Government.

† This city does not exist at the present day, but traces of it are to be seen in the ruins found in and about Ahmadábád. There is a Váv (well) at the village of Asárwá, about a mile from Ahmadábád, called Mátá Bhávání's well, which is said to be the oldest work near the city, and the only remnant of the old Ashával, near which Karan-Rájá is supposed to have built Karnávati.

works of public utility. The Mán-Sarovar, with several small temples on its bank, still to be seen at Viramgám, and the Malév tank at Dholká, were built by her orders. She also induced her son Siddh-Raj Jay-Singh to remit the tax levied at the village of Bhálod (now in the Rájpiplá State) on pilgrims proceeding to the shrine of Someshvar at the village of Koral, to which she is said to have presented an elephant and a gold figure called a "Tul Purush" (This probably means that she gave to the shrine gold equal to her weight). Several magnificent buildings, some of which exist even at the present time, are attributed to Siddh-Ráj Jay-Singh, who inherited his father's bountiful disposition. It was he who, after his conquest of Málwá, completed the temple of Rudra-Mál founded by the Solanki prince Mul-Ráj, and planted a victorious pendent of Mahádev on its summit. It was from this time that the town, which had hitherto been known by the name of Shri-sthal, obtained the name of Siddhpur in commemoration of the royal restorer of the Rudra-Mál. On this occasion he is said to have given the Bráhmans the grant of one hundred and one villages in the Bhál land in addition to the grant by Mul-Ráj.

Siddh-Ráj's reign was not so peaceful as that of his father. While engaged with his mother in the worship of Someshwar, the Málwá king, an old antagonist of Gujarát, invaded it from the North. The officer in charge of Anhilwár paid him a sum of money, and induced him to retire; but Siddh-Ráj did not approve of this, and began to make preparations to invade Málwá in his turn. In course of time he marched against that country, advancing stage by stage and subduing the chieftains of the places which came in his way. Siddh-Raj continued this war with the Málwá king for twelve years, during which he gained much renown, and at last took by storm the capital town of Dhárnagar, and captured the king Yashovámaan, grandson of the celebrated Rájá Bhoj. Thus, the standard of the king of Gujarát waved over the city of Bhoj.

On his way back from Málwá Siddh-Ráj attacked and drove away from their forts several chieftains who were in the habit of plundering travellers and pilgrims, and he thus made the country secure. From a valuable inscription, recently found at Dohad by Mr. D. P. Derásari and published* by Mr. H. H. Dhruva, Siddh-Ráj Jay-Singh appears to have stationed a separate commander-in-chief at Dohad on the frontier of Málwá and Gujarát. The inscription further shows that Dohad was then known by the name of Dadhipadra and that then as now it was subordinate to Godhrá (Godrahaka).

Some time after this Siddh-Ráj involved himself in a long war with Rá-Khengár, the king of Junágadh. This war arose in connexion with an interesting episode. The Rájá of Pawár in Sindh had a daughter born during the moon's passage through the Mul Nakshatra (constellation), whom the astrologers pronounced ill omened in consequence of the inauspicious moment of her birth. Accordingly the superstitious chief ordered the helpless child to be removed from his abode and placed beyond the limits of his territory, which order was duly carried out. Fortunately a man of the Od caste, the members of which are employed for the most part in building mud houses and digging tanks, noticed the infant, and, being himself childless, he took the girl to his home. His wife was delighted to nurse the little one as her own, and gave her the name of Ránik Devi. As the girl grew up, the fame of her beauty spread far and wide, and by means of a bard reached Siddh-Ráj's ears. That king at first refused to entertain the idea of any connexion with an Od's daughter, but, being convinced by the bard that she must have been born of princely

* Indian Antiquary, Vol. X pp. 158-162.

parents, he consented to the betrothal. The Od lived in Rá-Khengár's territory, and the Rá's sister's son Desal having represented to him that it would not be honourable for him to allow so great a beauty to leave his kingdom, the Rá forcibly married her. On this news reaching the ears of Siddh-Ráj, he became greatly incensed, and marched with an army against the Rá's capital, which he besieged. Though the siege lasted for twelve years without any successful result, the fort being impregnable and strongly defended, still Siddh-Ráj's pride would not allow him to withdraw his forces and retire. While he was wavering as to what should be done, some quarrel arose between Rá-Khengár and his nephews Desal and Visal, who turned traitors to their uncle the Rá. In secret treaty with Siddh-Ráj, they perfidiously introduced that king's army through one of the gates, which they had caused to be opened by treachery. Rá-Khengár, thus taken by surprise, fought desperately, but was at length slain. His consort Ránik-Devi with her two sons fell into Siddh-Ráj's hands and were conveyed to Wadhwán. Siddh-Ráj did his best by persuasion and then by threats to constrain Ránik-Devi to marry him; and went so far as to cause even her two innocent children to be put to death before her eyes. Ránik-Devi, however, absolutely refused to consent, and implored the king to allow her to become a Sati,* threatening him at the same time with a severe curse in the event of his witholding permission. In those days, a Sati's curse was much dreaded, and Siddh-Ráj, partly deterred by the threat and partly struck by Ránik-Devi's firm behaviour, eventually yielded to her entreaties. She cheerfully ascended the funeral pile that had been raised on the bank of the river Bhogáwá near the town of Wadhwán.† Over the spot where

* One, who immolates herself after her husband.

† Wadhwán is a very ancient town, now held by a second class Chief in Káthiáwár.

she immolated herself, Siddh-Ráj, repenting of his sins, built in her honour a temple the ruins of which still exist. Moreover, as a suitable punishment for the perfidious Desal and Visal, who had first induced Khengár to marry Ránik-Devi, and then betrayed him, he ordered that each should suffer the loss of his nose and ears. Thus the two brothers received the due reward of their treachery.

Siddh-Ráj was the most illustrious king of the Solanki dynasty. Notwithstanding his two long campaigns above mentioned and his expeditions against Kanauj and other places, he found time to superintend religious controversies not only between Bráhmans and Jains but between the Digambars and Swetámbars, two rival sects of the Jain religion. His territory extended beyond Abu to near Jhálor. Kachh, Saurásthra and Málwá were under his sway, and towards the south his dominion reached far into the Deccan. The kings of Ceylon and other countries sent ambassadors to his court, and, according to Colonel Tod, no less than twenty-two principalities owed him allegiance. Siddh-Ráj is also famous for his public works. In addition to the completion of the Rudra-Mál and the construction of other temples and of the Shahsra-Ling many noble reservoirs, palaces, and caravanserais are attributed to him. In short, so great was his fame both in the field and in the administration of his country that his name is still a household word amongst the inhabitants of Gujarát.

One story of his justice is worth recording. It appears that in A. D. 1100 some Muhammadans of Cambay, whose faction had been worsted in a fight between Hindus and Pársis on the one hand and Muhammadans on the other, made their way to Anhilwár (Pátan) and meeting king Siddh-Ráj Jay-Singh hunting in the vicinity, informed him that the Hindus had attacked the Musalmáns, killed eighty of them and destroyed their mosque and minarets. The King started for Cambay, and, wandering about the town in disguise, satisfied himself of the truth of the charge. On his return to Pátan he sent for two men from each class of the inhabitants, and ordered them to be punished. At the same time he made over to the Musalmáns money enough to rebuild all that had been destroyed.*

The above incident is recorded as showing that Musalmáns were resident in Cambay even before Alá-ud-din's conquest of Gujarát and that that town was at this period under the rule of the Anhilwár kings.

* Bombay Gazetteer, Vol. VI., p. 215.

CHAPTER V.

The reign of Kumár-Pál.

FROM 1143 to 1174 A. D.

After reigning forty-nine years, Siddh-Ráj died in 1143 A. D. He left no son, but in the line of Kshem-Ráj, son of Bhim-Dev, there were three sons, by name Mahi-Pál, Kirti-Pál and Kumár-Pál. The last of these was of noble bearing, and well fitted to succeed Siddh-Ráj. Owing, however, it is said, to an objection on the score of his mother not being descended from a princely family, Kumár-Pál was regarded with disfavour by Siddh-Ráj, who even tried to compass his death. Hence during that king's reign Kumár-Pál was obliged to lead a wandering life in the guise of an ascetic, and suffer great privations. Hearing, when in Málwá, of Siddh-Ráj's death he went direct to Anhilwár, where his maternal uncle Káhán-Dev was one of the ministers of the state. The latter received him kindly, but as the late king had made known his wish that Kumár-Pál should not be his successor, it was agreed that the appointment to the throne should be decided by election. With this object an open Darbár was convened, before which the three brothers appeared as candidates. The ministers first seated Mahi-Pál on the throne, but he was at once rejected on account of the effeminacy of his dress. Next Kirti-Pál was given the royal seat, and asked by the nobles how he would govern the eighteen regions left by his illustrious predecessor. His reply was "I shall govern them according to your counsel and instructions". This sounded tame. Kumár-Pál was then enthroned and was asked the same question, whereupon, starting to his feet, his eyes filled with martial fire, he half unsheathed his sword. Immediately the hall rang with acclamations, the nobles prostrated themselves before him, and in the presence of the assembled multitude declared him their chosen king. Thus Kumár-Pál ascended the throne of Anhilwár in A. D. 1143 in the fiftieth year of his age. By suitable presents he rewarded those who had assisted him in the days of his distress, and as his prime minister he appointed Vághbhat Dev, son of his predecessor's minister Udayan Mantri who had always helped him while under Siddh-Ráj's displeasure. However Udayan Mantri's other son Váhad, a great favourite of the late king, refused to obey him, and fled to Nágor (Ajmer). There he took service under the king Anák, grandson of Visal-Dev, and induced him to attempt an invasion of Gujarát. Intelligence of this duly reached Kumár-Pál, and his spies informed him further that the king of Málwá was also preparing to invade the country. Kumár-Pál's situation was, at this time, somewhat critical, for, besides these two powerful enemies, there were some disaffected nobles in his own service. He, however, made arrangements for preventing internal outbreaks, despatched two of his generals with an army to stop the progress of the Málwá king, and himself marched against Nágor. In the battle that ensued between the two armies, Kumár-Pál greatly distinguished himself by his valour and presence of mind. Observing that through the intrigues of Váhad some of his troops were about to desert, Kumár-Pál promptly ordered his Mahávat (elephant-driver) to urge the elephant to the spot where the king of Nágor was standing. The driver obeyed, when the deserter Váhad rushed between the two kings, and, with a view to kill Kumár-Pál, tried to step from his own elephant on to the head of that which bore the Gujarát king. The Mahávat, however, immediately forced his elephant back with his goad, and thus Váhad fell to the ground, and was seized by the Gujarát foot soldiers. Kumár-Pál then advanced towards Anák, and, wounding him with an arrow, brought him to the ground. Thus Kumár-Pál gained a complete victory.

Anák had to sue for pardon, which was granted on condition of his presenting a large number of elephants and horses, and giving his daughter in marriage to Kumár-Pál (A. D. 1167). Váhad was also subsequently pardoned and taken into service by Kumár-Pál.

After this, the king received tidings that the two generals whom he had sent against the king of Málwá had gone over to that king. Accordingly, immediately after the marriage ceremony with the Nágor king's daughter was completed, Kumár-Pál marched in person against the Málwá king, defeated him, and drove him back to his country. He then sent in the same year an army into the Konkan under one of his generals, who defeated and slew the king of that district and proclaimed Kumár-Pál's authority over it.

In civil matters, Kumár-Pál was just, religious and benevolent. Like his predecessor, he was fond of architecture, and under the advice of a celebrated Jain monk, named Hemáchárya,* he restored the ruined temple of Somnáth,† and also erected new shrines at Dilwárá, Cambay and Dhandukå. In later years he abstained, in accordance with Hemáchárya's advice, from the use of animal food and spirituous drinks, and tried to prevent, as much as possible, the slaughter of animals throughout his territory. He was indeed one of the most valiant soldiers of his time, and proved himself, both by his wisdom and his valour, a worthy successor of Siddh-Ráj. The

---

* Hemáchárya was born at Dhandukå, of Modh Wánià parents. At this place the king Kumár-Pál, while on his way to Satrunjáya on pilgrimage, erected a temple called the Cradle-Vihár.

† According to an inscription in the temple of Bhadra Káli at Dev Pátan, quoted in the Rás Málá, Valabhi year 850 (which corresponds with Vikram Samvat 1225 or A. D. 1169) is the year of the said restoration.

following inscription dated A. D. 1151, engraved on the Lákhan's Mandir at Chitor, and quoted in Tod's Western India, and from it in Forbes' Rás Málá, shews the high respect in which he was held even in countries not under his direct rule.

> " What was he like, who, by the strength of his invincible mind, crushed all his foes, whose commands the other sovereigns of the earth placed on their foreheads, who compelled the Lord of Sákambhari to bow at his feet, who in person carried his armies to Shiva Lok, making the mountain lords bow before him even in the city of Sálpura ?".

Chapter VI.

Ajáy-Pal, Bál Mul-Ráj, Bhim-Dev II.
surnamed Bholo and Tribhovan-Pál.

From A. D. 1174 to 1244.

Kumár-Pál died in A. D. 1174 after a reign of 31 years. He had no male issue, and was, therefore, succeeded by his nephew Ajay-Pál, son of Mahi-Pál. This king was a bitter enemy of the Jain religion, to which his illustrious uncle, Kumár-Pál had been converted by the monk Hemácharya, and although he conferred the office of prime minister on one Kapardi, who had been one of the favourites of Kumár-Pál, he caused a false charge of sedition to be brought against him, and had him cruelly put to death by immersion in a vessel of boiling oil. Another Jain leader, to avoid torture, killed himself by biting off his tongue. Ajay-Pál's tyrannical reign was however short, as within three years he was assassinated by one of his own gate-keepers in A. D. 1177. He was succeeded by his infant son known as Mul-Ráj II. or as Bál Mul-Ráj from the fact of his being, at the time of his accession, a mere child.

It was during the reign of this infant king that the Muhammadans, after an interval of about 160 years, again invaded Gujarát under Shiháb-ud-din Ghori, whose family had usurped the throne of Ghazni from Mahmud Ghaznavi's successors. This monarch in 1178 A. D. marched through Multán and the sandy deserts to Gujarát. He was however opposed by the young prince's uncle Bhim-Dev, a valiant and chivalrous youth, and defeated with much loss. Shiháb-ud-din Ghori had therefore to go back through the deserts, where his army suffered great privations.

In the following year the infant king Bál Mul-Ráj died,

and the kingdom of Gujarát devolved of right on the aforesaid Bhim-Dev who was destined to be the last of the Solanki kings. He was brave, but wanting in prudence, and hence he came to be popularly called Bhim Bholo,* that is Bhim the Simple. After he came to the throne he was involved in continual wars, some of which were the outcome of his own stubbornness, and though, through his valour and activity, he generally gained the day, still these conflicts tended to weaken his own and the neighbouring Hindu kingdoms. United, they might perhaps have been able to withstand a foreign foe, but divided as they were amongst themselves they were unable to face their common enemy, and fell one after the other before the Muhammadan invaders.

The ruler of Abu, by name Jetshi Parmár, had a daughter Ichani Kumári whose beauty was far-famed, and Bhim-Dev, being desirous of marrying her, sent an ambassador to the Parmár Rájá with a request for his daughter's hand. It happened however, that Ichani had, shortly before this, been betrothed to Prithvi-Ráj son of the Chohán king Someshwar of Ajmer, and her father could not with propriety break off the engagement. Moreover Bhim-Dev, like Kumár-Pál, observed the Jain religion, and this was another reason for reluctance on the part of the ruler of Abu, who accordingly expressed his inability to comply with the request that had been made.

When Bhim-Dev's ambassador conveyed this reply to him he was much enraged, and, declaring war with Abu, summoned his tributaries and vassals to join him. Bhim-Dev then left for Abu with a powerful army. The Parmár, on the other hand,

* The real meaning of the word "Bholo" is a simpleton, one who can be easily deceived or prevailed upon to believe anything. Hence, the appellation "Bholo" does not appear very applicable to Bhim-Dev, who was, on the contrary, headstrong and unyielding.

was aided by the Ajmer Chohán Prithvi-Ráj, and the contest between the opposing armies raged for several days. At length the Chohán and the Parmár retreated, and Bhim-Dev took the fort on the summit of Mount Abu (about A. D. 1190).

About this time a common enemy, Shiháb-ud-din Ghori, was threatening to assail the belligerents, and therefore several of Bhim-Dev's chieftains advised him to be content with the victory he had already gained on condition of the Parmár giving up his daughter. They also proposed that, instead of weakening and trying to ruin each other, they should unite their forces against the Mlechhas (Muhammadans). But Bhim in his arrogance would not listen to their sober advice, and said that he would march against the Ghori after he had stripped the Chohán chief of all his possessions. To effect this purpose he attacked the Chohán, who, however, by a sudden night attack led by his favourite bard Chand, succeeded in repulsing Bhim with great loss. So complete was the confusion that the Gujarát troops, failing to recognize friend from foe, came into conflict amongst themselves. Bhim Bholo, however, fought desperately till his sword was broken and his elephant killed, but at length he was compelled to retreat. Providence thus curbed Bhim Bholo's pride, and Prithvi-Ráj, after keeping a force to watch his movements, advanced with the main army against Shiháb-ud-din Muhammad Ghori, whom also he succeeded in defeating (A. D. 1191).

Thus Bhim the Bholo, by his obstinacy in disregarding the advice of his friends, lost even the advantage he had gained by his previous victory at Abu.

This defeat was still rankling in Bhim's mind, when another incident occurred which increased his rage against, and hatred of, the Chohán. His uncle Sárang-Dev had left seven sons, who, for some unknown reason, had gone into outlawry against Bhim-Dev. They removed to the mountains of Sorath, from whence they began plundering travellers and others, and became at length so powerful that Bhim was obliged to lead an expedition against them. One day while his elephant was bathing in a river they killed both it and its driver, whereupon Bhim declared that he would not rest content till he had avenged the insult in their blood. Terrified at this threat, the seven brothers took refuge with the Chohán of Ajmer, who gladly took them under his protection, and gave them lands for subsistence. However it so happened that one day as the Chohán king Someshwar's son Prithvi-Ráj was seated in Darbár, surrounded by his courtiers, among whom was his uncle Kun, the seven brothers presented themselves. They duly made their obeisance, and took their seats. In the conversation that ensued, a prominent topic was the Mahábhárat in which the warlike deeds of the Chohâns are related. As the recital proceeded, one of the unfortunate seven brothers, a noble youth, happened to twirl the ends of his mustache, most probably meaning nothing by the action. It was however construed as an insult by Kun, who at once unsheathed his sword, and cut the young man in two. The remaining brothers and their followers immediately attacked the assailant, but, being greatly outnumbered, they were soon overpowered and slain. Prithvi-Ráj was much displeased at this occurrence, but at the time could do nothing to prevent it.

The news of the murder of his seven cousins soon reached Bhim-Dev, who owing to the approach of the monsoon, could not at once advance to take revenge. He however marched with a powerful army at the earliest opportunity, and entered the Ajmer country. Someshwar left his son Prithvi-Ráj at Delhi, and himself marched against the invader. A fierce hand to hand fight ensued, in which many brave warriors were killed and amongst them Someshwar himself. The Gujarát king accordingly returned victorious to his capital.

Someshwar's son Prithvi-Ráj now ascended the throne, and after performing the obsequies of his father and giving large gifts to Bráhmans and donations to religious places, he marched against Gujarát to revenge his father's death. In due time Prithvi-Ráj entered Bhim-Dev's territory and sent forward Chand his favcurite bard to inform Bhim-Dev that he would not withdraw till vengeance had been taken. Chand took with him a net, a ladder, a spade, a lamp, an elephant goad and a trident. As illustrating the freedom of speech enjoyed in those days by Bards on the occasion of their conveying messages to rival kings, the following interesting account of the conversation between Chand and Bhim-Dev is given from the Rás Málá. On Chand's entering the Darbár and announcing the arrival of Prithvi-Ráj, Bhim asked the bard to declare the meaning of the strange emblems he had brought. Chand fearlessly replied that should Bhim seek escape by water the net would catch him, should he fly through the air the ladder would reach him, should he enter the depths of the earth the spade would disclose him, and should he seek the refuge of darkness the lamp would reveal him. The goad would bring him to subjection and the trident was destined to kill him. Bhim heard all this patiently and contented himself with advising the bard to be more modest in his utterances, and to reflect on what he, as king, had been able to accomplish in the war with Prithvi-Ráj's father. Chand thereupon replied that a mouse perchance might overcome a cat, a vulture might prey upon a swan, a deer might prevail over a lion, or a frog might chase away a snake, but such things happened only by some strange freak of fortune. Bhim-Dev was naturally incensed at hearing such insulting words, but, observing the respect due to a bard-messenger, merely remarked that he might please himself by fighting with words, and desired him to tell Prithvi-Ráj that none but a coward would fear his threats. Chand then returned and informed his king of what had passed, whereupon Prithvi-Ráj prepared for battle. In time both the armies came in sight of each other, and a fierce contest took place, in which, according to one account, Bhim-Dev fell desperately fighting. Though this version may not be altogether correct, it is certain he sustained a severe defeat. Thus ended the feud between two of the most powerful Hindu monarchs without bringing any substantial advantage to either, though greatly weakening both, and that, at a time of special danger from their common foe.

It may perhaps be considered foreign to the history of Gujarát to describe what happened at this time in the north of India, but as those events facilitated the Muhammadan invasion of that province, it seems advisable briefly to allude to them here. Though weakened by constant warfare, Prithvi-Ráj the Chohán was able, as already stated, creditably to sustain the first attack made in A. D. 1191 by Shiháb-ud-din Ghori, whom he engaged between Tháneshwar and Karnál and completely defeated. Two years later, in A. D. 1193, however, the attack was renewed. After a prolonged contest on the banks of the Sarasvati, the Hindus were completely exhausted, when, unexpectedly, a reserve body of fresh cavalry, 12000 strong and clad in steel armour, appeared as reinforcements for the enemy. The Hindus were unable to withstand their onset, and in the flight many of their best generals were slain. Prithvi-Ráj himself was captured, and cruelly put to death. The enemy then took possession of Ajmer, and the following year, after Kanauj and other places had been taken, Kutb-ud-din, whom Shiháb-ud-din had left as his lieutenant, invaded and conquered Gujarát (A. D. 1194). Before returning to Delhi, he appointed a Deputy-Governor for the province, but this officer was unable to maintain his hold of the newly acquired territory. Ultimately Bhim-Dev succeeded in regaining possession of Anhilwár, which town he held until his death, which took place, according to some writers, in A. D. 1215, and according to others, in A. D. 1242. It is not clear whether thereafter Gujarát passed at once into the hands of the Vághelás, or whether there were any later rulers of the Solanki dynasty. This much is certain, however, that the glory of that dynasty and of its kingdom passed away with Bhim-Dev.

Authors differ also in their statements both as to the name of Bhim's successor, and as to the length of his reign. The Mirát-i-Ahmadi mentions one Lakhumal-Dev, and gives the period of his reign as twenty years, and adds that "as Lakhumal-Dev had no child fit for the soverignty, it became the property of the Vághelás". From later researches however the name of Bhim's successor appears to be Tribhowan-Pál.

The table given in Appendix D has been drawn up after reference to several authorities and other available sources of information, and indicates, it is hoped, as correctly as is now possible, the name and period of the reign of each king of the Solanki dynasty.

The copper plate mentioned in Appendix D was engraved during the life time of Bhim-Dev II, and thus naturally supplies no information as to that king's successor. Mr. Forbes mentions A. D. 1215 as the year in which Bhim-Dev died. But this is contradicted by himself when he mentions that king as the contemporary of a certain Abu Chief in A. D. 1231. In the foot-note given on page 34 of Sir Edward Clive Bayley's History of Gujarát, Bhim-Dev is said to have reigned from 1178 to 1241 A. D., which period nearly corresponds with a statement in Mr. Mahipatram's "Short vernacular History of

Gujarat" where A. D. 1242/43* is given as the year of the close of Bhim's reign. The latter author states that Bhim-Dev was succeeded on the throne by Tribhowan-Pál who reigned from 1242 to 1244, and also mentions that in A. D. 1224 a Solanki chief named Jayant-Singh had taken Anhilwár, but that Bhim expelled him four years later.

If, then, we consider Bhim-Dev II. to have vacated the throne in A. D. 1215, the period of the Solanki dynasty reaches to 273 years, but if, on the other hand, it extends to the further limit, A. D. 1244, the Solanki dynasty must have lasted for 302 years (A. D. 942—1244).

* This year appears more reliable as an inscription dated Vikram Samwat 1290 (A. D. 1234) on the Mahá-Dev temple at Miáni mentions Bhim-Dev as the then reigning king. See Bhavnagar Prachin Shodh Sangrah by Mr. Vajeshankar Gavrishankar Ozá.

Chapter VII.

Vághelá dynasty.

From 1244 to 1295 A. D.

Whatever may be the correct date of the close of the Solanki rule in Gujarát, it is certain that, after the defeat of Bhim-Dev II. by Shiháb-ud-din Ghori, several of his tributaries and vassals took the opportunity of Bhim's weakened condition to revolt and shake of his yoke. This greatly affected his dominion and power though the sovereign title continued until the final usurpation of the capital by the Vághelás.

These were the most powerful of the Gujarát chieftains. Their ancestor Lavan Prasád had been minister of Bhim-Dev II., with whom he was also distantly connected, his grand-mother being the sister of Rájá Kumár-Pál's mother. He had received Vághel as the reward of his services, and seems to have possessed along with it the town of Dhawal-gadh (Dholká). In the days of Bhim's decline differences arose between him and Lavan Prasád, when the latter, it appears, rebelled and seized the parganás of Dholká and Dhandaká, and also the country between the Sábar and the Narbadá rivers. Lavan Prasád fixed on Dholká as his place of residence. He had an ambitious son, named Vir Dhawal, who extended his territory by annexing to it Cambay and Godhrá, whereby his importance was so greatly increased that some consider him as the first Vághelá king though he was not formally installed as such. His ministers Vastu-Pál and Tej-Pál, Porvál Vániás, founded in A.D. 1231 the most magnificent temples of Dilwárá, in which they placed an inscription describing their services and the confidence Vir Dhaval placed in them. In one of these temples Vir Dhaval is described as "Mahá Mandaleshwar" and "Ráná", but not as Rájádhiráj.

In connexion with Cambay, it would perhaps not be amiss here to mention that that city and its surrounding district appear generally to have been subordinate to the Anhilwár kings. The rule of one Kaliánrái, a Dasá Lád Vániá, deserves however a passing notice. It appears that some of the Pársis who had settled at Sanján were attracted to Cambay between 942—997 A. D., in consequence of its flourishing trade, and these in time became so numerous and important a class that they were able to compel the Hindu inhabitants to remove from Cambay. The Pársis thus remained in possession of the town for some time. Kaliánrái, one of the exiles, however, by trading in pearls in Surat, or more prabably Sauráshtra, amassed a large fortune which enabled him to obtain the assistance of a number of Rajputs and Kolis, who attacked the Pársis at night, and, putting most of them to the sword, burnt their houses. Kaliánrái then seems to have assumed the government himself and to have ruled with moderation. He increased the prosperity of the town very much by fostering trade, and is said to have built the town-wall with its seven gates and sally-ports, the Madulá tank and other buildings. The period during which this took place is not mentioned in Captain Robertson's Report, No. XXVI of Selections from the Records of the Bombay Government (new series), but it seems likely that the events here mentioned occured during the decline of the Solanki dynasty, and Vir Dhaval may have been the chief of the Rajputs and Kolis with whose assistance Kaliánrái drove away the Pársis from Cambay. In the Mirát-i-Ahmadi (Bird's translation, page 366) mention is however made of Sayyid-ud-daulat, a servant of Kaliánrái, having collected troops and seized Cambay during the confusion which followed the revolt of Muzaffar III. (A. D. 1583). If this be correct, the period of Kaliánrái's enterprise falls in the sixteenth century.

Vir Dhaval's son, Visal-Dév, succeeded him at Dholká on his death in A. D. 1242. He is said to have made an expedition against Anhilwár Pátan in A. D. 1244, and annexed it to his dominions.* He has, therefore, been considered as the first king of the Vághelá dynasty. He further assumed the title of Rájádhiráj after expelling the last Solanki King Tribhowan-Pál.

Visal-Dev was, indeed, the most illustrious king of the Vághelá dynasty. He successfully carried on a war against the King of Málwá, laid that country waste and made its ruler pay him tribute. He was a widely known patron of learning, and many poets besides the celebrated Nának-bhat, the court poet, flourished in his time. Performing a 'Yájná' (sacrifice) at Darbhávati (Dabhoi) the place of his birth, he formed† the following branches of the Nágars. Visalnagrá, Shatpadrá(Sathodra), Krishnapura (Krishorá), Chitrapuras (Chitrodas) and Prasnikás (Prasnorá) and built beautiful Brahm-Polls for them. During Visal-Dev's reign there was a severe famine, the evil effects of which he did his best to alleviate. He also repaired the town-wall of Visalnagar and the fort of Dabhoi.

Visal-Dev was succeeded on his death in A. D. 1262 by his son Arjun-Dev whose name occurs in an inscription,‡ dated A.D. 1264 in the temple of Somnáth at Dév-Pátan (Virával). Strange to say, this king is stated to have had two Muhammadan officers under him, by name Hormazd of Belakol (probably a Persian convert) and Khojá Ibráhim Nákhodá. The former is said to have built a mosque at Virával.

Arjun-Dev appears to have been suceeeded on his death in A. D. 1275 by Sárang-Dev who is mentioned in an inscription at Abu as the king of Anhilwár in A. D. 1294. His successor was Karan Rájá known by the surname Ghelo (mad), in whose time the Muhammadans finally annihilated Hindu rule in Anhilwár. The events leading up to this result will be related in the following Chapter.

---

* Vide Mahipatram's Short History of Gujarát, page 19.

† Indian Antiquary, Vol. XI, pages 98–108.

‡ See No. 106 of Bhávnagar Shodh Sangrah.

Chapter VIII.

Closing years of the Vághelá dynasty.

From 1295 to 1307 A. D.

For a long time subsequent to the defeat of Prithvi-Ráj of Delhi and the seizure of his kingdom by Shiháb-ud-din Ghori, the attention of the conqueror and his successors was engaged in consolidating and extending their power to the north and east. Gujarát consequently remained undisturbed. Indeed we find it mentioned by the great historian Ferishtá that, fifty years after the death of the celebrated Bhim-Dev, Ghiyas-ud-din the emperor of Delhi was advised by his ministers to undertake an expedition against Gujarát and Málwá, which had been annexed to the empire by Kutb-ud-din, but which had since shaken off the Muhammadan yoke. At that time however there was some fear of the Mughal Tátárs invading India from the north and this prevented Ghiyas-ud-din from turning his attention to Gujarát.

In A. D. 1295, Alá-ud-din Khilji ascended the throne of Delhi after treacherously murdering his uncle Jalál-ud-din. In 1297 he sent a large army under his brother Alaf-Khán and a general named Nasrut-Khan Jálesri to re-conquer Gujarát. Plundering and laying waste the country, the army appeared before Anhilwár, where Rájá Karan gave them battle. Being however defeated, he fled to Dev-Gadh in the Deccan. His treasure, elephants, baggage and even his wife named Kaulá-Devi, all fell into the hands of the victor. After this, Cambay, Somnáth and Siddhpur were successively plundered, and the idols in the last two places were mutilated. The treasure and jewels were sent to Delhi together with the captured queen Kaulá-Devi. She was admitted into the emperor's harem, and soon became, by reason of her great beauty and accomplishments his favourite queen.

Though Anhilwár and the neighbouring districts had thus fallen into the hands of the Muhammadans, still not all the country was subdued, and through the support of the Rájá of Devgadh the unfortunate Karan was able to hold out in the passes at the south-eastern corner of Gujarát. In A. D. 1307 Alá-ud-din sent another army to conquer the Deccan under one Káfur, a slave who had been captured at Cambay during its sack in A. D. 1297 but who had since been raised to high rank. It was at this time that the ill-fated Karan Rájá's further misfortunes began through the selfish devices of his own wife Kaulá-Devi. She represented to Alá-ud-din that she had two daughters by her former husband, that the elder girl had died, but that the younger, named Dewal-Devi, who was only four years of age when separated from her, was still living. Kaulá-Devi therefore begged of the emperor to obtain her, in order that she might have the satisfaction of again meeting her child. In compliance with this request, the emperor commanded Káfur to obtain Dewal-Devi, and to send her to Delhi with every mark of respect. Alaf-Khán the Governor of Gujarát also received orders to co-operate with Káfur. The latter encamped at Sultánpur, and sent orders to Karan Rájá, in his retirement in Bagláná, to deliver up Dewal-Devi. Karan Rájá however would not submit to such a dishonour, and accordingly refused to obey the order. Káfur then marched towards the Deccan, and the difficult task of obtaining Deval-Devi alive fell to Alaf-Khán. He accordingly led his army through the mountains of Bagláná, but Karan opposed him, and, fighting desperately for two months, foiled him in all his attempts to force a passage. In the meantime in the hope of inducing the Muhammadans to despair of obtaining Dewal-Devi, Karan Rájá readily consented to her marriage with the Hindu Prince of Devgadh, though under ordinary circumstances this match would not have been considered desirable. While the princess was being taken to that fort, a party of Alaf-Khán's soldiers, who had set off to explore the wonders of Ellora, accidentally met some Devgadh horsemen, and a skirmish ensued, in which the horse that carried Deval-Devi was wounded by an arrow, and the princess fell to the ground. A blow from one of the enemy's soldiers would have saved the honour of the Vághelá family, but the cries of Deval-Devi's female attendants caused them to recognise the prostrate figure, and they gladly took her off to Alaf-Khán. The latter knew well the influence which Kaulá-Devi exercised over the emperor, and, therefore, treating the princess with due respect, he took her to Delhi, where she soon found herself in the arms of her fond mother. In time Khizar-Khán, the eldest son of Alá-ud-din, became enamoured of Deval-Devi, and to him she was married under the name of Dával-Ráni. So tender was the love between them that it was made the subject of a long but beautiful Persian poem, Ashaki Báhár, composed by Amir Khushro.

After his final misfortune and disgrace nothing further is known of the unfortunate Karan Rájá, the last of the Hindu kings of Gujarát. It is probable, however, that he died of a broken heart.

Thus ended the reign of the last Vághelá king of Gujarát after the Hindu kingdom had existed for several centuries. Many of its kings may for bravery and enterprise take rank with the noblest sovereigns of their day; and the foregoing pages have but indicated some of their exploits and foreign conquests. The sway of Gujarát, during the period of its prosperity, extended to the neighbourhood of Jhálor beyond Mount Abu. It included Kachh as well as parts of the Deccan, and at one time even Málwá was a dependency of the Gujarát monarchs. Sindh also was subdued. In the midst of all the frequent wars, measures conducive to the prosperity of the inhabitants had not been neglected. It has been truly stated by the author of the Rás Málá, in appreciating the labours of the Gujarát kings, that their greatest monument is to be seen in the fact that when they took possession of the country they found it a waste, yet left it a land "flowing with milk and honey". When Van-Ráj first established himself at Pátan, large tracts of Gujarát had no other population than that of the wild aboriginal tribes, whereas, under his illustrious successors of the Chávadá and Solanki dynasties, the country soon became studded with wealthy towns and adorned with populous cities. Nor were architectural buildings and works of public utility neglected. Of this we have ample evidence in the noble shrines on Mount Abu and other places, and in the large reservoirs and wells with flights of steps, constructed in several parts of the province. It is further a matter of consolation that though the Hindus have ceased to reign as monarchs, some* of the subordinate branches of the original dynasties still continue, and, under the fostering control of the paramount British Government, enjoy their possessions in peace and prosperity.

It may not be out of place, before concluding the account of the Hindu period embraced in the foregoing pages, briefly to mention that the internal condition of the people of Gujarát, including Saurásbtra, appears, on the whole, to have been prosperous. At the time of Houen Tsiang's visit to India in the beginning of the seventh century, the inhabitants of the capital

---

* The Rájás of Lunáwádá claim descent from the Solanki kings of Anhilwár. The Thákors of Mánsá and Varsodá are said to be descended from the Chávadá Kings, and the Thákors of Pethápur, Limbodrá, Koth and Gángad from the Vághelá Kings, of Anhilwár. Bápá, the ninth in descent from the last Siláditya, is known as the founder of the present Mewár dynasty.

Valabhipur carried on a brisk maritime trade, as the province possessed several beautiful and important ports which still exist. It is said that immense treasure was accumulated by trade with foreign countries, and that there were at the capital no less than a hundred families with fortunes of one krore of rupees (one million of pounds). During the reign of the Solankis the prosperity of the country seems to have reached its culminating point.

The prevailing religions appear to have been Buddhism, Bráhmanism and Jainism, but except in the time of some intolerant prince, there does not seem to have been much religious persecution; and we find from an inscription of the first century before Christ in the cave at Násik that Usává-dátá, the son-in-law and vassal of the first Kshatrapa king Nahapána, though a Buddhist, made presents of villages and cows to Bráhmans, and defrayed the marriage expenses of their daughters. After this when we come to the time of the last Siláditya* (about the seventh century) we find that his twin-sister, who was married to the king of Broach, took the ascetic vow after her husband's demise, and her son Mul did the same. In reply to her son's enquiry as to whether Jainism had always been at the same low ebb in which he found it, the mother told him that it had once extended to every town of Gujarát, but that after the death of the famous religious preceptor Vir Surrendra, the Buddhists obtained the ascendancy. Mul accordingly proceeded to his maternal uncle Siláditya's court, and, defeating the Buddhists by his eloquence, obliged

* This Siláditya is said to have been the offspring of Surya Náráyan (the sun-god), and to have been provided by the latter with certain pebbles, by which he was enabled to kill his companions who jeered at him on account of his mysterious birth, and also to kill the king of Valabhipur and usurp his kingdom. See Rás Málá, Page 10.

them to quit Valabhipur, where Jainism again attained its ascendancy. We also find king Siddh-Ráj listening to Jain monks, and Kumár-Pál even adopted that religion under his preceptor Hemáchárya.

As regards Education it does not appear that there were any schools supported by the State for the primary education of the masses, who learnt merely to read and write in indigenous schools kept by Bráhmans. But it has been recorded that schools existed for imparting a knowledge of religion, poetry, and Sanskrit Grammar. These latter were kept up by learned pandits and monks, who were, no doubt, largely patronised by the Rájás who gave them grants of "Varsháshan" (annual allowances) or of lands, but the allowances were probably personal to the pandits, and do not appear to have involved any obligation to teach others. The undermentioned were some of the chief literary characters of the early period in Gujarát.

I. Hemáchárya, the author of Dayáshraya and of Sanskrit and Prákrit Grammars, who, as the religious preceptor of king Kumár-Pál, was the most conspicuous figure of his time.

II. Lakshmi Tilak Kavi, who made a commentary on Hemáchárya's work.

III. Lakshman, the author of the Ratna Málá, who flourished about the time of Bhim-Dev II.

IV. Merutang Achárya, a monk of the Jain convent at Wadhwán, and the author of the Prabandh Chintámani.

V. Shri Gunchandra Achárya, the author of a similar work.

VI. Nának-Bhat, the court-poet of King Visaldev Vághelá.

The system of collecting revenue from cultivators appears to have been the Bhágvatai, under which the Crown received a share of the produce from each cultivator through paid village "Mantris" (accountants) and in some cases through superior land-holders. In addition to land revenue, there were other sources of revenue, such as town and transit duties and "Verás" (taxes). A tax on pilgrims appears also to have existed. The village head-men were the Patels as at present.

PART II.

MUHAMMADAN PERIOD.

FROM 1297 to 1572 A. D.

CHAPTER I.

Viceroys from Delhi.

FROM 1297 to 1407 A. D.

The conquest of Gujarát and the final overthrow of Karan Vághelá have already been narrated. Subsequent to this the governors of the province were appointed by the emperor of Delhi. Alaf-Khán was the first nobleman honoured with this post, which he held for twenty years, ruling with prudence. He built the Friday mosque of white marble at Anhilwár (Pátan). It was then in the centre of the city, but, owing to the subsequent transfer of the capital to Ahmadábád and consequent decline of the population of the former town, the mosque is now isolated from the inhabited portion of the city. It is a magnificent building with pillars so numerous that in the mere counting of them one may easily make a mistake.

At the end of 20 years of good service and efficient management of the province, Alaf-Khán was recalled to Delhi on a false accusation of conspiring against the life of the king, which charge was brought against him and the heir-apparent Khizar-Khán through the intrigues of the slave Malek Káfur who had now risen to the rank of Minister. Alaf-Khán was unjustly put to death, and Khizar-Khán was confined in the fortress of Gwálior.

Soon after this act of injustice, Alá-ud-din's career was cut short by dropsy, to which he succumbed on the 19th of December 1316.

Malek Káfur, ignoring the right of Khizar-Khán and his

younger brother, placed a young boy, named Shiháb-ud-din Umar Khilji, on the throne, and deprived the unfortunate Khizar-Khán of his sight. The nobles, intensely disgusted with these cruel proceedings and with his gross abuse of authority, were able to effict Malek Káfur's death after his nominee had reigned for 45 days only. They then placed on the throne Alá-ud-din's younger son Kutb-ud-din Mubárik Sháh.

Meanwhile Gujarát had become a scene of great disorder after Alaf-Khán's recall to Delhi, and rebellions had broken out in every direction. Sultán Kutb-ud-din was therefore obliged, in the very beginning of his reign, to send a force under general Malek Kamál-ud-din to quell the disturbances, but the Malek was slain in action shortly after his departure from Delhi, and one Ainul Mulk Multáni was deputed as his successor. This officer, with the assistance of the army placed at his disposal, was able eventually to restore order in the province (A. D. 1318).

After this the sultán sent his father-in-law Malek Dinár with the title of Jáfar-Khán as Governor of Gujarát, who, within the space of about four months, completely settled the province and sent large sums of money to the royal treasury. However he too, like Alaf-Khán, fell a victim to the intrigues of those near the king, and being recalled was put to death on a false charge. One Khushro-Khán at this time enjoyed the king's confidence, and his brother Hisám-ud-din was sent as Governor of Gujarát. Both the brothers were originally Parmár Rajputs, and accordingly the Hindu chiefs, promising their assistance, incited him to rebel, but the plot was discovered in time by the Muhammadan commanders, who, after arresting Hisám-ud-din, sent him back to Delhi. Malek Vaji-ud-din Khoreshi, described as a brave and active officer, was then sent to Gujarát, and during his tenure of office the country enjoyed peace. In time he was rewarded with the title of Táj-ul-mulk and recalled to Delhi.

Khushro Khán the king's minister was then appointed to the Government of Gujarát. He however was not satisfied with this post, and, collecting his retainers around him, rebelled, and put the Sultán, his benefactor, to death (A. D. 1320). He then usurped the Government of Delhi, assuming the title of Násir-ud-din. His reign lasted for about four months, when a noble named Gházibeg Tughlak, indignant at his flagrant crime, collected an army and made him a prisoner. He afterwards gave orders that Násir-ud-din's body should be cut to pieces and sent to the capital.

There was now no survivor of Alá-ud-din's family, and accordingly the nobles elevated to the throne this Ghásibeg, who assumed the sovereignty under the title of Ghiyás-ud-din Tughlak Sháh (A. D. 1321).

Gujarát being still in a disorderly condition, the new Sultán appointed one Táj-ul-mulk to be the Governor of that province with instructions to bring the country into complete subjection. Sultán Ghiyás-ud-din was, however, killed in the fourth year of his government by the falling of the roof of a summer-house. He was succeeded by his son Sultán Muhammad Tughlak in A. D. 1325. In his reign Malek Mukbil, the son of a celebrated musician, held the Government of Gujarát under the title of Khán Jahán. While he was marching to Delhi by way of Baroda and Dabhoi with treasure and horses, certain Mughal chiefs plundered him and obliged him to flee to Anhilwár. The Sultán, on hearing this, marched to Gujarát with an army to avenge the insult. His stay in the country was protracted to two years, during which he attempted, though it appears without success, to capture the strong fort of Junágadh. He however met with better fortune elsewhere. Mokheráji, the chief of Piram, an island near Goghá, took that town from its Musalmán Kasbáti. The Emperor accordingly sent an army against Mokheráji. This chief made a bold defence, but was at last slain, and the fort of Piram was destroyed (A. D. 1347). After the withdrawal of the imperial army, Mokeráji's son Dungarji succeeded in repossessing himself of Goghá, and his younger brother, Sámarsinghji fled to Rájpiplá to his maternal grandfather, Chok Ráná*, whom he eventually succeeded.

It is interesting to note that the Mokheráji here mentioned is the ancestor of the present Mahárájá of Bhávnagar. His grandfather Sejakji claims descent from Sáliváhan (A. D. 78). Sejakji was driven into Káthiáwár by the Ráthods from his ancestral seat at Kherghad on the Luni in Márwár (A. D. 1260–1290). He had given his daughter Wálam Kunvarbá in marriage to the son of the then Ráv of Junágadh named Kawád. The Ráv treated Sejakji kindly and granted him Sháhpur and twelve villages. Sejakji built a new town on the lands of Sháhpur and calling it by his own name made it his capital, whence he conquered some more villages, which he annexed to his territory. He was succeeded by his son Ránáji (A. D. 1290–1309), who, strengthening Sejakpur with a fort, changed its name to Ránpur. Ránáji's son the Mokheráji above mentioned extended the power of his clan and moved southwards (A.D. 1309) taking Bhimrád, Umrálá, Khokhrá and the island of Piram which last was then in the possession of a Báriá Koli chief. He further attacked Goghá, but this venture drew on him the expedition of Muhammad Tughlak referred to above.

On Muhammad Tughlak's death in A. D. 1351, his nephew Sultán Firuz Sháh was crowned king of Delhi on the 24th of March 1351. After attending to more urgent affairs of state and

* Chok Ráná was the son of Saidamat king of Ujjáin. He quarreled with his father and settled at Juná (old) Rájpiplá.

conquering Nagarkot, he visited Gujarát in A. D. 1361, when he displaced Nizám-ul-Mulk and appointed one Jáfar Khán to the government. This officer died in A. D. 1371, and his elder son Dariá Khán was nominated to succeed him, but Shams-ud-din Dangháni having offered to give the Sultán 40 lacs of Tankahs*, one hundred elephants, twentytwo hundred Arab horses and fourhundred slaves over and above the usual collection received from Gujarát, the Sultán's choice eventually fell on him.

Shams-ud-din was however unable to fulfil his agreement and went into rebellion in which he was slain. One Malek Muzaffar was then appointed Governor, and subsequently obtained the title of Rásti Khán (A. D. 1387).

The last named officer's administration was, however, felt to be so tyrannical that the inhabitants of Cambay complained to the Emperor who, in the month of February 1391 A. D., sent Jáfar Khán with the title of Azim Humáyun to depose the existing Governor. Jáfar Khán accordingly proceeded to Pátan and sent the Sultán's order to Rásti Khán, but the latter would not submit. A battle took place near the village of Kambbu in the Pátan district between Rásti Khán and the imperial troops, in which the former was defeated and slain (A. D. 1391). At the place of the victory, a village, named Jitpur, was founded by the victorious viceroy. He then returned to Pátan, redressed

---

* The value of a Tankah is variously estimated. If a silver Tankah it must have been about ½ of a rupee.

As regards the copper Tankahs, the Mirát-i-Ahmadi says there were a hundred Tankahs to the rupee in the time of Mahmud Begadá. In another place, in or about A. D. 1512, the value of a copper Tankah has been given at two pice or half an anna. Stanley Lane—Poole in his recently published life of Aurangzeb, "Rulers of India Series", states, "The fiscal unit of the native returns is the dám, and forty dáms went to the rupee" (p. 121) and further "the terms Dám and Tankah are interchangeable, as is proved by the inscriptions on the coins themselves" (p. 156).

the grievances of the Cambay people and of others whom the late Rásti Khán had oppressed, and by his conciliatory and firm behaviour established his authority througout the province.

Jáfar Khán's father Sáhárán and uncle Sádhu belonged to the family of Tánk Rájput chieftains then holding Thásrá in the Kairá district. Here prince Firuz Tughlak, one day happened to come, having lost his way while on a hunting excursion. The two brothers, though unaware of his princely rank, treated him most hospitably. While staying with them, the prince was charmed by the beauty of their sister, whom they readily gave in marriage to their guest after learning who he really was. Firuz took them with him to Delhi, where he induced them to embrace the faith of Islám, and in A. D. 1351 on his accession to the throne he conferred on Sáhárán the title of Vaji-ul-mulk and on Sádhu that of Samsher Khán. They subsequently rose to high eminence, and Vaji-ul-mulk's son Jáfar Khán was eventually granted, as above mentioned, the vice royalty of Gujarát with the title of Azim Humáyun.

Jáfar Khán, after having spent some time in settling the country, led a warlike expedition in A. D. 1393 against the Ráthod chief of Idar*, who had refused to pay the customary tribute. After enforcing his demand on Idar, Jáfar Khán met Adil Khán Asiri of Burhánpur, who had invaded Gujarát, and compelled him to retire. He then marched against Junágadh and exacted tribute from the Ráv (A. D. 1394). His next expedition was against Somnáth, and destroying the temples there, he introduced the Muhammadan faith into that intensely Hindu

---

* Idar, formerly known as Ildrug, is a very ancient town and is said to have been in the Dvápur Yug, or third age, the residence of Elvan the Rákhshas and his brother Vatápi. It has, except during short intervals, always been under Hindu chiefs of one dynasty or another. The present Mahá Rájá Sir Kesrisinghji Javánsinghji K.C.S.I., is a descendant of the celebrated Jodhpur family. See Bombay Gazetteer Vol. V. page 446.

district. After making further raids on other smaller towns, he returned to Pátan in A. D. 1397.

The affairs of the Delhi empire had, in the meantime, become involved in utter confusion, and its authority was well-nigh shattered owing to the imbecility and follies of successive emperors. In the short space of the 96 years during which the Tughlak dynasty lasted there were no less than six kings notorious alike for tyranny and folly. Rebellion after rebellion took place, troops mutinied and the governors of Bengal, Oudh and other places declared themselves independent. A succession of disasters overtook the kingdom, the last and most serious of which was the invasion of India by Timur (Tamerlane), the terrible and ruthless Mughal chief, who, after conquering Persia and Transoxiana, and after ravaging Tartary and portions of Russia, led his wild troops against India, already distracted by internal dissensions. He defeated the imperial troops before Delhi on the 17th of December 1398, and the city surrendered on promise of protection. It was, however, none the less mercilessly pillaged during five days, after which Timur gave orders to his army to return into Central Asia. Muhammad Tughlak, then emperor of Delhi, had fled for safety to Gujarát and thence to Málwá, but he eventually succeeded in regaining possession of the capital after the death of Ekbál Khán, who on Timur's departure had assumed sovereignty over Delhi and other adjacent districts (A. D. 1400).

Shortly before the invasion by Timur, Tátár Khán, the son of Jáfar Khán and governor of Pánipat, was defeated by Ekbál Khán, and had to flee to Gujarát to seek his father's protection. He strongly urged the latter, after Timur had withdrawn, to march on Delhi in order to expel Ekbál Khán and assert his own claim to the throne, but Jáfar Khán, having clearer foresight, refused to follow his advice. This led to much wrangling, and Jáfar Khán either resigned his power to his ambitious son or was compelled to yield to him, and forthwith Tátár Khán, assuming the name of Muhammad Sháh, proclaimed himself king of Gujarát. He fixed his capital at Asáwal, and after subduing the chief of Nándod (Rájpiplá) marched against Delhi to revenge himself on Ekbál Khán, who, on hearing of his approach, became greatly alarmed. But Tátár Khán fell ill on the road, and before reaching Delhi died in the month of Shabán A. H. 806 (A. D. 1403). His dead body was taken back to Pátan, where it was interred with due honours. Tátár Khán's death is attributed by some to a slow poison administered by one of his father's friends, but the early historians state that Jáfar Khán mourned for his son until the day of his own death.

On receiving the sad tidings, Jáfar Khán at once joined the camp, where, being welcomed by the army, he resumed the government of Gujarát. The disorders at Delhi continued to increase and, accordingly, after the lapse of some six years, Jáfar Khán, who out of respect for the throne of Delhi had hitherto refused to call himself king, assumed that title in A. D. 1407/8 at the request of his nobles, and, taking the name Muzaffar Sháh, struck coins in his own right. Thus was established the separate Muhammadan kingdom of Gujarát, which lasted until A. D. 1573, when the great Akbar conquered it and reannexed it to the empire of Delhi.

CHAPTER II.

The reign of Sultán Muzaffar I.

FROM 1407 to 1410 A. D.

Some of Muzaffar Sháh's exploits while he was yet vice-regent in Gujarát have been already mentioned. After formally assuming the title of king, he learnt that Diláwar Khán, the vice-regent at Málwá, with whom he had been very intimate when both were at Delhi, had been poisoned by his son Alp Khán. Accordihgly he marched against that country with the object of chastising the ungrateful son. The latter opposed him, but was defeated and taken prisoner (A. D. 1407/8). Muzaffar Sháh then himself appointed a governor over Málwá, and kept Alp Khán in confinement for upwards of a year, but eventually pardoned and reinstated him in his dominions. To do this, however, it became necessary to send an army under the command of the Sultán's grandson Ahmad Khán, inasmuch as one of the Málwá chiefs, named Musá Khán, had grown sufficiently powerful to gain possession of the capital Mándu. Muzaffar Sháh then sent an army against the Hindus of Kanth-Kot in Kachh and subdued them (A. D. 1409/10).

At the end of the month of Safar, A. H. 813, A. D. 1410, the Kolis of Asával and its vicinity, having become disobedient, commenced plundering on the highways. Muzaffar Sháh, therefore, sent an army against them under his grandson Ahmad Khán. This young prince, who had already gained renown in the expedition against Málwá, encamped at the Khán Sarovar (lake) outside Pátan. Here he summoned an assembly of men noted for piety and learning, and questioned them as to whether the son of a man who had been unjustly murdered ought or ought not to exact retribution. Not understanding the real object of the prince in putting this question, all replied in the affirmative.

Ahmad Khán then took their written reply and kept it with him. The next day he went into the city, made Muzaffar Sháh prisoner, and gave him a cup of poison to drink. The old man, much struck by this conduct of his grand son whom since the death of Tátár Khán he had nominated his successor, and to whom he had given a princely training, addressed him as follows: "My child, all that I have is but in keeping for you, why such unseemly haste for your inheritance?" These gentle words seem to have had no effect on the heart of the young man, who, believing, whether rightly or wrongly, that his father had been murdered, was burning with a desire for vengeance. He accordingly replied "All men have their time appointed, and when the hour is come they cannot delay or advance it a moment". Muzaffar Sháh, after counselling him on various topics, and after cautioning him against indulgence in wine, raised to his own lips and drained the bitter cup of death. The founder of the Muhammadan Sultánat of Gujarát thus departed from this world (A. D. 1410) after a just and wise reign of eighteen years, eight months and fourteen days, in which period is included the term of his vice-regency. His remains were buried in the mausoleum erected in the centre of Pátan.

Chapter III.

The reign of Sultán Ahmad I.

From 1410 to 1441 A. D.

Ahmad Khán ascended the throne of Gujarát on the 14th of Ramzán A. H. 813, (A. D. 1410), under the title of Sultán Ahmad Násir-ud-din. About that time his cousin Moid-ud-din, Governor of Baroda*, having gained over some of the chieftains of that district to his interest, excited a rebellion, and accordingly an army was sent against the insurgents. Dissensions soon broke out among them, and Moid-ud-din went away to Cambay, where he was joined by Ahmad Sháh's uncle Masti Khán, Governor of Surat. The Sultán himself therefore marched against them, whereupon they fled to Broach, but were pursued thither by the Sultán, who proceeded to besiege the town. Here the army of Moid-ud-din, and also that of Masti Khán, surrendered to the Sultán. The monarch, after having sent for Moid-ud-din, generously forgave him, and returned victorious to Ahmadábád.

It was on his march back from this expedition that Ahmad Sháh, at the suggestion of his spiritual adviser Shekh Ahmad Khattu Ganj-Bakhsh, originally a native of Khattu near Nágor, who had settled at Sarkhej, determined to found the city of Ahmadábád and make it his capital. Before doing so, however, the Sultán had to defeat and extirpate the followers of a famous chieftain, named Asá Bhil, who infested the neighbourhood. Having cleared the country of robbers and highwaymen,

---

* Baroda is now the seat of the Gáekwád Government. The original name of this ancient city was Chandanávati, the city of sandal-wood. Subsequently it received the name of Varávati (the abode of warriors), and still later that of Vat-patra (Leaf of the Vad)—Anglicé Baroda—from some fancied resemblance to the leaf of the banian tree.

Bombay Gazetteer Vol. VII. page 529.

Sultán Ahmad carried out his arrangements about the founding of the city. In this he was assisted by three other Ahmads, by name Shekh Ahmad Khattu Ganj-Bakhsh, Kázi Ahmad and Malek Ahmad, who, as well as the Sultán, superintended each division aided by twelve persons, called Báwás* or Bábás (A. H. 814, A. D. 1411-12). For his new capital, Sultán Ahmad built a citadel of much strength and beauty, which is known by the name of the Bhadar (propitious), and which is still the quarter where the Government offices are located. A fine mosque, called after Ahmad Sháh, was also built and appears to have been set apart as a chapel for the Royal family. He further erected a palace and other magnificent buildings. Though these do not now exist in their entirety, portions of them have been thoroughly repaired and are now used as public buildings. For the city itself the Sultán laid out fine broad streets and caused noble edifices to be constructed, the marble and stones for which were brought from Pátan, Chandrávati, Dhrángadhrá and other places. With a view to secure an adequate supply of water for the inhabitants, the Sultán diverted the course of the river Háthmati so as to make its waters flow into the Sábarmati. He also built in the heart of the city a superb Jumá (Friday) Mosque, which is one of the largest in India, the exterior dimensions being 382 feet by 238 feet with a height of 49 feet. The minarets were originally of a great height but portions of them fell down during the severe earthquake of A. D. 1819. A

Finished in A. H. 820. A. D. 1417.

Completed in A. H. 817, A. D. 1414.

Commenced in A. H. 815. A. D. 1412. Completed A. H. 827, A. D. 1423.

* These Báwás must not be confounded with Hindu ascetics. They were Muhammadan holy personages, such as Báwá Ali Sher, whose mosque is at Sarkhej, and Báwá Lului who is buried in the mausoleum near the Rushi ford on the eastern bank of the Sábarmati near the city.

strange architectural phenomenon was noticeable in these minarets, which has been described in some detail by Colonel Monier Williams who visited the mosque on the 31st May 1809.

> "We found on examination today that the minarets of the Jumá Masjid shook just as much, or even more than any of the others, and that one communicated the motion to the other fully to as great a degree as those of the Bibi Sáhebs. Indeed, we tried the experiment upon every perfect pair of stone minarates within and about the town to-day, and the effect was just the same with them all.
>
> "As the motion that one of the minarets receives from the shaking of the other might be supposed to be communicated to the whole intermediate building, I lay down on the terraced roof, equidistant between the two minarets, while people above were shaking them; but I was not sensible of the smallest motion or agitation whatever in the building under me."
>
> (Quoted in Grindlay's "Costume and Architecture of India", page 6).

Sultán Ahmad gathered merchants, weavers and skilled craftsmen from many different places and settled them advantageously in the new city, giving them every encouragement. By bestowing much attention and sparing no expense on the city, he made it a centre of trade and manufacture, which it continues to be upto the present day.

Popular tradition has an amusing story of a certain difficulty encountered by the Sultán in erecting the town-walls. It is said that a saint named Máneknáth Godariá lived in a shed near the river, who, with a view to thwart the Sultán in his attempt to found the new city, used to busy himself in stitching threads in a quilt during the daytime while the work of building the ramparts was progressing, but each evening, after all the workmen had dispersed to their several homes, Máneknáth used to unravel the threads from the quilt, when lo! all the portions of the wall built during the daytime would crumble to the ground. The Sultán was extremely annoyed by this repeated misfortune, and on making enquiries learnt that the saint possessed magical powers, so he sent for Máneknáth, and asked him what further wonders he was able to perform. He replied that he could enter a *badná* (a vessel shaped like a teapot) and come out through its spout. The Sultán asked him to satisfy his doubts by doing this. Máneknáth immediately entered the vessel, but before he could ever issue from its spout the Sultán covered it with his finger, and thus effectually prevented Máneknáth's exit. Máneknáth exclaimed, "Oh king, you have committed treachery." The king replied "You do not like good work, and are by magic hindering us in building the city, so treachery must be met by treachery." Having spoken thus, he refused to allow him to come out, and Máneknáth was smothered to death. Before death, however, he begged the Sultán to do him the favour of immortalizing his name by connecting it in some way with the city. The king was pleased with this request, and complied. Hence the south-western tower of the Bhadar, which is supposed to contain the foundation stone of the city, is called, even at the present day, the Mánek Buruj, and the square in which the chief market is held is known as the Mánek Chok. The saint's tomb or small pagoda (Dehri) is still to be seen in a corner of the square, and an annual allowance of five Rupees is still paid by Government to its custodian.

That Máneknáth actually possessed such supernatural powers as are ascribed to him by tradition is certainly beyond belief, but inasmuch as his name is so intimately connected with the city, and the tradition is still in vogue, some mention of it has seemed desirable. Tradition further supplies two reasons for the founding of the city at the place on which it stands. The first, and perhaps the most powerful, was the king's love for Asá Bhil's daughter. The second was his admiration of the courage displayed by a hare which, while the king was hunting on this spot, fiercely attacked his hounds. This has given rise to the popular saying :—

"જબ કુત્તેપર સસા આયા, તબ બાદશાહને શહેર બસાયા."

"When a hare attacked a dog, the king founded the city."

The city of Ahmadábád contains an area of upwards of two square miles, and is surrounded with a semi-circular wall of about five miles in circumference, and has, besides, numerous suburbs. The population, according to the census taken in February 1891, is 1,48,412 souls*.

In A. H. 814 (A. D. 1411–12), while Ahmad Sháh's attention was engaged with the founding of his great city, his cousin Moid-ud-din's cupidity was again excited, and entering into conspiracy with several chiefs, amongst whom were Ran-Mal, Rájá of Idar, and his uncle Masti Khan, governor of Surat, he again revolted. They gained over the officer who had charge of the fort of Modásá, and encamped at Rangpur, a village 5 kos (about 7½ miles) distant from that fort, belonging to Ran-Mal Rájá. The Sultán marched against them and besieged Modásá, which he took by

---

* There is no reliable record of the population of the city before it came under British rule. Some idea of the large increase of population during the last 75 years may be formed from the following figures :—

Population in A. D.	1817	about	80,000 souls.
"	1824	"	88,000.
"	1832	"	90,000.
"	1845	"	95,000.
"	1872	"	1,16,873.
"	1881	"	1,27,621.
"	1891	"	1,48,412.

storm. Ran-Mal and Moid-ud-din then fled to Idar, and the other chiefs dispersed in different directions. The Idar Rájá next hit expedient of purchasing peace, and with this view he collected the elephants and horses of his unfortunate allies, and, sending them as a present to the Sultán, caused their baggage to be plundered. This mollified the Sultán, who was content to return to his capital after exacting from the Idar Rájá a suitable tribute. Both Moid-ud-din and Masti Khán took shelter with their uncle Shams Khán who ruled at Nágor*, but were killed in an action which took place between Shams Khán and the Ráná of Chitor.

In those troubled times, however, neither the king nor the country was destined to enjoy a long continued peace. In A. H. 816 (A. D. 1413) certain high-placed Muhammadan officers of Anhilwár Pátan, the former capital, opened a secret correspondence with Sultán Hoshang, king of Málwá, inciting him to invade Gujarát. They further won over several Zämindárs (landholders), and induced them also to revolt.

The ungrateful Hoshang despatched a force under several officers towards Gujarát. The Sultán, hearing of this, sent his troops in different directions to attack the rebels, and, himself marched towards Chámpáner,† and thence also sent an army under a general named Imád-ul-mulk to engage the Málwá King. The latter was greatly alarmed and, on the pretext that it would be a disgrace to fight with any one not his equal, retreated. Imád-ul-mulk was thus enabled to devastate a portion of Málwá without

---

* Now in the Jodhpur State.

† This ancient city is said to have been founded by Chámpá, the minister of Van Ráj in the 8th Century of the Christian era (Journal of Asiatic Society of Bengal, Vol. 9 page 199). It is now in a deserted state, the only inhabitants being a few Náekrás and Bhils who gain their subsistence by carrying the litters and baggage of gentlemen visiting the Pávágadh hill. The climate has for years been very unhealthy.

opposition. The other generals, of whom one was Latif Khán (the Sultán's own brother), drove the insurgents of Pátan and Satarsál the chief of Jháláwár before them as far as the province of Sorath. Accordingly in the year (A. H. 817 A.D. 1414) the Sultán marched against the strong fortress of Girnár in that province. The chief, Ráo Mandlik, also assembled his army near the base of the mountain and gave battle to the Sultán, but was defeated. The Ráo fled to the fortress, deemed impregnable, and the Sultán contented himself with taking the lower fort of Junágadh and subduing several Zamindárs upon whom, as well as on the Ráo Mandlik, he imposed an annual tribute. Thereafter Ahmad Sháh returned to Ahmadábád.

The next year, A. H. 818 (A. D. 1415), he employed his army in destroying the temples and idols in the town of Siddhpur, a place held especially sacred by the Hindus.

Nasir-ain-ul-mulk, ruler of Asir and Burhánpur, having dared to attempt an encroachment on the Gujarát king's border-towns of Sultánpur and Nandarbár, Sultán Ahmad proceeded thither in order to punish Nasir (A. D. 1416). Considering this a fit opportunity for assailing Sultán Ahmad, Sultán Hoshang again marched on Gujarát with the connivance of the chiefs of Idar, Nandod, and Jháláwár, and halted at Modásá. Nothing daunted, Sultán Ahmad at once left Nandarbár, although it was now the rainy season, and within seven days arrived at Modásá. He pitched his camp within five kos of Sultán Hoshang's army. The latter, seeing this, was much amazed, and not less alarmed. Upbraiding his allies for not having kept him properly informed regarding the Gujarát king's movements, he fled by night, leaving to their fate the unfortunate Rájás above named, who forthwith beat a precipitate retreat. Sultán Ahmad then destroyed Nándod, and the chief, Harising was driven into the jungles and became an outlaw. He was however pardoned and his estate was restored to him after twelve years.

Thus Sultán Hoshang himself gained nothing by his treachery, but his arrival had inspired false hopes in the minds of the chiefs of Sorath, who now withheld their tribute, and Nasir of Burhánpur was also induced to renew his sedition. Ahmad Sháh. however, by dividing his forces, was able to meet his enemies separately, and defeated them all.

After this the Sultán, fully bent upon effectually subduing Hoshang, marched on Málwá (A. D. 1417). At that time, all the Rájás who had previously aided Hoshang in his invasion of Gujarát sent envoys to crave pardon on their behalf from Sultán Ahmad which that king from motives of policy was glad to grant. He then proceeded towards Málwá by regular stages, and, on his arrival at the banks of the Kaliádá river near Ujjain, he found Sultán Hoshang in a camp, which he had already strongly entrenched. Shortly afterwards a severly contested battle ensued, in which the Gujarát army proved victorious, and all the enemy's treasure and baggage fell into its hands. Sultán Hoshang fled to the fort of Mándu, whither, however, he was followed by the Gujarát king, who, halting in its vicinity, ravaged the country round about. He then set out for his capital, which he entered in triumphal procession.

Thereafter, although his mind was engrossed with the project of reducing the strong fort of Mándu, the Sultán delayed taking action. He marched, however, on Chámpáner (A.D. 1418), the Rájá of which district he compelled to pay tribute, and turned next towards Sankhedá Bahádurpur, which he took (A. D. 1419). Here he subsequently built a fort and a mosque. Further, with a view to establishing the Muhammadan faith in that district, he appointed a Kázi and other religious teachers to reside in the place. Leaving with them a garrison for the maintenance of order, the Sultán at length proceeded towards Mándu. On his arrival at Dhár, however, he was met by envoys from Sultán Hoshang, who tendered ample apologies. These the Sultán graciously accepted, and retracing his steps, he arrived at his capital in the month of Rabi-ul-Akhir.

The next year (A. H. 823, A. D. 1420), the Sultán busied himself in establishing order throughout his dominions. He destroyed Hindu temples and erected mosques in their places; he organized military posts, and built forts in several towns, amongst others at Dohad on the frontier of Málwá. He also repaired the fort at Kadi, which had been built by Alp Khán while governing Gujarát on behalf of Alá-ud-din in A. D. 1304. Sultán Ahmad now sent an army to Gohelwád to levy tribute. The amount not having been paid in full, Sárangji the minor chief was taken as a hostage to Ahmadábád, his uncle Rámji remaining in charge of his district. Sárangji however succeeded, after having remained in confinement for two years, in effecting his escape through the assistance of a potter of the village of Bhandário, who with the aid of some Gosains conveyed him in a donkey's panniers to his fathers sister's husband the Phatai Ráwal of Chámpaner. She paid his ransom to the Sultán, and her husband kept Sárangii with him until he attained the age of twenty years, when, with the aid of some troops furnished by the Ráwal, Sárangji returned to Goghá and compelled* his uncle Rámji to restore to him all his father's territory save only the Tapás of Ukharlá, Bareli, Aghiáli and Monpur.

In A. D. 1421 Sultán Ahmad had again occasion to march on Málwá *via* Chámpáner. Having taken the fort of Mesur, the army pushed on to Mándu and besieged it for fortyeight days,

* From this time Sárangji assumed the title of Ráwal according to the advice of the Phatai Ráwal.

but without success. The rainy season having set in, the Sultán halted at Ujjain, once the capital of Málwá, and situated in the very heart of that country, a great part of which he subdued.

At the end of the rainy season, Mándu was again invested, but Sultán Hoshang had in the interim materially strengthened it, and accordingly Sultán Ahmad, feeling himself unable to effect its capture, marched on Sárangpur, another fortress of Málwá. He had hoped by this change in his plans to draw Hoshang out of his stronghold, but that king now employed new tactics. He sent ambassadors to the Sultán with instructions to represent to him emphatically the impiety of his attacking and laying waste the country of Islám, at the same time asking on Hoshang's part forgiveness for all his offences, and promising henceforth to behave loyally. Sultán Ahmad, moved by this appeal to his religious feeling, and acting on the advice of his ministers, pardoned Hoshang and gave orders for the troops to return to Gujarát. However, on the 26th of December 1422, when the generous minded Sultán Ahmad was about to start on the return journey, Hoshang perfidiously made a night attack on his camp, and even penetrated as far as Ahmad Sháh's own tent, which was guarded by 500 Rajput soldiers under the command of Sámant, a Garásiá of Dhandhuká. These brave soldiers, taken by surprise, were nearly all killed, but Ahmad Sháh effected his escape. The Gujarát troops would have taken to flight but for Ahmad Sháh's intrepidity. He hovered about the skirts of the camp until daybreak, when he led a small but resolute band against the Málwá soldiers while they were engaged in plundering. A hand-to-hand conflict ensued, and both the kings were wounded, but eventually Sultán Hoshang being defeated fled to the fort of Sárangpur. The Gujarát army not only recovered all they had lost, but captured twentyseven of Hoshang's elephants. Ahmad Sháh then returned thanks to the Almighty, and retraced his steps towards Gujarát. Hoshang however pursued him, and Ahmad Sháh was thus compelled to halt and give him battle. On this occasion Hoshang was again defeated, and he fled a second time to Sárangpur, while some noble elèphant's which he had brought with great trouble from Jijnagar, fell into the hands of the Gujarát king, who now returned victorious to his capital midst the glad greetings of his subjects.

For the next three years the army enjoyed rest, and the king devoted his sole attention to the internal management of his kingdom. In A. H. 820 (A. D. 1426) he marched against Ráv Punjá the Rájá of Idar, who was in secret correspondence with the Málwá Sultán. Ahmad Sháh drove the Ráv to the hills and plundered his capital. He then founded, on the confines of his territory and on the bank of the Háthmati river, a strong-walled town, which he named Ahmadnagar (A. D. 1427), and which still exists about eighteen miles distant from Idar. Punjá, however, did not give up his hostile projects, and the very next year attacked a foraging party sent by the Sultán. He assailed it while off its guard, and captured one of the elephants, but the party rallied as soon as Punjá retired, and, pursuing him, overtook him and his men near a defile on one side of which was a hill and on the other a deep ravine. Between these was a narrow pass, along which Punjá tried to make his way. Taking advantage of this spot, the Mahâwat (driver) of the captured elephant very pluckily turned the animal at Punjá's horse which was close behind, whereupon the latter shied, and falling with his rider into the ravine both were killed (A. D. 1428). A few days afterwards Ráv Punjá's head was brought to the king by a wood-cutter, and was duly recognised. After this Ráv Punjás son Nárandás agreed to pay an annual tribute of Rs. 3000, and in this way purchased peace.

Nárandás having however failed the next year to pay his tribute, Sultán Ahmad again marched on Idar, and carried by storm that strong fortress on the 14th of November 1429, where he now built a magnificent mosque.

The thorn in the Gujarát king's side being removed by the death of Ráv Punjá, he again confined his attention to the management of his territories, and for two years there was no foreign war. But after that period, Sultán Ahmad Báhmani, king of the Deccan, having, on the death of the Governor of Mahim (near Bombay) dared to seize that fort, Sultán Ahmad sent an army from Gujarát under the command of his son Jáfar Khán, and also a squadron from Cambay, Goghá and Diu to recapture it. Success attended this expedition, and the fort was retaken in A. D. 1429.

In 1431 A. D., taking opportunity of Ahmad Sháh's advance upon Chámpáner, the Báhmani king laid waste the country round about Baglánà, and seized Támbol, a fort in that province. Ahmad Sháh, on hearing of this, marched to its relief and defeated the Báhmani king. Before returning to his capital a treaty was entered into with the Rái of Mahim, according to the terms of which the latter king gave his daughter in marriage to Ahmad Sháh's son, prince Fateh Khán. The Sultán next imposed a tribute on the states of Bundi and Kotá in Mewár, and then returned to Gujarát.

In A. D 1435 prince Másud Khán, grandson of Ahmad Sháh's old antagonist Sultán Hoshang, fled to him for protection against his father's minister Mahmud Khilji, who had poisoned his master Ghiráni Khán Bin Hoshang and usurped the throne. The Sultán, moved by pity, espoused his cause and marched with an army (A. H. 841, A. D. 1437) to chastise the usurper and reinstate Másud on his fathér's throne. On this expedition, however, the Gujarát monarch was nòt attended by the same good fortune that had marked his former campaigns. He succeeded indeed in laying siege to the capital Mándu, and defeated the usurper Mahmud Khilji in a hard contested battle consequent on the latter's sallying out of the fort with a view to a secret night attack on the Gujarát camp, but an exceedingly severe pestilence broke out which in two days, carried off several thousands of his soldiers. Sultán Ahmad was thus compelled to beat a hasty retreat to Ahmadábád, where, at the age of fiftytwo years he breathed his last in A. H. 845 (A.D. 1441). His remains were interred in the mausoleum* in front of the Friday mosque. During Sultán Ahmad's brilliant reign of thirtytwo years and six months, victory often accompanied his standard, and the army of Gujarát overcame the troops of Málwá, the Deccan, Burhánpur and Mewár. Though the greater part of his life was spent in warfare, yet he did not neglect the civil administration of his country. The method adopted by him for the payment of his army was recognized even by his enemies as one calculated to attach his soldiery to their country. Instead of the officers and men being treated as mere mercenaries, it was Sultán Ahmad's policy to pay them a moiety of their salary in land, and the remainder in money. The payment in land was especially advantageous as providing a means of employment and subsistence for the soldier's family during his absence on service.

---

* An urus (fair) is annually held here in the Sultán's honour on the 4th of Rabi-ul-Akhir, for the expenses of which a sum of Rs. 83 is paid from the Government Treasury. A party of musicians is regularly stationed on the upper storey over the gateway leading to the mausoleum. These beat the nobat (kettle-drum) and sing verses three times a day, at dawn, in the evening and at midnight. On Thursdays and Fridays, in addition to the above, the songs are repeated at 9 A. M., at midday and at 3 P. M. The annual cost to Government on this account is Rs. 426. An additional sum of Rs. 2,032 is annually paid for issuing cooked Khichadi (rice and dál) to the poor under the supervision of a committee of Muhammadan gentlemen appointed by Government.

With a view to the collection of the revenue, and prevention of fraudulent combination, it was a rule with the Sultán to appoint joint revenue officers*, of whom one was in the Sultán's pay, but the other a man of independent means and good family. Ahmad Sháh was very rigid as regards the administration of justice. On one occasion his son-in-law in the passion of youth killed a personal enemy, whereupon the Sultán himself is said to have given orders that the murderer should be hanged before his own house. The Kázi had sought to satisfy the relatives of the murdered man by the payment of twentytwo gold mohurs, but the Sultán indignantly declared that such a compromise would tend only to encourage evil disposed and wealthy persons in the commission of crime.

On another occasion, the Sultán was seated in the balcony of a pleasure house on the banks of the Sábarmati, when he noticed that the water was disturbed and that a black object was floating down the stream. Orders were given to bring it to the river-side, when it was discovered to be a jar containing a dead body. The Sultán ordered all the potters of the city to be collected, and ascertaining from one of them that he had sold that jar to the Mukhi (head-man) of a village in the neighbourhood of the city, the latter was sent for. It was eventually proved that he had murdered a merchant, and with a view to conceal his crime had put the dead body into the jar and set it adrift. The Mukhi was publicly executed. These severe examples served their purpose as an effectual restraint on crime.

---

* The same system prevails up to this day in regard to villages. The Talátis (accountants) are stipendiary servants, and the Patels belong to the villages themselves, and are either hereditary employees or serve by rotation according to the custom of the village.

CHAPTER IV.

The reigns of Muhammad Sháh, Kutb-ud-din and Dáud Sháh.

FROM 1442 to 1459 A. D.

On the death of Ahmad Sháh his son Muhammad Khán ascended the throne on the 3rd Rabi-ul-Akhir A. H. 846 (12th August 1442) under the title of Muhammad Sháh. He spent much of his time in ease and pleasure, and being exceedingly lavish in his gifts, soon acquired the surname of "Zar Baksh" (Giver of Gold). In A. H. 849 (A. D. 1445) he led an expedition against Ráv Bhán the Rájá of Idar, whom he drove to the hills. From thence the Rájá sent ambassadors asking for forgiveness, and a treaty was eventually concluded, by which the Rájá's dominions were restored to him, and his daughter was given in marriage to Muhammad Sháh. From Idar the Sultán carried his army into Wágad, which he plundered, and thereafter returned to his capital.

The same year witnessed the death of the holy saint Shekh Ahmad Khattu Ganj-Bakhsh, on whose advice Sultán Ahmad had founded the city of Ahmadábád. He was buried at Sarkhej, where Muhammad Sháh caused a superb mausoleum* and mosque to be erected in his memory.

In A. H. 854 (A. D. 1450) the Sultán marched against Chámpáner, at which place the Rájá Gangádás gave him battle. Being defeated, however, the Rájá retreated to the strong fortress,

* The mausoleum was completed by Muhammad Sháh's successor Kutb-ud-din, and is an object of great interest to travellers. An uras (fair) attended by some four thousand pilgrims from far and near is annually held there on the 14th of Shawál and the two following days in honour of this saint. The village of Okáf of the estimated annual revenue of Rupees 2,200 has been assigned for the support of the mausoleum.

which the Sultán fortwith invested. At length the Rájá having been reduced to great straits sent secret emissaries to the king of Málwá the inveterate enemy of Gujarát entreating him to march to his assistance, and promising a large sum of money to meet the expenses of his troops. The Málwá King Mahmud Khilji eagerly seized this opportunity of revenging himself upon Sultán Ahmad's successor, and marched with a large army towards Gujarát. On Mahmud's arrival at Dohad the Gujarát Sultán raised the seige of Chámpáner and removed to Godhrá. Falling ill he was taken to Ahmadábád, where he died in the month of Muharram A. H. 855 (A. D. 1451), his remains being interred close to his father's tomb in the mausoleum at Mánek Chok. The Mirát-i-Sikandari attributes this king's death to poison administered to him by some of his nobles because of his cowardice in retreating before the Málwá King, and thus proving himself an unworthy son of his illustrious father.

Sultán Muhammad was succeeded by his son Sultán Kutb-ud-din, who ascended the throne on the 11th of Muharram A. H. 855 (13th February 1451). Mahmud Khilji, encouraged by his recent success, marched without delay against Gujarát *via* Sultánpur and Baroda. Kutb-ud-din set out from Ahmadábád to oppose him, and encamped at Khánpur on the bank of the Mahi river. On hearing this Mahmud Khilji advanced on Ahmadábád *via* Kapadvanj, near which town the armies met in a fiercely contested battle, in which Mahmud Khilji's army was able at one time to penetrate to the rear of the Gujarát force, and carried off from Sultán Kutb-ud-din's pavilion his crown and jewelled girdle of immense value. In the end, however, the Málwá King suffered a severe defeat on the 1st day of Safar A. H. 856 (22nd February 1452). Sultán Kutb-ud-din, thus victorious, returned to the capital, and completed the mausoleum of Ganj-Bakhsh, which had been commenced by his father. About that time he also caused to be constructed the Hauz-i-Kutab or the Kánkariá tank with the garden called Naginá (jewel) in its centre, and the Ghatá-mandal, a palace for the summer retreat of the king and his family. It may be as well to mention that no trace of the Ghatá-mandal remains, but the tank has survived the vicissitudes of the time and still exists. It covers an area of 72 acres of land, and is a regular polygon of thirtyfour sides, each side 190 feet long, so that the entire perimeter is more than a mile in length. It was, when originally completed in 1451, quite surrounded by tiers of cut stone with six sloping approaches flanked by cupolas and an exquisitely carved water-sluice. In the centre of the tank*, connected with the margin by a fortyeight arch viaduct, was an island with the Naginá garden.

Sultán Kutb-ud-din's later expeditions were against the Ráná of Chitor to humble whom Mahmud Khilji had entered into a combination with the Gujarát king. The latter marched against the Ráná Kumbhá in A. H. 861, (A. D. 1456-57) and took the fort of Abu, which he made over to its rightful

* Portions of this tank are said to have been repaired during the rule of the Maráthás by the Subá Káká Sáheb (A.D. 1800—1810), but it again fell into utter disrepair. The approaches and their cupolas were in ruins, the sides of the tank broken, the bridge fallen in and the garden a waste, when in A. D. 1872, Mr. A. A. Borradaile, Collector of Ahmadábád, caused the whole to be admirably restored at a cost of no less than 83,832 rupees from the Municipal funds, and it now affords a delightful recreation ground for the citizens of Ahmadábád. The Naginá Vádi has also been entirely reconstructed and the masonry wall surrounding the island has been rebuilt as also the central fountain. The bed of the tank being of Kankar (from which probably is derived the name Kánkariá), the monsoon water collected in it is soon absorbed, and therefore, with a view to keep a continual supply in the tank, a canal eleven miles long has been constructed, connecting this tank with the Khári river and supplying water to the Chandolá tank which irrigates about 291 acres of rice land.

Mr. Borradaile's name as the restorer of both the Kánkariá tank and the Sháh Alám mosque will long be held in grateful remembrance.

owner Khátiá Deoráh, the Rájá of Sirohi, from whom it had lately been usurped by the Ráná. Sultán Kutb-ud-din then advanced on Kumbhalner which he plundered. Near Chitor the Ráná and Kutb-ud-din met in battle for five days, in which the Ráná was eventually defeated and put to flight. He was, however, pardoned by the Sultán on his binding himself to pay tribute and never again to molest Nágor.

Some six months later, however, the Ráná, disregarding his treaty obligations, advanced against Nágor, but the Sultán, on obtaining information of this, at once proceeded against Kumbhalner, whereupon the Ráná retreated to his capital.

In A. H. 862 (A. D. 1457) the Sultán went to Sirohi, and thence entering the country of the Ráná of Chitor and devastating it, returned to his capital. Here, on the 6th of Rajab A. H. 863 (13th May 1459 A. D.), after a short reign of eight years and a half, he fell sick and died. He was buried in Sultán Ahmad's mausoleum in the Mánek Chok by the side of his father and grandfather.

The third day after the death of Sultán Kutb-ud-din, his uncle Dáud ascended the throne in May 1459, but by showing a disposition to raise to power men of low rank who had been his friends while he was yet a prince, and by exhibiting extraordinary meanness in reducing the grain allowance for pigeons, and the oil for lights, he soon proved himself unfit for the management of a kingdom, and the nobles, within seven days dethroned him, placing on the throne Muhammad Sháh's second son Fateh Khán, a young prince of much promise, who had received his education under the illustrious Saint Sháh Alam. Dáud Sháh, hearing the noise of trumpets, enquired the reason, and on learning that Fateh Khán was being brought to the palace in order to be installed as king, fled through a wicket facing the Sábarmati, and spent the remainder of his life as a devotee and disciple of Shekh Adhan Rumi.

Chapter V.

The reign of Sultán Mahmud Begadá.

From 1459 to 1511 A. D.

Sultán Mahmud was enthroned at Ahmadábád on the 12th of Shábán A. H. 863 (18th June 1459 A. D.). He was born on the 20th Ramzán A. H. 849 (A. D. 1445), and was thus only fourteen years of age when the cares of a large kingdom devolved on him. But he proved himself equal to the difficulties he had to encounter, and added glory and lustre to his throne. Benefiting by the instruction he had early received from his religious preceptor Sháh Alam, son of Kutb-ul-Alam of Batwá, he displayed, even in youth, singular soundness of judgment.

Some months after his accession, several of the nobles who were enemies of the minister Imád-ul-Mulk, otherwise named Shábán, repaired early to the king's private audience chamber, and there represented to the Sultán that Imád-ul-Mulk was meditating treason and intended to raise his own son to the throne. Imád-ul-Mulk, in complete ignorance of their designs, presented himself at the usual hour, and the nobles feigning zeal and fidelity at once openly accused him to the king. The minister was accordingly fettered, and confined on the roof of one of the gates of the Bhadar under the custody of 500 soldiers, whom the nobles had won over to their cause. The king, in the hurry and confusion of the moment, felt unable to interfere, but, recognising the gravity of the situation, he determined upon a strict investigation in order to ascertain the truth. At night he learnt from the Darogá in charge of the elephants that the nobles had treacherously conspired against Imád-ul-Mulk the faithful Vazir. The Sultán next consulted his mother, herself the daughter of a prince in Sindh, and other trusty advisers, and from the information he obtained, having good reason to suspect that the persons who had calumniated Imád-ul-Mulk were themselves the real traitors, he gave instructions to the Darogá to bring out all the elephants fully equipped to the approaching Darbár. He then ordered Imád-ul-Mulk to be summoned, ostensibly for punishment, but as soon as he came near caused his fetters to be struck off. When the nobles heard what turn affairs had taken, they assembled their adherents and followers, and marched towards the chief gate of the Bhadar in battle array. The young king, however, was equal to the emergency, and, acting on the advice of Malek Shábán, at once gave orders for the elephants, some six hundred in number, to charge the rebels. This was done, and the Amirs with their rabble fell into confusion and fled out of the city in different directions. In course of time each of the chief conspirators was apprehended, and severe examples were made of some. The head of one was hung up near the Bhadar gate, another was trampled to death under the feet of an elephant, while others were imprisoned. So deep was the impression caused by the young Sultán's firmness and courage that no one thereafter dared to disobey his orders. While punishing the refractory, he did not, on the other hand, fail suitably to reward those who were faithful to him.

After satisfactorily arranging the internal affairs of his kingdom the Sultán was at pains to increase the efficiency of his army, which he raised to double its former strength. Thus supported, he advanced towards the Deccan in A.H. 866 (A.D. 1461-62)at the urgent request of its ruler Nizám Sháh Báhmani, whose country had been invaded by Mahmud Khilji of Málwá. The latter, as soon as he heard that the Gujarát Sultán was marching to the relief of the Deccan by way of Burhánpur, immediately retreated *via* Gondwáná. His troops, however, before reaching their own country, suffered severely from want of water and from attacks by the hill tribes. The Gujarát king also returned to his capital, having received the thanks of Nizám Sháh for his timely succour.

The next year Mahmud Khilji again marched on the Deccan, when Sultán Mahmud not only frustrated him a second time, but wrote him a letter couched in such threatening terms that he never afterwards ventured to disturb the Deccan.

In A.H. 871 (A. D. 1466-67) Sultán Mahmud being desirous of capturing the stronghold of Girnár in Sorath, equipped a large army and besieged the fort. After engagements extending over several days the Ráo Mandlik tendered his submission through his ambassadors, which the king accepted, and his troops returned to Gujarát after amassing immense booty from the plunder of Káthiáwár.

The next year (A. D. 1468) having heard that the Ráo Mandlik had visited a certain temple with all the insignia of royalty, the Sultán sent a force of forty thousand horse and several elephants in order to humble that chief's pride. The Ráo, however, on hearing of this expedition, immediately forwarded his royal umbrella and gold-worked dresses to the king, and thus averted the threatened attack. The Sultán is said to have given away the rich dresses to his musicians.

His ambition, however, does not appear to have been satisfied, and in A.H. 874 (A.D. 1469-70) he again made known his intention to attack Girnár. So deeply, however, was the Ráo impressed with the Sultán's strength that on this occasion he himself unexpectedly appeared in the royal camp, and implored, in the most abject manner possible, to be informed of the reason for this long continued hostility. Mahmud sternly replied that there could be no greater fault than infidelity, and that before he could hope for peace he must acknowledge the unity of God. The unfortunate

Mandlik Rájá begged for time to consider what answer he should give and fled by night to the fort of Girnár. The latter was forthwith besieged by the king's troops, and its garrison and people were reduced to the utmost straits. At length the Rájá delivered up the keys of the fort to the king's general and accepted the faith of Islám. The title of Khán Jahán was subsequently conferred on him, and he became a follower of Hazarat Sháh Alam. Thus the fort of Girnár, considered one of the strongest in all India, and well nigh impregnable, surrendered to the Gujarát Sultán in A. H. 877 (A. D. 1472-73)*.

The Sultán now busied himself in settling the newly conquered territory of Sorath, and, calling together Sayyids and learned men from every quarter, induced them to take up their residence in that country. He rebuilt the fort and laid the foundation of a grand palace. His nobles also, following his example, began to erect magnificent buildings, and thus there soon arose a new city to which the Sultán gave the name of Mustafábád.

In A. H. 878 (A. D. 1473-74) Mahmud Begadá marched on Sindh, the Zamindárs of which province assembled a force of about 24000 men, and took up a strong defensive position. But as soon as the Gujarát army approached, they sent envoys to offer their submission, which was accepted on the ground that they were Muhammadans. The Sultán, however, finding that they still clung to many Hindu customs, took several of them with him to Junágadh that they might receive instruction which should enable them, on their return to teach their fellow countrymen the true faith of Islám. He also defeated and subdued the Hindu chief of Kachh.

The next year the Sultán subdued the Hindu Zamindárs

* Some authors mention this conquest as having taken place two years earlier *i. e.*, A. H. 875, A. D. 1470.

of Sindh, and sent many of their women and children as captives to Junágadh. In that same year, some pirates of Jagat (Dwárká) and Sankhodhar (Bet) plundered a ship belonging to a Muhammadan Mulláh of Samarkand, and seized his wives and property. The Sultán, on the Mulláh's complaint, marched against Jagat on the 17th of Julhaj. On his approach the inhabitants fled to the island; the place was given up to plunder, the temples were destroyed and their images broken up. The Sultán then attacked the island with his fleet, but was obstinately opposed. At length, however, the arms of Islám prevailed, and Mahmud landed victorious. Immense booty in pearls, rubies and rich stuffs fell into the conquerer's hands. The captive members of the Mulláh's household were released. After spending some time on the island, where he laid the foundation of a mosque, and appointing a Deputy to govern in his name, the Sultán left for Junágadh, taking with him as prisoner Bhim Ságar the Rájá of Jagat on the 13th of Jumádul-awal A. H. 878 (A. D. 1473). Mahmud had, meanwhile, ordered the Samarkand Mulláh to come from Ahmadábád to meet him. On his arrival his family was made over to him, and with them the captured Bhim Rájá. At the Mulláh's request Bhim was sent to Ahmadábád, where he was barbarously murdered, and portions of his body were hung over each gate of the city as a fitting punishment for his having plundered a holy man and imprisoned his family. On his way back, the Sultán received at Junágadh the submission of several Sorath chiefs, after which, it having been brought to his notice that some Malbáris who lived by piracy were harassing the Gujarát ports, he went to Goghá and there equipped some vessels, which he sent against the pirates, himself returning by way of Cambay. The Sultán entered Ahmadábád in triumph and spent the next few years in peace.

In A.H. 880, A.D. 1475, Sháh Alam, the religious preceptor

of the Sultán died, and a beautiful mausoleum* was erected to his memory by Táj Khán, a nobleman of Mahmud Begadá's Court. To this building several additions have been made from time to time, and Asaf Khán, brother of the celebrated Nurjahán Begam, wife of the emperor Jahángir, ornamented the dome with gold and precious stones in the beginning of thé sixteenth century.

In 1479, during one of his hunting excursions, being much pleased with a site on the bank of the river Vátrak, the Sultán founded there the town of Mahmudábád (Mehmadábád) twelve kos south-east of Ahmadábád, and, having fortified some rising ground on the river-side, he ordered some noble palaces to be built, the ruins of which are still to be seen. The Bhamariá† well, constructed in the time of this Sultán as a hot weather retreat in the vicinity of Mahmudábád, is an object of special interest. It is 74 feet long by 24 feet broad with entrances from four winding flights of stairs, and has eight underground chambers, four large and four small.

In 1480 A.D. while the Sultán was at Mustafábád (Junágadh) some of his nobles and officers at Ahmadábád, tired of the constant wars, and dreading the Sultán's contemplated expedition

---

* This mausoleum is an object of interest to travellers. Several villages have been set apart for its maintenance and the support of its custodians. The present Pirjádá is Musá Mián Sáheb Valade Ahmad Mián Sáheb.

Government a few years ago sanctioned Rs. 5,300 for the repairs of this mausoleum, and Rs. 5,000 for the Rojá of Ganj-Bakhsh at Sarkhej. Both these tombs are now in good condition.

An Urus (fair) is annually held here on the 20th Jamádi-ul-Akhir and four following days, at which about 50,000 people attend from Bombay, Surat, Cambay, Káthiáwár and other places.

† The well is now in a ruinous condition, and might well be restored from the sum annually set apart by Government for the restoration of ancient buildings.

against so strong a fort as Chámpáner, entered into a conspiracy to seat the Sultán's son prince Ahmad on the throne, but through the fidelity of the Prime Minister Imád-ul-mulk the conspiracy was detected in time, and the king returning to Ahmadábád severely punished the conspirators.

In 1480 A. D. the Sultán's commandant at Morámli (Rasulábád) on the frontier of Chámpáner, having made several forays into the dominion of the Chámpáner chief, the latter in his turn attacked and defeated the commandant, capturing two elephants and several horses. This gave the Sultán a sufficient pretext for invading Chámpáner, then held by Chohán* Rajputs, the ancestors of the present Rájás of Chhotá Udaipur and Báriá. Accordingly he marched with a powerful army against that fort by way of Baroda. His advance guard reached the foot of the Páwágad hill on the 17th of March 1483, when the Rája, Phatai Ráwal Jaysingh, son of Gangádás mentioned as the opponent of Sultán Muhammad I., sent ambassadors to ask for pardon, but the Sultán refused to listen to any terms. The Rájá then prepared for defence, and, as on a previous occasion when besieged by Muhammad Sháh I., wrote to Ghiyás-ud-din of Málwá for assistance. Sultán Mahmud, however, having determined to make a detour on Mándu, the Málwá king thought it more politic to withhold his aid from the unfortunate Ráwal. The latter none the less offered a stubborn resistence, and defended his fort for some time. At length, in a moment of dispair, having first consigned to the flames the women of his household and all his valuables, he made a fierce charge on the besiegers, in which he was wounded and seized along with his minister Dungarsi on the 17th of November 1484†. They were

* The Chohāns appear to have usurped Chámpáner from its former possessors of the Tuár dynasty in or about 1297 A. D.

† The Hindu date preserved by the bards as given in the Rás Málá is Sunday the 3rd of Posh month, Samvat 1541.

urged to accept the religion of Islám, but, unlike the Mandlik Rájá, declined the proposal, and were accordingly executed.

Chámpáner, another great bulwark of Hinduism in Gujarát, thus fell into the hands of the Muhammadans, though not until six of the Rájás, who had assembled for its defence, fell, and a large number of the besiegers as well as the besieged were killed. So greatly was Sultán Mahmud pleased with the place and its surroundings that he made it for some time his capital, caused a mosque and other beautiful buildings to be constructed, and gave orders that the town should henceforth be known by the name of Mahmudábád Chámpáner. Either in this his new capital, or in Mustafábád (Junágadh) or in Ahmadábád, the Sultán spent the greater part of the next five or six years, free from foreign embroilments.

Besides the foreign expeditions mentioned in the foregoing pages, Mahmud Begadá's annihilation of the small chieftainship of Ránpur, situated about 112 miles south-west of Ahmadábád at the confluence of the Bhádar with the Gomá river, merits mention. That town was, as has been already stated, founded by Gohel Ránáji, son of Sejakji the ancestor of the present Bhávnagar ruling family. Ránáji's descendants appear to have been in peaceful enjoyment of their estate for upwards of a century, but in the time of Ránáji II. ill-feeling arose between that chief's wife and her sister. The latter being married to Mahmud Begadá, the chief's wife regarded her as having lost caste, and accordingly refused an invitation to dine with her. The Sultáná, on her return to Ahmadábád, complained to her husband of the insult. At this time Ránáji also happened to be in Ahmadábád, and the Sultán, obtaining under some slight pretence certain symbols belonging to that chief, treacherously sent them to his sister-in-law by a discharged servant of Ránáji with a message that the latter wished her to join him in Ahmadábád. The lady obeyed the summons, and appeared before her lord, who immediately perceived some plot was brewing. He promptly substituted another woman for his wife, and took her back in safety to Ránpur. Here however he soon afterwards killed a young Muhammadan lad, who with his mother was proceeding on pilgrimage, and who, early one morning, happened to cry aloud the call to prayer. The injured mother retraced her steps and laid her complaint before the Sultán, who forthwith sent a force under his sister's son Bhanderi Khán against Ránáji. Bhanderi Khán's marriage had been celebrated only that day, yet against the earnest entreaties of his friends he volunteered to lead the expedition. Ránáji II opposed the Sultán's army at Dhandhuká, but was beaten and driven back to the gates of Ránpur. Hence he sent word to his wives that if they saw his umbrella go down they should understand that he had been slain. It happened that the umbrella-bearer, feeling thirsty, set it down for a moment to take a drink of water. The unfortunate Ránis believing their lord to have fallen, threw themselves into a well in the fort and perished. Shortly afterwards the chief, who had continued the battle, also fell, and the Sultán's troops took possession of the fort, though with the loss of their chivalrous young commander Bhanderi Khán. Mahmud Begadá afterwards presented Ránpur to the deceased Ránáji's sister's son, Háloji Parmár of Muli, who embraced the faith of Islám, and his descendants, now divided into five families, still hold nine of the villages under the Tálukdári tenure.

In A. D. 1494 the Sultán had occasion to march against Bahádur Khán Giláni, a vassal who had revolted against the Báhmani king of the Deccan, and who, from his fort of Dábhol in the present Ratnágiri district, was committing piracy on Cambay and other Gujarát ports. The Sultán prepared and sent a fleet against the rebel, but the Báhmani king, fearing that the invasion of his territory by the Gujarát troops would lead to disastrous results, himself took the field against his refractory vassal, and having succeeded in capturing him and his fleet, delivered over the latter to the Sultán, to whom he also sent the head of the rebel.

The next year the Sultán marched on Wágadh and Idar, from the Rájás of which provinces he exacted large offerings, and returned to Mahmudábád Chámpáner.

In A. H. 904 (A. D. 1498) Adil Khán Faruki of Khándesh having neglected to send the usual tribute, a force was despatched against that country. As soon however as the Sultán reached the banks of the Tápti, Adil Khán paid up the tribute in full, offering excuses for the delay, and the king, accepting this apology, returned with his troops to Ahmadábád.

In A. D. 1507, the Sultán led an expedition against the Portuguese*, who, having become powerful on the western coast of India, had of late usurped the dominion of the sea, and had attacked the Gujarát possessions of Mahim and Bombay. On his arrival at Diu, however, the Sultán learnt that Malek Aiáz, his deputy at Sorath, had already collected a fleet, and with the aid of a squadron sent by the Sultán of Turkey, who was jealous of Portuguese influence in India, had inflictedon the Portuguese a terrible defeat and sunk one of their largest vessels. This was a most splendid achievement on the part of Malek Aiáz, and the Sultán, conferring high favours on him, sent him a robe of honour in recognition of his services, and, after a stay of a week

* The Portuguese were the first Europeans to settle in India. Their emissary Covilham reached Calicut about A. D. 1487 by land, and a fleet under Vasco-da-Gama cast anchor off the same city on the 20th May 1498. Goa was seized in A. D. 1510, and has since remained the capital of Portuguese India. (Sir W. Hunter's Indian Empire, Pages 356-357).

only at Bassein, returned to his capital on the 1st Muharram A. H. 914 (A. D. 1508).

The same year, at the request of his daughter's son Alam Khán, the Sultán interfered in the matter of the succession to the Khándesh Government, which he caused to be conferred on Alam Khán declaring him to be the rightful claimant, and presented him at the same time with four elephants and three hundred thousand Tankáhs.

About this time a certain Sayyid, calling himself Muhammad Junpuri, came to Ahmadábád. He claimed to be the Imám Máhdi, and, taking up his abode in the mosque of Táj-Khán near the Jamálpur gate, began to gain disciples in large numbers. On this the Ulemás (learned men) of the city took offence at the pretender, and desired that he should be put to death. But the Sayyid escaped to Pátan, where he continued his ministrations. Some Muhammadans in Pálanpur became his followers, and even now adherents of this Máhdi sect are said to be found in that town.

In the month of Julhaj A. H. 916 (A. D. 1510) the Sultán went for the last time to Pátan. There he gave the usual royal entertainments, and informed his nobles that he felt his life was near its close. On his way back he visited the tomb of Shekh Ahmad Khattu Ganj-Bakhsh at Sarkhej, and inspected his own tomb, which was built in a separate mausoleum at the foot of that of the holy saint. He then went to Ahmadábád, sent for his eldest son Prince Khalil Khán, Governor of Baroda, admonished him to rule with righteousness and justice, to protect his people, to succour the oppressed and to punish the oppressors. He rallied, however, from this illness, but died three months afterwards on Monday the 3rd of Ramzán A. H. 917, A. D. 1511, at the age of sixtyseven years, and was buried in the mausoleum at Sarkhej.

The most wonderful stories are current regarding the enormous quantities of food Sultán Mahmud was capable of eating. His daily allowance is stated in the Mirát-i-Sikandari, to have been one Gujaráti maund of 40 lbs. weight. This must of course have included much that remained over. In the morning after his prayers it is said that he used to take a cupful of honey and another of butter, and along with these a hundred plantains. Even if the latter were of the smaller kind, still the allowance above stated would be altogether extraordinary. There are other curious legends relating to him, one of which is that sundry poisonous drugs produced no effect upon his system. His skin, it is stated, was itself so saturated with poison that if a fly chanced to settle on his hand it fell to the ground dead. To show how fond he was of the display of grandeur, the traveller Varthema narrates that every morning when the Sultán left his bed there was a parade of fifty elephants in front of his palace which returned to their stables after doing him reverence. They did him the same reverence at the hour of dinner. About fifty kinds of musical instruments were played during the time occupied in dining. He had very long mustaches, which were twisted like a cow's horns. To this fact some have attributed his surname of Begadá; but another and more plausible origin of the name has been conjectured, *viz.*, that having conquered and annexed to his territories the two (Be) strong fortresses (Ghad) of Girnár and Chámpáner, he became widely known as the Begadá. Mahmud Begadá was very fond of trees and encouraged their growth throughout his dominions. The abundance of mango groves and of other fruit trees in and about Ahmadábád, and the long avenue of mango trees near the village of Bág Fardosh*, commonly called Amrai, are ascribed to his care and encouragement. It is further stated

* Heavenly garden. Lands in the vicinity of this once favoured spot have, for the last few years, been turned by the Ahmadábád Municipality into a night-soil depot.

that most of the elegant handicrafts and arts carried on in Ahmadábád were introduced under this monarch's favouring protection. He was, moreover, a great lover of architecture, and built magnificent caravanserais and lodging places for travellers. He also founded several colleges and mosques. His generous example was followed by his nobles and officers, who vied with one another in the splendour of their architectural buildings, to which the numerous mausoleums in and around Ahmadábád bear ample testimony. The beautiful Wáv (a well with galleries and flights of steps) at Asárvá about a mile from Ahmadábád, known as the Dádá Hari's well, was built by a lady named Bái Hari of Mahmud Begadá's household. The Sanskrit inscription on one of the galleries of this well shows that it was built on Monday the 13th of the light half of the month of Posh Samvat 1556, which corresponds to A. D. 1499-1500. The cost is estimated at about three lacs of rupees. A similar well at Adálaj on the road to Disá dates from A. D. 1499, having been constructed by Rudbai Ráni, the consort of one Vir Singh Vághelá, then Thákor of Kalol, at a cost of about five hundred thousand Tankáhs. Here it will perhaps not be amiss if we deviate shortly from Mahmud Begadá's time to trace the origin of Vir Singh. He is supposed to have been a descendant of the old Vághelá dynasty of whom two brothers Warsoji and Jetoji had been driven into outlawry by the loss of their estates. One day in their despair they intercepted and attacked the carriages of Sultán Ahmad's chief queen and her female companions while they were going one Friday to the mausoleum of Shekh Ahmad Khattu Ganj-Bakhsh and the escort was lagging behind. On the queen's earnest entreaties and on her promises to have their grievances redressed, the brothers allowed her and her companions to go unmolested. The queen, true to her word, interfered on their behalf. They also gave their sister Lálán in mariage to the Sultán, who was pleased to grant them five hundred villages in the Kalol district for their support. Vir Singh took as his share Kalol and two hundred and fifty villages in the neighbourhood of Sánand. The latter, owing to its splendid wheat crops, eventually became a very valuable possession. Kalol was lost in A. D. 1728 by Vir Singh's descendant Bhagat Singh, who retired to Limbodrá, which is still held by his descendants.

Most of Sultán Mahmud Begadá's military exploits have been already mentioned. He was the most renowned of all the Gujarát Sultáns, and during his reign the splendour of Gujarát was greatly increased. Even the Emperor of Delhi sent him presents, and thus virtually acknowledged Gujarát as a separate kingdom.

Chapter VI.

The reign of Khalil Khán, entitled Muzaffar Sháh II.]

From 1511 to 1526 A. D.

Khalil Khán ascended the throne on Friday the 17th of Ramzán A. H. 917 (A. D. 1511) under the title of Sultán Muzaffar, and distributed presents and titles according to custom. In this year one Mir Ibráhim Khán came as an ambassador from the king of Persia, bringing costly presents for the Sultán. After his reception with due honours, the Sultán proceeded to Baroda, to which place he gave the name of Daulatábád*. About this time intelligence was received of troubles having again arisen in Málwá. Khwájá Jahán, the Minister of the late Mahmud Khilji had, on the demise of its king Násir-ud-din, ousted the elder son Sultán Mahmud, otherwise called Shihábuddin, and placed his younger brother Sultán Muhammad on the throne. The latter, however, having been defeated in a battle on the plains of Mándu, fled for protection to Gujarát. Sultán Muzaffar received him kindly and kept him as his guest, promising to march to his assistance after the rainy season was over. In consequence, however, of an affray between the followers of the Persian envoy and of the Málwá prince, in which the latter was to blame, Sultán Muzaffar became somewhat estranged from Sultán Muhammad, owing to whose folly he had to make good to the Persian envoy some six lacs of Tankáhs for the loss of his property, and to appease him with large presents, fearing lest the matter should be reported to the king of Persia.

The Málwá prince, either ashamed at his conduct or not

* Probably Muzaffar Sháh built a new town close to the old one. This view is confirmed by the traveller Mandelslo in 1638 and by Mr. Oglivy's Atlas V. 214 (1660—1680).
Vide Baroda Gazetteer P. P. 529-530.

viewing the action of the Gujarát king in its proper light, suddenly left for his own country, having received an invitation from some of his nobles, and a battle took place between him and his brother's minister named Medni Ráe in which the former was defeated. The victorious minister had already gained great influence over Mahmud and the whole power of Mándu now fell into his hands. He entrusted even the household affairs of the Sultán to the management of his own relatives and friends, and caused the death of the Musalmán nobles one after the other, plundering their property and confiscating their estates. On every side the tokens of idolatry increased. When all this was represented to Sultán Muzaffar he was much moved by religious zeal, and at once prepared (in the month of Shavál A. H. 918, A. D. 1512), to march against Málwá in order to crush the power of Medni Ráe and restore Muhammadan supremacy. After his arrival at Godhrá, however, at which town he had ordered his troops to concentrate, he was obliged to march back against Idar, the chief of which state, Ráv Bhán, had rebelled and had defeated the king's officer sent against him. On reaching Modásá, the Sultán gave orders that Idar should be entirely destroyed. The Rájá, hearing of this, at once sent apologies and the tribute of twenty lacs of Tankáhs said to be equal to twenty thousand rupees, one hundred horses and other presents, which were accepted the more readily as the affairs of Málwá still demanded the Sultán's attention (A. D. 1513).

Sultán Muzaffar next returned to Godhrá, and thence went on to Dohad. Having given orders for the repair of the fortress of that town, he continued his march towards Málwá. On the way thither, he heard that Medni Ráe had carried his protégé to Chanderi. The Sultán then publicly proclaimed that in undertaking the present expedition, his object was not to annex Málwá to his territories, but simply to drive away

Medni Ráe and other infidels, and to reconcile the two brother princes. As one of the two, however, had already invoked the aid of the king of Delhi, the Sultán declared that he would wait and see the result of this appeal and act as the occasion might require. The fame of the palaces and hunting park of Málwá's former capital Dhár had spread far and wide, and accordingly the king proceeded thither with a light detachment, and devoted himself for a while to the chase. Then, after visiting the deer park at Dilwára, he returned* to Ahmadábád, being unwilling to assume the responsibility of interfering further in a quarrel in which one of the parties had solicited the assistance of the Delhi king.

The subsequent events in Málwá appertain to the history of that province. It is enough here to state that in A. H. 920, (A. D. 1514), having heard on his return from Málwá that Ráv Bhán the Rájá of Idar was dead, and that his grandson Raimal had, through the asssistance of his father-in-law, the Ráná of Chitor, assumed the sovereign power to the exclusion of the Rájá's son Bhármal, the Sultán took offence at the intervention of the Ráná, and ordered the Jagirdár of Ahmadnagar to expel Raimal and seat Bhármal on the Idar throne. This was effected with much trouble, and led to several engagements with varying results between the Sultan's army and that of the Idar chief, A. H. 923, (A. D. 1517).

In this year several nobles from Málwá fled to Gujarát, and represented to Muzaffar Sháh that on his return to Ahmadábád, the Delhi troops had also gone back, and that Medni Ráe

---

* According to the account given in the history of Mándu by a Subaltern (name not given) and published by Col W. Kincade the reason of Muzaffar's return from Dhár was the defeat of a portion of his army by Medni Ráe near Mándu, A. H. 919, A. D. 1513-14.

had, in the mean time, become supreme in power. They further stated that Mahmud was now king in name only, and stood in hourly danger of being blinded or imprisoned. The Sultán accordingly promised to march to their assistance at the close of the rainy season. In the mean time, Mahmud himself, disgusted at seeing the whole resources of his kingdom in the hands of Medni Ráe, left Mándu on the pretext of going on a hunting excursion, and by bribing the guard escaped at night with his wife to Gujarát, where the king furnished him with tents, elephants, horses and all that was necessary for a royal guest. He then advanced towards Málwá on the 18th of November 1517. At this time Medni Ráe, who had been repairing the fortress at Dhár, fled to Chitor to obtain assistance from Ráná Sánga, and Dhár readily opened its gates to the Gujarát army, which then advanced and laid siege to Mándu. After several months that strong fortress was taken by storm on the 2nd of Safar A. H. 924 (A. D. 1518), but not until nineteen thousand Rajputs had been slain. On this occasion their wives and children performed the Johár ceremony (immolating themselves on a vast funeral pyre) in order to prevent their falling into the hands of the enemy.

This conquest having been effected at the cost of the lives of some two thousand of the Gujarát soldiers, the officers of Sultán Muzaffar's army advised him to retain the country which had so often been a source of annoyance to Gujarát. Muzaffar Sháh, true to his word, said that he had undertaken the expedition to oblige a brother king, and not to deprive him of his kingdom. Fearing, however, lest he might be further tempted to annex the country, he did not even stay in the fort, though cordially invited by the Málwá king, but returned to his encampment.

On Muzaffar's departure, Mahmud, in token of his gratitude,

sent to him by his son the jewelled sword-belt which his predecessor Mahmud Khilji I. had captured from the royal pavilion in the battle at Kapadvanj in A. D. 1452. He accompanied it with an invitation to a superb banquet, which was accepted. The Málwá Sultán treated his deliverer with noble hospitality, and placed at his disposal all his jewellery and even his harem, but the pious Muzaffar refused all, saying it was a sin even to look at what is unlawful. He reinstated Mahmud on his ancestral throne, which was thus a second time at the disposal of the Sultán of Gujarat, and leaving an auxiliary force with Mahmud departed for Gujarát, the king of Málwá accompanying him as far as Deolá. Muzaffar Sháh devoted the following few days to hunting, after which he entered Idar in trimuph, where he spent the hot season and the rains in pleasure, his army also enjoying its well earned repose.

In A. H. 925 (A. D. 1519) there was a great battle between Ráná Sánga of Chitor and the Málwá King, in which the latter was wounded and taken prisoner. Sultán Muzaffar had therefore to send an army to occupy Mándu. The Ráná, however, on this occasion, acted very honourably, and allowed Mahmud to return to his capital after recovering from his wounds.

The next year, A. D. 1520, the Sultán went from Mahmudábád to Idar, where he occupied himself for some time with the chase. Before going thence to Ahmadábád, the Sultan appointed one Nizám-ul-mulk in charge of Idar*. In his presence a wandering bard one day extolled the Ráná of Chitor, and affirmed he would soon come to Idar in order to restore the government to Ráe Mal. Nizám-ul-mulk, feeling annoyed,

* It is said that during the occupation of Idar by the Muhammadan commanders, the Ráos lived with their families in the hill country on the borders of Mewár. Forbes' Rás Málá, page 297.

not only said that Ráná Sánga was a dog*, but even called a dog of his by the Ráná's name and tied it at his door, and then taunting the bard, bade him go and tell the Ráná all that he had seen and heard. The Ráná, when informed, was fired with rage, and marched with an army of forty thousand horse on Idar. Nizám-ul-mulk at once sent messengers to the Sultán stating that his garrison did not consist of more than a thousand soldiers. Some of the ministers were, however, inimical to him, and, misrepresenting matters to the Sultán, delayed sending reinforcements, so that the Ráná was able without difficulty to enter Idar. Nizám-ul-mulk, abandoning the capital with great reluctance went to Ahmadnagar, where small reinforcements arrived. A brilliant battle took place, in which the Muhammadans showed great bravery, but they were at length overpowered by superior numbers. The Ráná then took Ahmadnagar, which he gave up to plunder. He next went to Wadnagar with a view to sack it also, but the earnest entreaties of the Bráhmans of that place caused him to desist. Accepting a large present from them, he shaped his course for Visalnagar, which town he pillaged. Soon, however, the news came that the Sultán's forces were on their way from Pátan and Ahmadábád, and accordingly the Ráná immediately retreated towards Idar and thence returned to his own country. Thus the enmity of the ministers against Nizám-ul-Mulk resulted in disgrace to Gujarát and the loss of many lives.

Eager however to retrieve his honour, Muzaffar Sháh sent a large army (A. D. 1521) under Malek Aiáz Sultán, governor of Sorath, to invade Chitor. They ravaged the district of Wágar the Rájá of which state had joined the Ráná in his previous expedition, and the capital Dungarpur was reduced to ashes

---

* "Sag" is the persian for a dog.

Malek Aiáz then advanced, and laid siege to the Ráná's fort of Mandesar, the walls of which were ten feet thick. Here the Ráná sent overtures of peace, apologizing for his behaviour and offering to return all he had taken in his former invasion, to pay an increased tribute, and to pass a written agreement promising submission and obedience for the future. There being at this time dissensions in his army, Malek Aiáz thought it prudent to rest content with the success already achieved, and, accepting the proposed terms of peace without the Sultan's full confirmation, marched back to Gujarát. Sultán Mahmud Khilji of Málwá, who had come to the Gujarát Sultán's assistance, also returned to his country on receiving from the Ráná a suitable present. His son, whom the Ráná had held as a hostage ever since the Málwá king's defeat in A. D. 1519, was also restored, and accompanied his father back to Málwá.

Sultán Muzaffar was displeased at this termination of the war, and, sending back Malek Aiáz to his government of Sorath, gave out his intention of renewing the campaign after the rains. He was, however, dissuaded from his purpose by a submissive embassy headed by the Ráná's son in person, who brought the stipulated tribute and presents.

The next few years the Sultán passed in Gujarát, strengthening the fort of Modásá and other frontier posts, and improving the administration of the country. He fell sick and died at Ahmadábád on the 2nd of Jumád-al-Akhir, A. H. 932 (A. D. 1526), after a reign of fourteen years and nine months. He was buried beside his father in the mausoleum at Sarkhej. While none of the Gujarát kings exceeded Muzaffar in learning and wisdom, he proved himself also a brave and able general. He is still known by the name of Muzaffar the Clement, on account of the mercy he was wont to show to all, and especially to any in distress. Many instances of his benevolence and charity are recorded in the Mirát-i-Sikandari, from which we select one only. It is said that the people of Jháláwár having complained to the Sultán that they had not sufficient pasturage owing to a large tract of country having been brought under cultivation, Muzaffar Sháh at once ordered a portion of the cultivated land to be left waste, notwithstanding the fact that the Government revenue from the land would of course be thereby seriously diminished.

Chapter VII.

The Reign of Sultán Sikandar.

1526 A. D.

On the very day of his father's death, Sultán Sikandar ascended the throne at Ahmadábád. He procceded to Chámpáner three days afterwards, where he distributed presents and titles (April 1526). At that time his foster brother Imád-ul-mulk, who had been expecting to be nominated prime minister, was grievously disappointed in consequence of Sikandar retaining his father's prime minister Khudávand Khán in that post. Imád-ul-mulk from that moment began conspiring against Sikandar, and, feigning sickness, did not attend the King's Darbár for several days. On one occasion when the Sultán had returned from playing Chaugan*, and retired for a little rest, the wretch entered the palace and ordered his attendent Páhárá to kill the Sultán in his sleep, an order which was immediately obeyed (14th Shábán A. H. 932 ; 26th May 1526). Great were the consternation and regret of the people of the town when the corpse of the Sultán was borne through the market to Hálol, only two hours after he had passed through it with royal pomp and pride, little dreaming that the angel of death was so near, and that the slave whom his kind hearted mother Bibi Ráni had nourished as her own child and to whose care she had on her death bed recommended her son, should prove his murderer. The only event of importance in this Sultán's short reign of one month and sixteen days was an expedition against his half brother Latif Khán, who laid claim to the throne and held possession of the mountainous country about Sultánpur and Nandurbár. It is said that the Sultán was informed of Imád-ul-mulk's treacherous intentions, but, considering him incapable of conspiring against his life, he took no heed of him, and spent his days in ease and enjoyment.

* This game resembles polo.

After murdering Sultán Sikandar, the villain Imád-ul-mulk took from the harem a son of the late Muzaffar II, named Násir Khán, then five or six years of age, and proclaimed him king under the title of Mahmud Sháh II. The nobles, however, were greatly displeased with Imád-ul-mulk, and, thirsting for revenge, sent secret messages to Muzaffar Sháh's second son Bahádur Khán, apprising him of all that had taken place, and asking him to return and govern his father's kingdom, promising at the same time their hearty assistance and co-operation. It is necessary here to state that Bahádur Khán, a brave and enterprising prince, had, during his father's life time, left Gujarát in disgust in A. D. 1524, owing partly to the insufficiency of his Jágir and partly to jealousy entertained towards him by his elder brother Sikandar, the heir apparent. Muzaffar Sháh was much distressed when he heard of his son's departure, and endeavoured, but without avail, to persuade him to return to Gujarát. Bahádur Khán first went to Bansvárá and thence to Chitor, where the Ráná treated him very kindly. One day, however, an unhappy incident occured. The Ráná's nephew gave Bahádur Khán an entertainment, at which a dancing girl of great beauty was summoned to perform. Seeing that the Gujarát prince was much struck with her exquisite dancing, the Ráná's nephew told his guest (probably without intending any insult) that she was the daughter of the Kázi of Ahmadnagar, and had been carried away by him when the Ráná sacked that town in A. D. 1520. Roused to sudden anger at seeing the daughter of a Kázi forced into concubinage, Bahádur Khán at once unsheathed his sword and cut down the unfortunate Rajput prince. A great uproar ensued, and the Rajputs rushed at Bahádur to kill him on the spot, but the mother of the Ráná, with singular presence of mind, ran forward holding a drawn dagger, and declared that she would stab herself if any one dared to touch Bahádur Khán, who was their guest, and whom she had called her son. Thus his life was saved by her timely intervention. The Ráná also said that his nephew was to blame for having provoked the Gujarát prince to sudden anger. Bahádur Khán, however, saw that he was looked upon with distrust by the people of Chitor, and thought it wise to leave that town. Accordingly, after taking leave of the Ráná, he went to Mewát, whose chief offered to assist him should he desire to attack Gujarát. Bahádur Khán, however, thankfully declined the offer, and said he could not meditate such treachery as to attack his father. He next proceeded as far as Delhi. It happened that at that time the king Ibráhim Lodi had gone to Pánipat to repel an invasion of his territory by Bábar king of Kábul. Ibráhim was therefore glad to avail himself of Bahádur Khán's services. On one occasion that prince greatly distinguished himself. In a skirmish between the Mughal and Afghán troops some of the latter were captured, and were being taken off the battle-field with their hands tied and with ropes round their necks. Though the king was himself present, no one dared to attempt their rescue. Prince Bahádur, the gallant grandson of Mahmud Begadá, heedless of the danger, dashed upon the Mughal troops with his small party and, defeating them, released the prisoners. This enterprise greatly redounded to prince Bahádur's fame, and the Delhi nobles even thought of making him their leader. This however excited jealousy in the mind of Ibráhim Lodi, and Bahádur Khán therefore abruptly left for Juánpur, whither the Delhi nobles sent envoys, inviting him to take command of the army, and stating that they were ready to acknowledge him as their king. The prince was about to accept this invitation, when the messengers from Gujarát arrived with letters from the nobles of that province. Bahádur Khán therefore resolved to return to his native country and avenge the murder of Sikandar. Accordingly after spending four days in the usual rites of mourning, he left Juánpur and set out for Ahmadábád.

Chapter VIII.

The Reign of Sultán Baháдur.

From 1526 to 1537 A. D.

Baháдur Khán procceded *via* Chitor, the Rájá of which state received him kindly. Here he was met by the Afghán, Ali Sher, an officer in the Gujarát army, who informed him of all that had taken place subsequent to Sikandar's death. From Chitor he marched to Dungarpur and thence to Kapadvanj, where several other officers and nobles joined him. Baháдur Khán then proceeded to Modásá, which fort had been strengthened by Imád-ul-mulk, but its garrison soon submitted to Baháдur Khán.

On the 20th. of Ramzán A. H. 932 (August 1526) he was received at Anhilwár by Táj Khán and other nobles from Ahmadábád. Thence he advanced with royal pomp towards the capital, which he entered without meeting with any resistance, and, after making his obeisance at the tombs of his ancestors in the Mánek Chok, he took up his abode in the palace in the Bhadar. On the 27th he held a public Darbár, and on the day of the Id (the Muhammadan new year's day), conferred distinctions on the nobles and officers. He further caused the Khutbáh (public prayers) to be read in his name.

After the Id ceremonies were over, Sultán Baháдur marched from the Ghatámandal palace on the Kánkariá tank to Mahmúdábád, where he was joined by additional troops, to whom the traitor Imád-ul-mulk had given an advance of pay in order to induce them to remain firm in his cause. Baháдur Sháh next crossed, though with difficulty, the Shedhi river, at that time in flood, and halted at Nadiád. The Sultán left that town on the 16th of Shawál, and crossed the river Mahí at the Khánpur ford. Thence, leaving his main army behind, owing to the difficulty of making forced marches in the rain, he went to Mahmudábád Chámpáner with only four hundred horse and a few elephants. After visiting the tomb of his brother Sikandar at Hálol, Bahádur Sháh sent an officer named Táj Khán to plunder Imád-ul-mulk's house at Chámpáner and take him captive. This order was carried out, and the villain, as a fitting punishment for his crimes, was ordered to be ignominiously executed along with two of his companions. The accomplice Páhárá, whose hand had given the fatal blow to Sikandar Sháh, was flayed alive, and his corpse was exposed on a gibbet. Sultán Bahádur now formally mounted the throne at Mahmudábád Chámpáner on the 14th of Jul Kadah A. H. 932 (22nd August 1526), and, bestowing the usual dresses and honours, ordered a present of one year's pay to be given to the army.

While the Sultán was thus engaged, prince Latif Khán, whom Imád-ul-mulk had secretly invited but who, owing to the celerity of Bahádur Shah's movements, had been unable to join the rebel, caused disturbances near Nandurbár, in which he was aided by Bhim Dev, chief of Rájpiplá, and others. An army was therefore sent against him. In the fight which took place Bhim Dev was slain, and the unfortunate Latif Khán received wounds, from the effects of which he died while being taken as a captive to the Sultán's camp. A few days afterwards, the infant Násir Khán also died (December 1526), having been, according to the Mirát-i-Ahmadi, poisoned. The bodies of both the princes were buried close to that of Sikandar in the vault at Hálol. Soon thereafter intelligence was received that Bhim Dev's son and successor Rai Singh had plundered Dohad; a force was therefore sent against him, which spent some months in ravaging his dominions.

At the close of the year A. H. 932 (A. D. 1526), Bahádur Sháh went on a hunting expedition in the direction of Cambay, where news was brought him that the Governor of Sorath was in treaty with the Portuguese to surrender Diu. Bahádur Sháh accordingly went to that port, where he stayed for a month, and then replacing the Governor of Sorath as well as the commander at Diu by other more trustworthy officers, he returned *via* Talájá and Goghá to Mahmudábád, where Vikramájit, son of Ráná Sanga of Chitor, waited upon him with suitable presents. After spending a month at Mahmudábád and three months at Ahmadábád in ease and pleasure, the Sultán went to Nándod, where he received the submission of the Rájá of that state. He then proceeded to Surat, and, returning thence to Mahmudábád, gave the son of the Chitor Ráná leave to depart.

About this time it became evident that the Portuguese were endeavouring to establish themselves on the coast of Sorath, and to acquire possession of the fort of Diu. In order to frustrate their designs Sultán Bahádur was under the necessity of devoting much of his time and attention to that island, and he frequently visited it as also Cambay and Goghá*. He further gave orders for the construction of a fort at Broach (A. D. 1527) on the opposite coast of the gulf of Cambay. On representations made by his sister's son Muhammad Khán Adil Khán, Ruler of Khándesh, Sultán Bahádur sent an army into the Deccan in aid of the chief of Gáwel, a fort in the Berárs, who had been persecuted by Nizám Sháh of Ahmadnagar. The latter was defeated and his capital plundered (A. D. 1529) and the Khutbáh was read in the Gujarát Sultán's name. It is said that in this expedition the Sultán's force consisted of not less than one hundred thousand horse and nine hundred fighting elephants.

Sultán Bahádur was of a very restless disposition. After paying one more visit to Diu and Cambay and purchasing for

---

* This fine sea-port town was twice burnt by the Portuguese, once in 1531 and again in 1546 A. D.

his own use the entire cargo of a ship containing amongst other merchandise no less than thirteen hundred maunds of rose-water, the Sultán marched to Wágar A. H. 937 (A. D. 1531). Here the Dungarpur Rájá Prithviráj waited upon him, and his son embraced the Muhammadan religion. The Sultán brought Wágar into submission, and posted garrisons in strong places. He gave half of its territory to Prithviráj and half to his brother Chagá, and bestowed the village of Sanilah on the newly converted prince.

Ambassadors from Ráná Ratansingh, the son and successor of Ráná Sánga, also waited upon the Sultán with presents, and complained of the conduct of Mahmud Khilji of Málwá in attacking his territories. Sultán Bahádur had himself reason to be displeased with the Málwá king for having, notwithstanding the obligations under which he stood to his father, harboured his brother Chánd Khán when aspiring to the throne of Gujarát. Mahmud however sent ambassadors expressing friendship and a desire to see Bahádur Sháh, who consented to the interview, but delayed from day to day, and the Gujarát Sultán accordingly marched on Mándu in conjunction with the armies of Chitor, Bhilsá and Raisen. The Governor of Dhár also came over to him. Sultán Bahádur posted his allies in the surrounding districts, and himself invested Mándu with the main body of his army, whose attacks were several times bravely repulsed by Mahmud Khilji, though his garrison did not exceed four thousand men. They were, however, at last worn out by fatigue, and Bahádur Sháh, with a select band on the 9th of Shabán A.H. 937(28th March 1531),escaladed the fort at the point where it was known to be most difficult of approach. Trusting to the inaccessibility of the fort at that point, the garrison had left it unguarded, and hence the storming party, after it had once succeeded in gaining the heights, met with but little opposition. The army then proceeded to invest the palace, whither Mahmud had retreated with a view to defend it to the last, but he was overpowered and compelled to surrender together with his seven sons. Sultán Bahádur, it is said, was inclined to treat him with kindness, and even to restore him his kingdom, as had been done by his father, but Mahmud in his pride and arrogance insulted Bahádur Sháh to his face, whereupon he was ordered to be confined and sent to Chámpáner together with his sons. The Gujarát prince Chánd Khán fled towards the Deccan during the confusion.

On the road to Chámpáner the party escorting the unfortunate Khiljis was attacked by a band of Bhils and Kolis, supposed to have been mercenaries of the Rájpiplá chief, and the guard, fearing lest their royal prisoners should escape, killed them all. The Khilji family of Málwá thus became extinct, and that important province was annexed to the kingdom of Gujarát (A. H. 937, A. D. 1531).

Bahádur Sháh spent the rainy season at Mándu, and appointed a Governor and other officers to the province. He also treated the former nobles with kindness, and confirmed them in their Jágirs.

In the same year, hearing that Rájá Mánsing of Jhálávár*, a dependency of Gujarát, had sacked several of the Gujarát towns and killed the commandant of the Dasádá outpost, the Sultán sent an army against him, which took, and permanently severed from the Jhálá's territories, the parganáhs of Viramgám and Mándal, which now form part of the Ahmadábád district.

The Sultán then proceeded to his nephew Muhammad Faruki's territories of Burhánpur and Asir, (9th Safar A. H. 938

* Now under the Káthiáwár Political Agency.

(A. D. 1532), and conferred on him the title of Sháh. Názim-ul-mulk, the ruler of Ahmadnagar, also received from him the title of Názim Sháh.

The Sultán now sent a force against a Rajput Chief named Silhádi who held the strong fortress of Ráisin and who had been of service during the campaign against Mándu. For this service the Sultán had rewarded him with the grant of the city of Ujjain, the parganáh of Ashtá and the district of Bhilsá, and three lacs of Tankáhs. The Sultán, on his return from the Deccan, sent an officer to summon Silhádi, but the latter, suspecting evil, hesitated, and presented himself only after much delay. Bahádur Sháh became much displeased, and making him prisoner on the 17th Jumád'l-aval, compelled him to embrace the Muhammadan faith, and marched on the fortress of Ráisin. Silhádi's brother Lakhshman offered a stubborn resistance, and Silhádi obtained permission to go and persuade his garrison to submit. After he had entered the fort, however, Silhádi's wife and officers so completely won him over by their entreaties and arguments that he did not return to the Sultán. He fell in the defence of his fort, and his wife, together with seven hundred other females of his harem, immolated themselves. The fort was ultimately taken on the 30th of Ramzán A. H. 938, 10th May 1532.

About this time Sultán Alam Lodi had been driven by Humáyun Pádisháh of Delhi from Kálpi, and sought an asylum with Sultán Bahádur. The latter, to his own misfortune, granted his request, and for the support of his army, consisting of twelve thousand horse, gave him the newly conquered provinces of Ráisin, Bhilsá and Chanderi. He then went to Gondwáná on an elephant-hunting expedition, and succeeded in obtaining a great number of elephants. Having subsequently reduced the forts of Islámábád and Hushangábád, he appointed Imád-ul-mulk to conquer the rest of the country about Mandásar, and himself returned to his capital Mahmudábád on the 15th of Safar.

Soon after this, intelligence was received from Diu that the Portuguese were coming with a large fleet to capture that fort. The Sultán therefore, about the end of A. H. 937, A. D. 1531, proceeded to Cambay, and the Portuguese fled on hearing of his approach. The Sultán, however, still proceeded on his way to Diu, and as his heart was embittered against Chitor because the Ráná of that place had sent a force in aid of Silhádi, and had thus caused much trouble and delay in the taking of the Ráisin fort, the Sultán despatched for the siege of Chitor an immense Egyptian gun brought by his Turkish General Rumi Khán, and with it one hundred other smaller guns*. He then returned to Ahmadábád via Cambay, and after visiting the tombs of his ancestors and paying his respects to his spiritual preceptor Sháh Shekh jiu at Batvá, he journeyed in a single day to Mahmudábád Chámpáner. Here he married a daughter of Jám Firoz, king of Sindh, who, on his defeat by the Mughals, had taken refuge with him in the month of Ramzán A. H. 935 (A. D. 1529).

At Mahmudábád the Sultán enlisted several thousand picked soldiers, and, being aware of the strengh of the fortress of Chitor, he collected a vast supply of arms and ammunition and proceeded to Mándu, where he concentrated his troops and sent them on towards Chitor. At Mandásar they were met by envoys, who begged forgiveness for the Ráná, and communicated his readiness to carry out whatever order was given by the Sultán. The latter, however, refused to retire, and the army marched on to Chitor (Rajab A. H. 939, A. D. 1533). After plundering the suburb attached to the fort, the force under

* This is the first mention of the regular use of artillery in Gujarát. Tod's Rájasthán Vol. I, p. 330.

Tátár Khán (son of Alam Khán Lodi) carried the Parkotah (outer gate) on the 6th Rajab. Two days afterwards the siege train arrived with the big gun, which speedily caused great havoc by levelling ramparts and buildings. All the arrangements of the besiegers were excellent, and were so effectively carried out that in a short time the garrison was reduced to the utmost straits, and the fall of the fort seemed inevitable. In this emergency the grandmother of the Ráná, who had saved Bahádur Sháh's life when he was a refugee at that court in A. D. 1524, wrote a very impressive letter to Bahádur Sháh, offering to surrender to the Sultán all those towns and villages of Málwá which had been in the Ráná's possession since his predecessor Ráná Sanga's victory over Mahmud Khilji in A. D. 1519. She further promissed to present him with a golden waist-band and jewelled crown of priceless value, taken from the same Mahmud Khilji, and also agreed to pay five lacs of rupees, one hundred horses and ten elephants in token of submission. The Sultán, out of gratitude for her past services, acceeded to her prayers, and raised the siege of Chitor on the 27th of Shábán A. H. 939 (24th March 1533), but only to renew the attack two years later.

From Chitor Bahádur Sháh sent a portion of his army under trusted officers to Rantambhor and Ajmer to reduce the fortresses in those towns. He then went to Mándu, whither the remainder of his army followed and there enjoyed a well earned rest.

Gujarát had now reached the zenith of its prosperity. Its territory was both large and well defended. The kingdom of Málwá was annexed, while Chitor was trembling and destined soon to fall. The kings of Delhi sought and obtained protection from its brave ruler, and the kings of Khándesh, Berár and Ahmadnagar in the Deccan were compelled to acknowledge his supremacy. From the fact of the kingdom of Gujarát having a sea-board with no less than eighty-four ports, even Sikandar Lodi of Delhi used to say, "the magnificence of the kings of Delhi consists of wheat and barley, whilst that of the kings of Gujarát has its foundation on coral and pearls."

After a brief period of inaction and without any provocation on the Ráná's part, the idea of annexing Chitor to his kingdom again took possession of the mind of the ambitious Sultán Bahádur. A controversy, however, which eventually proved ruinous to the Gujarát Sultán, arose between him and the Emperor Humáyun of Delhi. It has already been stated that the Sultán had given offence to Humáyun by sheltering his opponent Ibráhim Lodi, and now another political refugee Muhammad Jumál Mirzá, husband of Humáyun's sister, after intriguing against the Emperor, fled to Gujarát and sought the Sultán's protection (A. H. 940, A. D. 1533-34). Humáyun wrote several letters to Bahádur Sháh, couched in very courteous terms, asking him either to surrender the fugitive or to expel him from his dominions, but Bahádur Sháh, puffed up with his victories, not only declined to comply with the request, but expressed his refusal in very offensive terms*.

The infatuated Gujarát Sultán, moreover, in his mad desire to annex Chitor, marched against that fortress instead of rather reserving all his forces to cope with the powerful enemy he had in his arrogance created. Humáyun left Agrá for Chitor (A. H. 941, A. D. 1534), but recognising that by attacking Bahádur Sháh while the latter was engaged in the siege, he

---

* It is said that Bahádur Sháh not being able to read or write had employed as his Munshi a man dismissed by Humáyun. Accordingly this Munshi, in order to slight the Emperor, worded the replies in an unbecoming style.

would be indirectly assisting an infidel, and thus acting contrary to the dictates of religion, he halted at Gwálior, patiently allowing Sultán Bahádur to go on with his operations against Chitor and fatigue himself. That fortress, though bravely defended, fell at length on the 31st of March 1535 before the superior strength of the Gujarát artillery, which was ably commanded by the Turkish general Rumi Khán, and worked by the Portuguese whom the commandant Kiwám-ul-mulk had captured in or about A. D. 1528 and afterwards converted to the Muhammadan faith.

The capture of Chitor was, however, not effected until thirty-two thousand of its brave defenders and nearly all the chiefs of the neighbouring states, which had come to its aid, had fallen in its defence. On this occassion the horrors of the Jauhár ceremony, in which thirteen thousand females headed by the Ráná's mother perished in the flames, were again witnessed. As an instance of the courageous devotion of Rajput women, the queen-mother Javáhir Bái, clad in armour, had headed one of the sallies from this fort, and thus met a glorious death*.

After the fall of Chitor, Humáyun, whose army had already inflicted a severe defeat on the Gujarát troops sent to make a demonstration against Delhi, advanced to attack Sultán Bahádur. The latter also moved forward his army, but halted on reaching Mandásar, where he entrenched himself behind his artillery, being influenced largely by the advice of Rumi Khán in whom he placed entire confidence. This general, however, had taken offence at Bahádur Sháh having broken his promise to give him the command of Chitor, and therefore did every thing in his power to mislead the Sultán. He even sent secret messages to Humáyun offering his services, and advised him to keep a body of cavalry ready to intercept supplies.

* Tod's Rájasthán vol. I, p. 331.

This was accordingly done, and the Gujarát troops were almost reduced to starvation. The opposing forces remained in sight of each other for some days, but the Sultán's army became so weakened as to be quite unable to cope with the formidable Afgháns. To add to the disaster Rumi Khán secretly went over and joined the enemy. At last, when supplies were exhausted, Sultán Bahádur, hitherto unaccustomed to reverses, lost heart, and in despair caused all his diamonds and other jewels to be destroyed. His guns were next blown up, the bullocks having no strength to pull them, and the trunks of two of his best fighting elephants were cut off, in order to prevent them ever being of service to the enemy. He then, with a few of his followers, fled by night to Mándu. The army, on hearing the next morning (25th March 1535) of the Sultán's flight, fell into great confusion, and the Emperor taking this opportunity to advance, the camp became a scene of plunder and massacre. Humáyun then exultingly entered the Sultán's tents, which were all covered with embroidery and interwoven with gold, and exclaimed, "These are the equipments of the lord of the sea," referring by this epithet to the Gujarát Sultán's sway over the eighty-four seaports.

Midst the melancholy history of Sultán Bahádur's misfortune, an amusing story has been recorded by the author of the Mirát-i-Sikandari, whose father accompanied Humáyun in this expedition in charge of his library. He relates that when the victory was complete, the Emperor seated himself on his throne and held a general reception. Nobles and officers stood before him with their hands folded, when a parrot which had been found in the plunder of Bahádur Sháh's camp was brought to him in its cage. The Emperor was greatly amazed at its utterances. At that time Rumi Khán entered, and the king said kindly to him "Rumi Khán, come here." The instant the parrot heard the name, it began to call out in Hindustáni "That scoundrel Rumi Khán", repeating these words several times. Rumi Khán hung down his head abashed, and the Emperor, still further surprised at the bird's talk, yet unwilling to destroy so strange a creature, remarked to Rumi Khán, "If any rational being had spoken thus, I should have had his tongue cut out, but what can I do to a senseless animal?"

It may be that the above is not mere idle gossip, for, those who are aware of the power to talk possessed by these birds will not find it difficult to believe that after Rumi Khán's desertion from Sultán Bahádur's camp, the men of his army being accustomed to speak of that foreigner in terms of disrespect, the parrot may have caught up these expressions from them. Hence, as in the story just related, when it heard Rumi Khán's name, it at once began to utter the disrespectful phrases it had learnt, and in this way shamed the traitor.

Sultán Bahádur, after his flight to Mándu, shut himself up in that strong fortress, whither the Emperor Humáyun followed him after a short delay in collecting the spoils at Mandásar. Here Rumi Khán added to his perfidy by persuading Bhupat Rái, under the pretext of avenging the injury inflicted on his father Silhádi, to open one of the city gates, of which he was in charge at the time of assault. This agreement was carried out, and Sultán Bahádur, considering his case hopeless, departed for Gujarát (A. H. 942, A. D. 1535) leaving his officers to defend the remaining five gates as best they could. Some of Humáyun's men, observing his flight, pursued after him, but the Sultán, on being overtaken, turned and fought with such bravery that they were driven back. Humáyun's generals, on defeating the troops left to defend the citadel, entered it in triumph, after which a general massacre took place, streams of blood flowing in the streets of Mándu.

From that town, Humáyun marched on Chámpáner, whither Sultán Bahádur had fled on his way to Cambay and Diu. Chámpáner had been left in charge of trusted officers, who defended the fort with valour. At last, however, some Kolis, foolishly sent out to procure provisions, the fort still containing plenty of grain, fell into Humáyun's hands, and in order to save their lives, showed him a path not known either to the besiegers or to the besieged. By this the troops entered, and succeeded in taking Chámpáner, which might otherwise have held out for a much longer time (Safar A. H. 942, August 1535 A.D.).

From Chámpáner Humáyun went to Cambay, where he spent a few days in making excursions into the neighbourhood, but having been molested by Kolis, who, in their night attacks, even entered his pavilion and carried off his baggage and books, he gave the unoffending town up to plunder. Humáyun left Cambay for Ahmadábád, whence he visited the tomb of Kutub-ul-Alam Burhán-ud-din at Batwá, and encamped his army at the village of Ghiáspur, two kos to the south of the city. Bahádur Sháh, on the other hand, after leaving Cambay, went to the port of Diu. He sent off to Mediná his family, and with them 300 iron chests, containing treasure and jewels. On this occasion he is said to have also despatched an ambassador to Constantinople with costly presents, including the jewelled belt he had obtained from the Chitor Ráná's mother, the value of which has been estimated at three krores of Ashrafis.* None of this immense treasure ever found its way back to Gujarát, but it remained with the Grand Signior of Constantinople, who, from its possession, became entitled to the appelation of Sulimán the Magnificent (Briggs's Ferishtá vol. IV. p. 141).

Thus it came to pass that the reigning Sultán of Gujarát,

* The Ashrafi is a coin of variable value, but is commonly reckoned as equal to one gold mohur (30 shillings).

who had hitherto always been victorious and able to command obedience from the kings of the Deccan, Khándesh and Berar, who in Málwá had overthrown the powerful rule of Mahmud Khilji and only a few days previously had conquered Chitor, one of the best fortified towns in India, not only lost all his newly acquired territory,* but within the short space of six months, had to destroy or part with the greater portion of all that he himself and his predecessors had amassed. His family moreover became exiles in a strange land, while he himself was obliged to seek safety in flight. All this, as is evident, was owing to his own arrogance and ambition. Had he been content with humbling the Ráná of Chitor, his army and resources would not have been so utterly exhausted and, more especially, had he treated with becoming courtesy the Emperor Humáyun, the latter, embarassed as he was by revolts and troubles in other quarters, would not have thought of attacking him. But to his cost Sultán Bahádur failed to adopt right measures, and his annihilation would have been complete had the Emperor Humáyun been able to follow up his victories, and march against Sorath. Fortunately however for the Sultán, Sher Sháh the Governor of Bengal revolted at this very time, and hence the Emperor was obliged to return to his own capital. He accordingly left his brother Mirzá Askari and other officers in charge of Gujarát, and himself hastened to his capital in order to suppress the revolt.

Availing themselves of the opportunity thus afforded them, Malek Amin Darwish, Commandant of Rantambhor, Malek Burhán-ul-mulk of Chitor, and Shamsher-ul-mulk of Ajmer

---

* Chitor was regained by the Ráná Vikramájit during Sultán Bahádur's flight before the emperor Humáyun. The capital was removed from Chitor to Udaipur at the end of the sixteenth century.

effected a junction, and collecting a force of about forty thousand horse, proceeded towards Pátan, whence they sent information to Sultán Bahádur Sháh, who joined them with his men. The Emperor's Commander Yádgár Násir retreating to Ahmadábád, the Sultán followed, but on his approach the enemy encamped at Ghiáspur. This they left at night for Kanij, three Kos from Mahmudábád, where they were joined by troops from Broach. At Kanij a well contested battle was fought between Sultán Bahádur and the imperial troops, in which the latter were defeated. They were pursued as far as Chámpáner, at which place the Sultán halted, sending on, however, his nephew Muhammad Sháh' Asiri to drive them from Málwá, which he effected (A. H. 942, A. D. 1535–36). Thus both Gujarát and Málwá were relieved of the Mughals after they had occupied these provinces for about nine months, and Sultán Bahádur Sháh regained his kingdom.

Another enemy destined soon to arrest the further course of this energetic Sultán was, however, springing up in the west. During the days of his misfortune, while Bahádur Sháh was staying at Diu, the Portuguese, who had become known in this country by the name of Firangis (Franks), had tendered him their service and promised him assistance at their ports. Under the straitened circumstances in which he was placed, the Sultán accepted their overtures. In return for their supplying him a force of five hundred Europeans to assist him in recovering his kingdom, he gave them leave to build a factory at Diu. Instead of a factory, however, the Portuguese erected a strong fort, in which, after furnishing it with guns and muskets, they took up their residence. Sultán Bahádur, on regaining possession of Gujarát, greatly regretted having granted them any permission at all, and began devising means for turning them away by artifice. He therefore proceeded to

Diu, and had an interview with Nuno-da-Cunha the Portuguese Viceroy, who had recently arrived there with a fleet. Remonstrances and explanations took place, and it is admitted both sides meditated treachery. The Governor, when invited to see the Sultán, feigned sickness, but sent a return invitation to Sultán Bahádur. The latter, accompanied by only a small guard, visited the Governor on board his vessel on the 14th of February 1537, and was received apparently with much honour, but, on leaving, an affray took place, in which Sultán Bahádur and his attendants were killed and thrown overboard. The Portuguese represent this affray as accidental, and the Muhammadans as designed, but the evidence seems to warrant the latter conclusion.

Thus on the 3rd of Ramzán 943 (February 14th, A. D. 1537) the career of the brave and illustrious Sultán Bahádur was closed at the early age of thirty-one years, and after a short but glorious reign of eleven years, during which the power of Gujarát had attained its culminating point.

The ungrateful Mirzá Mahmud Zamán, who has been mentioned above, and whom the Sultán had granted a Jágir at Awán near Diu, did not scruple to aspire to the throne of his benefactor on his death, whereupon a battle took place between his troops and the Sultán's army, which ended in the defeat and exile of the Mirzá.

Chapter IX.

The Reigns of Sultán Muhammad Faruki and Sultán Muhammad III.

From 1537 to 1554 A. D.

After the murder of Sultán Bahádur, his ministers and nobles wrote to his sister's son Muhammad Sháh Faruki, king of Asir and Burhánpur, whom that Sultán had during his life time nominated as his heir. Acquainting him with what had happened, they invited him to come to Ahmadábád and assume its government. The Faruki Muhammad Sháh was so greatly attached to his uncle, with whom he had co-operated in several of his brilliant campaigns, that the shock of the news of his death brought on an illness which in seventy days terminated fatally. No heir was now left except the son of the late Sultán Bahádur's brother Latif Khán named Muhammad Khán. This prince, whom Bahádur Sháh had ordered to be kept in confinement, was accordingly released, and the nobles installed him as king under the title of Muhammad Sháh III.

The splendour of Gujarát had, however, passed away with Bahádur Sháh. On his death the Portuguese had regained possession of Diu,* and subsequent to it no tribute reached the capital from the Deccan or from any of the ports held by Europeans. The Portuguese also attacked and took Cambay in A. D. 1538, when they sacked and burnt the town and carried off immense booty, the town being then one of the richest in India.

Sultán Muhammad bin Latif Khán being only eleven years

* It appears on a reference to Lethbridge's History of India that Muhammad III besieged this fortress in 1538 and 1545, but was bravely repulsed by the Portuguese on both occasions, but neither the Mirát-i-Ahmadi nor the Mirát-i-Sikandari mentions anything of these two expeditions.

of age when he ascended the throne (A. D. 1537), the sovereign power was divided between Imád-ul-mulk the Prime Minister and one of the nobles named Dariá Khán, these two carrying on the Government between them, while the young king was kept under surveillance. The conjoint rule, however, did not long prevail, and one day Dariá Khán took the Sultán on the pretext of hunting some miles away from Ahmadábád, and there assembling a large army commanded Imád-ul-mulk, in the name of the minor Sultán, to depart to his Jágir in Jháláwár. Although Imád-ul-mulk obeyed, Dariá Khán none the less led an army against him, and, defeating him in a battle at Pátri, compelled him to take shelter first at Burhánpur and then at Mándu.

Dariá Khán thus acquired the entire control of the Sultán and of the government. For some five years the Sultán bore his treatment at the hands of Dariá Khán with fortitude, but at the end cf that period he began to grow impatient, and entering into league with one Alam Khán Lodi, Jágirdár of Dhandhuká, fled to that town. But Dariá Khán was in possession both of the treasure and of the capital, hence he elevated another boy, a descendant of Sultán Ahmad, to the throne, and, having given him the title of Sultán Muzaffar, caused coin to be struck and the public prayers to be read in his name. He also collected fifty thousand horse, and went out to oppose Alam Khán Lodi and the Sultán, defeating both at the village of Dábar, about seven kos from Dhandhuká. The Sultán fled to Ránpur, and Alamkhán to Sádrá, seventeen kos north of Ahmadábád.

Dariá Khán then returned victorious to Dholká. Public feeling was, however, on the side of the Sultán, and some large bands, as well as some deserters from Dariá Khán, joined his camp. The Sultán therefore again joined Alam Khán, and the united forces marched on Ahmadábád. Dariá Khán had already proceeded thither and had forcibly gained admittance, the inhabitants having closed the gates of the city against him. Recognising however that he would not be able to hold Ahmadábád, he sent forward his wives and treasure to the fort of Chámpáner, and himself fled to Asir in the vain hope of obtaining assistance there (A. H. 950, A. D. 1543).

The Sultán, after a few days stay in Ahmadábád, advanced on Chámpáner, which he besieged. He carried the fort by storm, and in doing so shewed an intrepidity and courage well worthy of a descendant of Sultán Ahmad. Here the Sultán rested for three months, and appointed Alam Khán his Commander-in-chief, and Burhán-ul-mulk, an upright and prudent officer, his Prime Minister. Imád-ul-mulk, the former minister, who had been dismissed by Dariá Khán and was residing at Mándu under the protection of its then ruler Kádir Sháh, was also recalled, and the Sirkár of Broach as well as the fort of Surat were given him in Jágir. For some time prosperity attended the young Sultán, but unhappily he took into his confidence and made a favourite of one Chárunji, who, originally a bird keeper, had assisted the Sultán in his days of adversity by carrying messages between him and Alam Khán Lodi at Dhandhuká. This individual of mean origin induced the Sultán to hang two officers of high rank, Alá-ud-din Lodi brother of Sikandar Lodi king of Delhi, and Shuját Khán, and to order their bodies to remain exposed for three days. This enraged the nobles, who demanded that the low-born knave should be deliverd up to them. The Sultán declined, but invited the noblemen into his presence. They obeyed, but seeing Járji, on whom the proud title of Maháfiz Khán (protector) had been conferred, standing at the Sultán's side, they forthwith cut him to pieces. The Sultán strove to save him, but failing in the attempt, was about to plunge a dagger into his own heart, when the weapon was wrested from him after having inflicted only a slight wound. Perceiving that unworthy persons could influence the Sultán for evil, the nobles, placing him under restraint, removed him to Ahmadábád. They soon, however, were tired of keeping guard over him, and a conspiracy was formed to blind him, and either put a minor on the throne, or divide out the kingdom among themselves. Fortunately for the Sultán, this design was not accomplished, as he obtained timely information regarding it from a noble named Tátár-ul-mulk, with whose aid and that of other officers he took the conspirators completely by surprise, and, issuing out one day with a body of horse, ordered the houses of the chief rebels to be plundered. According to a preconcerted arrangement, this was done so expeditiously in the early morning while these nobles were yet asleep, that they had time only to escape with their lives.

It would be tedious to relate in detail the later history of the banished nobles, but it suffices to say that they were ultimately expelled from Gujarát (A. H. 952, A. D. 1545) though with considerable difficulty, and eventually sought refuge with Sher Sháh of Delhi.

Sultán Muhammad III. having rebuilt the castle of Surat (A. D. 1543), next devoted his attention to the administration of the kingdom, and appointed as his Prime Minister one Asaf Khán, who had been minister of Sultán Bahádur and had taken the family of that prince to Meccá. The army was also put on a proper footing. The Sultán then expressed a desire to seize Málwá, but the minister rather unwisely suggested that he might obtain a country equal in extent to Málwá by merely attaching the Wántá* lands then

---

* Wántás, or portions of village lands had been assigned as a conciliatory measure by Sultán Ahmad I, the founder of Ahmadábád, to the original Rajput Chiefs Much of the Wántá land is still enjoyed either free from assessment or subject to a quit-rent.

possessed by the Rajputs, Garásiás and Kolis in Gujarát itself. The order was accordingly given, and the chiefs of Idar, Sirohi, Dungarpur, Bánsvárá, Lunáwárá, Rájpiplá and the villages on the banks of the Mahi river began to raise disturbances (A. D. 1546). The forces at Sirohi and several other outposts thereupon received orders to extirpate every Rajput and Koli except those Government servants and traders who wore a particular mark on the sleeves of their coats. This order appears to have been rigidly carried out, and the turbulent Garásiás were thus forcibly reduced to submission. No Hindu was permitted to ride through the city or to dress himself in fine clothes; even the observance of the Diváli and Holi festivals was, prohibited, and thus the minds of the Hindus, and those of the military classes particularly, were quite alienated during the latter part of this Sultán's reign. A striking evidence of the destestation in which he was held is afforded by the fact that when he was assassinated by his own Muhammadan servant, the Garásiás made a stone image of the murderer, and worshipped it as that of their deliverer.

In A. D. 1546 the Sultán proceeded on a pleasure trip to Mahmudábád, where he laid out a magnificent deer park six miles in extent. At each corner of the park was a palace with gilded roofs. On the right hand side of the door leading to each of the palaces was a market, in which everything was provided that could contribute to pleasure. Here Sultán Muhammad, following the practice of his predecessors, used to celebrate the nativity of the prophet from the first to the 12th of Rabi-ul-Aval, when all the Ulemás, Shekhs and learned men attended and rehearsed the traditions of Islám. One night during these celebrations in A. D. 1554, the Sultán retired to rest after taking leave of the' assembly. After a short sleep, feeling thirsty, he asked for a little sherbet, when one Burhán* gave him a poisoned draught, which the Sultán drank. Feeling uneasy soon after, Burhán said it must be owing to fatigue, and accordingly gave him some Májam (an intoxicating drug) by which the Sultán grew drowsy, and, as he was on the point of going to sleep, he was stabbed to the heart by this villain. Thus on the 12th of Rabi-ul-aval A. H. 961, A. D. 1554, ended the career of Sultán Muhammad III at the age of twenty-eight, after a reign of eighteen years.

Not content with the foul murder of his sovereign, Burhán concealed in the ante-chamber a body of armed men with instructions to kill every one who entered. He then sent his attendants to call the Prime Minister Asaf Khán and other nobles on the pretext that the Sultán wanted to consult them on urgent business. Asaf Khán, Afzal Khán and some others came, and were all assassinated one by one. After this the wretch laid his hand on the royal treasure and effects, and, dressing himself in princely attire, and binding on his neck a jewelled collar of great value which the Sultan had frequently worn, he seated himself, like a dog, on the royal chair. He then gave away the Sultán's best horses with their saddles and gold and silver head ornaments to his vile companions.

Meanwhile the rumour of what had occurred spread through the city, and forthwith two of the surviving leaders went to the palace. On Burhán addressing one of these named Sherwán Khán with a view to gain him over, he was fired with rage, and thrust Burhán through the shoulder with his sword, so that the villain fell dead at his feet. Others with him were also put to the sword. The nobles then caused the body of the deceased Sultán to be removed to Sarkhej and buried in the mausoleum of Mahmud Begadá.

* This Burhán was a man of low birth whom the Sultán had raised to a post of trust in his kitchen, and who, having been detected drinking wine in the deer park on the feast day in honour of the Prophet's birth, feared punishment at the Sultán's hands.

Chapter X.

The reign of Ahmad Sháh II.

From 1554 to 1561 A. D.

After the murder of Muhammad III, the nobles, after consultation together, raised to the throne a descendant of Sultán Ahmad the founder of Ahmadábád, by name Ahmad Khán, who forthwith assumed the title of Ahmad Sháh II, (15th of Rabi-ul-aval A. H. 961, 28th February 1554). As he was only a minor, it was agreed that Itimád Khán, the Prime Minister, should carry on the government in the king's name, the country being parcelled out among the nobles, each one of whom agreed to protect the frontier and preserve the public peace. Seeing the kingdom thus divided, Mubárak Sháh, king of Khándesh, took the opportunity of marching on Gujarát in order to assert his own claims, but the nobles banded against him, and the armies encamped on the opposite bank of the Narbadá. Here negotiations were opened, and a peace was concluded, after which the Khándesh ruler returned to his country and the Gujarát nobles to Ahmadábád. Unity did not, however, prevail long among them, and a party headed by Ikhtiár-ul-mulk raised another prince named Sháhu to the throne. A battle shortly ensued in which Sháhu was defeated, whereupon the nobles agreed to the following division of the province.

For Ahmad Sháh's private expenses.	Ahmadábád and the Daskrohi subdivision.
For Itimád Khán and his party.	Kadi, Jháláwár, Petlád, Nádiád, Bhál, Rádhanpur, Sami, Munjpur, Godhrá, and the country of Sorath.
For Sayyid Mubárak and his party.	Pátan, Cambay with the Chorási, Dholká, Goghá, Dhandhuká, Chámpáner, Sarnál, Bálásinor and Kapadvanj.

For Imád-ul-mulk Rumi and his party.	Broach, Barodá, Surat as far as Sultánpur and Nandurbár frontier.
For the Gujarát nobles under Itimád Khán.	Modásá and other districts.

The king was, however, always at the mercy of one noble or another, and dissensions springing up between them, Itimád Khán fled to Mubárak Sháh of Khándesh, who again led an army against Gujarát. The other nobles made a treaty with Mubárak Sháh, according to which the districts of Sultánpur and Nandurbár were given to the ruler of Khándesh (A. D. 1560), and these parts thus became permanently alienáted from Gujarát. Itimád Khán also regained his supreme influence. Quarrels, however, continued to arise, and eventually Imád-ul-mulk, Jágirdár of Broach, marched on Surat to take possession of that city, but was assassinated by its Governor Khudávand Khán Rumi. Changiz Khán, the son of the murdered nobleman, attacked Surat in order to avenge his father's death, but, failing to gain the fort, he sought the assistance of the Portuguese. Thus strengthened, he effected the submission of the city, and put to death Khudávand Khán. The Portuguese were rewarded for their services by a grant of the districts of Daman and Sanján (A. D. 1560). Thus two more districts were lost to Gujarát.

The king was, meanwhile, growing more and more impatient of Itimád Khán's control. At times he would cut down plantain leaves and say "See, I have beheaded Itimád Khán and have cut the body of Imád-ul-mulk to pieces". Itimád Khán's assistant Wajih-ul-mulk thus came to regard the Sultán with suspicion. One day he sent a message to the Sultán, offering to compass the death of Itimád Khán on condition of his being made Prime Minister. To this the Sultán consented, whereupon Wajih-ul-mulk at once gave the information to Itimád Khán. The latter declared he would not believe it to be true unless with his own years he should hear evidence of the Sultán's complicity. Wajih-ul-mulk therefore concealed the minister in an ante-chamber, and then, inviting the Sultán to his house on some slight pretext, renewed the proposal. The Sultán at once reiterated his former promise. On hearing this, Itimád Khán entered the apartment, and asked the king what harm he had done him that he should wish to murder him. The Sultán, utterly astonished, could make no reply. He was immediately killed by Itimád Khán's attendants, who cast out the body on the sands of the Sábarmati river. Subsequently, however, it was removed and buried in the mausoleum of Sultán Ahmad I, (A. H. 968, A. D. 1561).

Chapter XI.

The reign of Sultán Muzaffar III. the last of the Gujarát Kings, and the surrender of Ahmadábád to the Emperor Akbar.

From 1561 to 1573 A. D.

After the murder of Sultán Ahmad II. the Prime Minister Itimád Khán, who was now all powerful, seeing that there was no member left of the late Sultán's dynasty, produced a young boy of the name of Nathu, and swore that he was the son of Sultán Muhammad III. He explained that the mother had been entrusted to him for the purpose of procuring an abortion, but that she had none the less given birth to the boy, who had in consequence been reared secretly. All giving credence to this story, the boy was formally installed king under the title of Muzaffar Sháh III (A. H. 968, A. D. 1561). He was however a king in name only, the kingdom being partitioned among the several nobles as follows :—

Musá Khán and Sher Khán Faoládi.	The Sirkár of Pátan.
Changiz Khán.	The districts of Surat, Broach, Chámpáner and Barodá.
Sayyid Hamid, grandson of Sayyid Mubárak.	Dhandhuká, Dholká and other districts.
Amir Khán Ghori.	Junágadh with the country of Sorath.

These nobles, after they had oppressed the country for a considerable time, began fighting with one another, and, to add to the general distress, certain Mirzás, who had opposed the Emperor Akbar and had been expelled from Delhi, Málwá and other provinces, now entered Gujarát with the remnant of their forces. By promising to give assistance to the contending nobles, they gained a footing and possessed themselves of several districts. This increased the disorder in Gujarát, so that at length the entire province fell an easy prey to Akbar the Great, who annexed it once again to the empire of Delhi, as will be narrated further on.

The victories of the Emperor Humáyun over Sultán Bahádur and the return of the former to his capital in consequence of the revolt of the Governor of Bengal, have already been alluded to in Chapter VIII. Humáyun met with many reverses after his return from Gujarát, and had to flee through the desert of Sindh as an exile to Persia. It was during this flight that his famous son Akbar was born to him in A. D. 1542 at the petty fort of Umarkot. After the lapse of fourteen years, Humáyun regained his kingdom in India in A. D. 1556. He died however the same year, and was succeeded by Akbar, who from early boyhood was distinguished for justice, prudence and valour. This prince gradually recovered several of the former possessions of Delhi, and gladly availed himself of the dissensions prevailing in Gujarát to despatch an army on the 20th of Safar A. H. 980, (A. D. 1572) to invade that province, himself following a short time afterwards. On the road the Rájá of Sirohi, having invited the chief officer commanding the expedition to a Pán-Supári entertainment, treacherously wounded that officer. This brought ruin on Sirohi, and the traitors as well as several of the inhabitants were put to death.

The Imperial army then encamped in the neighbourhood of Pátan, and an officer was sent to offer words of assurance to the Prime Minister, Itimád Khán. That nobleman had, in consequence of Sultán Muzaffar having left his protection and besieged Ahmadábád, not only communicated to the Emperor the state of affairs, but had also invited him to take possession of the country. The imperial troops continued their march, and on reaching Disá intelligence was received that Sher Khán Faoládi had abandoned the siege of Ahmadábád, and, after sending his family to a place of security, had taken to flight. Ibráhim Husain Mirzá, who had come from Broach to assist Itimád Khán, also departed on learning that the latter intended to submit. Officers were sent to seize Sultán Muzaffar and the family of Sher Khán. The latter, however, had safely passed the mountainous defiles of Sorath, and the troops could merely plunder the baggage following them. Sultán Muzaffar was found concealed in a grain field, and was brought to the Emperor, who delivered him over to the charge of an officer, named Karam Ali. After this all the nobles tendered their submission to the Emperor, and orders were given that coins should be struck and the Khutbáh read in the name of Akbar Sháh.

The Emperor, solicitous of settling and protecting the country, assembled the nobles on his arrival at Kadi, and took security from each of them. The army then encamped at Hajipur, where some vagabonds spread the report that the Emperor had given orders for plundering the Gujarát camp. While this was proceeding a great tumult arose, whereupon the Emperor caused the most careful inquiries to be instituted, and the offenders were seized with the property they had plundered. Akbar then mounting a throne gave a general audience to the people, and ordered all concerned in the plunder to be trampled under the feet of wild elephants, while the articles recovered from the plunderers were all restored to the rightful owners. Confidence and tranquillity where thus speedily re-established, and the Imperial colours were planted soon after within sight of Ahmadábád on the 14th of Rajab A. H. 980 (18th November A. D. 1572) The inhabitants of the city at once came out in crowds to pay their respects to the victorious Emperor.

Thus Gujarát was conquerred and the capital city surrendered to Akbar without even a battle having been fought. The province, however, was not completely subjugated till some twenty years later (A. D. 1593).

PART III.

From the conquest of Gujarát by the Emperor Akbar till its occupation by the Maráthás.

(FROM 1573 to 1753 A. D.)

CHAPTER I.

Government of Mirzá Aziz Koká and return of the Emperor to his Capital.

(FROM 1573 to 1575 A. D.)

Some days after the arrival of the Emperor at the Capital, Amir Khán Ghori, who had charge of the province of Sorath, sent him a letter of submission and also tribute, which were accepted, but the tribute from Ibráhim Husain Mirzá of Broach was refused, as the Emperor did not consider it was proffered in good faith. The government of Ahmadábád, with the settlement of the country, was now entrusted to Mirzá Aziz Koká, and the remaining parganás of Barodá, Chámpáner, Surat and others, then in possession of the Mirzás, were assigned to the Gujarát nobles, who undertook the task of driving out these foreigners.

On the 2nd of Shabán A. H. 980 (December A. D. 1572), the Emperor proceeded to Cambay, where he appointed one Husain Khán to be Governor of the fort. Thence he went to Barodá and sent the major portion of his army to capture Chámpáner. Soon after the troops had departed for this purpose, Akbar learnt that Ibráhim Husain Mirzá was still at Broach, and was thinking of sallying forth in order to disturb the country, and accordingly the Emperor, though left with only a few men, determined to oppose him. At the village of Surtál on the Mahi river, the troops came in sight of each other, and an action took place, in which, although the Mirzá's position was favourable, he sustained a defeat, and his men were scattered in different directions.

The army was then sent against Surat, and encamped before it on Monday the 17th of Ramzán A. H. 980 (19th January A. D. 1573). Here, early in the campaign, some huge elephants and certain effects, which the Mirzás in their confusion had sent to Ráná Rámdev of Rájpiplá, fell into the hands of the Imperial troops. Further, Mirzá Ibráhim Husain, who had taken the bold alternative of marching on Delhi with the object of drawing the Emperor in that direction, died in the vicinity of Multán. Both of these were fortunate occurrences for Akbar.

The besieged in the fort of Surat, seeing no other way of escape, asked assistance from the Portuguese of Goá then considered powerful on the sea-coast. These shrewd people, however, when they saw the magnitude and resources of the Imperial army, soon deputed ambassadors to visit Akbar, and solicited his favour by a present of many valuable articles from Europe. In the meantime mines were being laid in the direction of the city, and the work had advanced as far as the gates. The commander, learning this, and despairing of assistance from other quarters, surrendered with his men on condition of their lives being spared (A. H. 980, A. D. 1573). Being however a notable talker, he offended the Emperor by his conversation, and was, in consequence, doomed to lose his tongue.

Akbar, after enternig the fort, entrusted the charge of it to one of his officers named Kalij Khán, and on Monday the 4th of Zulkad (6th March A. D. 1573), marched back towards Ahmadábád. When on his way thither he arrived at Broach, the mother of Changiz Khán, Jágirdár of that district under the old régime, craved justice from the Emperor against Suját Khán Habshi, who, under the cloak of friendship, had treacherously murdered her son during the dismemberment of Gujarát in the reign of Sultán Muzaffar. Akbar accordingly instituted inquiries, and, the complaint being proved true, the Habshi was trodden to death under the feet of an elephant. The Emperor with his troops then continuing the march reached Ahmadábád on the 31st of March 1573, and soon after he began to effect a settlement of the province.

On adjusting the conquered territory, the Emperor divided it among his nobles, and conferred the Viceroyalty on his foster brother Mirzá Aziz Koká. He then started for his capital on Monday the 10th April 1573, Mirzá Aziz Koká and the other nobles accompanying him as far as Siddhpur.

As soon, however, as the Emperor had turned his back, Sher Khán Faoládi, Ráv Náráyan chief of Idar, and the refractory Mirzás commenced creating disturbances. Mirzá Muhammad Husain besieged Surat, but so effective were the defensive measures taken by the Commandant of the city, that the siege was soon abandoned. The Mirzá then turned towards Broach, which he took, as also the town of Cambay, whence he marched to Ahmadábád. Here during two months the rebel troops came into frequent conflict with the Imperial army, but no decisive engagement took place, inasmuch as the Emperor's instructions to the governor were not to risk a battle save under urgent necessity, but to forward immediate information. Mirzá Aziz Koká accordingly communicated the state of affairs to the Emperor, and remained on the defensive.

The Emperor, on hearing of the disturbances, marched with a picked army towards Gujarát on Sunday the 24th July 1573. He also arranged with several officers in Málwá to join him. By forced marches the Emperor arrived at Disá within a single week. Here he was met by the troops from Pátan, and the Emperor proceeded with all despatch to Ahmadábád. At Jhotáná some of Sher Khán Faoládi's men ventured to oppose his progress, but they were driven back with loss, and the march was continued. On Wednesday the 3rd of August, the Emperor arrived within three kos of Ahmadábád and prepared for battle after sending forward a messenger to inform Mirzá Aziz Koká of his arrival.

The enemy appear to have been completely ignorant of the Emperor's approach, and accordingly, when they heard the sound of trumpets, some believed that their own confederate Sher Khán Faoládi had advanced to their assistance, while others thought that the troops which had come up were those of the Emperor's Commandant at Pátan. Soon, however, the truth was known, and, the Mirzá at once prepared for battle. Some of the Emperor's officers, seeing the numerical superiority of the enemy, advised a postponement of the attack, but Akbar, favouring an immediate engagement, gave orders to cross the river, which was forthwith done, and the Imperial army thus gained a position on rising ground. A brisk engagement ensued, in which the Emperor had two or three narrow escapes. At length a general charge was made, in which Muhammad Husain Mirzá was taken prisoner, and a complete victory was gained by the Imperial troops. Their loss amounted to only one hundred men, while that of the enemy was reported at twelve hundred. The captured Muhammad Husain Mirzá was killed in the confusion that followed the battle, and the heads of the officers and rebels who fell in this conflict were collected and built into a pyramid in order to strike terror into the hearts of the disaffected.

Akbar now entered Ahmadábád in triumph, and issued a proclamation to all the neighbouring districts announcing his victory. Detachments were then sent to Broach, whither Sháh Mirzá had fled, and an army was also despatched under the command of Rájá Bhagvándás of Jeypur to punish the Rájá of Idar, Ráo Nárandás.

Having arranged for the government of the whole province, the Emperor eleven days later left Ahmadábád for his capital

(14th August 1573). Halting at Dholká, he there gave leave to Mirzá Aziz Koká to return to Ahmadábád, but himself went on to Siddhpur, where he remained until news was brought him of the capture of Wadnagar by Rájá Bhagvándás. He then continued his journey, but as he found that the country was groaning under the weight of the oppressive assessment to which ever since the time of Sultán Bahádur, who appears to have introduced the farming system, it had been subjected by revenue farmers, he deputed his minister Rájá Todar Mal to make full inquiry and fix a suitable rate of assessment for agricultural land. This reform was duly carried out.

Rájá Todar Mal also induced the Chief of Dharampur, then called Rámnagar, to acknowledge himself as a vassal of the Emperor, and to agree to serve the Gujarát Viceroy with one thousand five hundred horse (A. D. 1576). On this occasion the Rájá presented Todar Mal with four horses and 12,000 rupees. A tribute of rupees 35,556 is also stated to have been imposed on Rájpiplá, but this is doubtful, as the chief in 1609, when a post was established at Rámnagar, furnished a contingent of one thousand men.

The Emperor now conferred high honours on Itimád Khán and the other nobles of Gujarát who had remained loyal to him, and appointed one Wajih-ul-mulk Gujaráti as the first Diwán of the province.

Mirzá Aziz Koká ruled as viceroy for about two years, when some differences of opinion arising between him and the Emperor regarding certain marks to be worn by the Imperial Cavalry, he was recalled to the capital, and resigned in A. D. 1575.

CHAPTER II.

Government of Mirzá Khán with Wazir Khán as his Deputy. Fresh disturbances created by the Mirzás. The governments of Shiháb-ad-din Ahmad Khán and Mirzá Khán. Disturbances by Sultán Muzaffar III. His capture and suicide.

FROM 1576 TO 1592 A. D.

Subsequent to the resignation of Mirzá Aziz Koká, the Emperor Akbar conferred the government of Gujarát on Mirzá Khán, the son of his faithful minister Behrám Khán. The latter had gained the battle of Pánipat for Akbar's father Humáyun, and, while Akbar himself was a minor, had held the reins of the Empire. Behrám Khán was however killed at Anhilwár Pátan, while on his way to Meccá, by a fanatic Patlián whose father he had killed in action. As Mirzá Khán was quite a young man, the Emperor associated with him as his Deputy one Wazir Khán, and an experienced Hindu officer named Prágdás was appointed Diwán. Rái Sing and Sayyid Hashim were also stationed at Nándod to maintain the peace in that district, and a strong army was sent to subdue Idar. The Rájá of this last place fled to the hills, but, having at length ventured a battle, was defeated and Idar was taken in A. D. 1576.* Intelligence was also received at the same time of the capture by the Commandant at Pátan of the fort of Sirohi.

Fresh disturbances were, however, created about this time by Muzaffar Husain Mirzá who, with his mother Gulrukh Begam had fled to the Deccan in A. D. 1573. He now returned with his mother and with some rebels, and gained possession of Baroda, which city yielded without any show of resistance.

* Following his conciliatory policy, Akbar restored Idar to the Ráv on his submission, and made him a commander of 2000 infantry and 500 cavalry.

Troops were accordingly sent against the insurgents, but ill success attended them. Hearing of this, Todar Mal, who was about to start for the capital, his survey and settlement work being now completed, returned to Ahmadábád, and induced the Viceroy to leave the city and proceed against the enemy. His army was within four marches of Baroda, when the rebels fled to Cambay, where the Commandant was wounded in action. That town was next besieged, but on the approach of the Imperial troops the rebels withdrew towards Junágadh. They were, however, overtaken at Dholká, where an engagement took place, in which the rebels were defeated and put to flight. Strange to say, amongst the prisoners and slain on this occasion were several women, who, wearing men's dress, had fought in the battle as archers.

Rájá Todar Mal sent, under the charge of his son Sidhári, all the prisoners and plunder to the Emperor at Delhi. He himself also subsequently departed for the capital, after which robber bands under Muzaffar Husain plundered the rich town of Cambay. The Deputy Governor Wazir Khán went in pursuit of them, but, learning that they were gathered in great force, and suspecting at the same time the fidelity of his own troops, he returned to Ahmadábád, which the enemy closely invested. The city, however, held out bravely though sore pressed. On one occasion the enemy had even scaled the walls, when their leader fell, struck by a shot from the garrison. The rebels, falling into disorder, took to flight, and the city was saved. Husain Mirzá now fled to Khándesh, but was there seized, and with his surrender to the Emperor, the rebellion of the Mirzás came to an end (A. H. 986, A. D. 1578).

The Emperor was not wholly satisfied with the administration of Wazir Khán, and accordingly transferred the Governor of Málwá Shiháb-ad-din Ahmad Khán to Gujarát at the end of

A. H. 985, A. D. 1577. The latter officer created several new military posts and strengthened the old ones. Under the Emperor's order he also made a redistribution of the twenty-five districts then under Gujarát, a list of which is given in Appendix H. Shiháb-ad-din, however, involved himself in war with Amir Khán Ghori ruler of Sorath, being instigated to this by Amir Khán's commander-in-chief Fateh Khán, who had grown disaffected towards his master. The Viceroy was however unsuccessful, and his nephew Mirzá Khán, to whom the expedition had been entrusted, returned wounded to Ahmadábád. Shiháb-ad-din was accordingly recalled to Agrá, and Itimád Khán, the Prime Minister of the late Sultán, was appointed to the post of Viceroy. About this time Sultán Muzaffar, to whom, while a state prisoner, the emperor Akbar had indulgently granted a Jágir, managed to escape to Gujarát (A. D. 1583). After a short stay at Rájpiplá, he crossed over to Sorath, where he was joined by about seven hundred discontented soldiers, whom Itimád Khán had, agreeably to orders from the Emperor, refused to entertain. Muzaffar Sháh, being thus strengthened, marched with about three thousand horse on Ahmadábád (A. D. 1583). He took the city after a brief contest with the son of Itimád Khán, the father having at this juncture incautiously gone to Kadi to persuade his predecessor Shiháb-ad-din to come to his aid. These two now approached Ahmadábád, but were attacked and totally defeated with the loss of their baggage. Thereupon the major portion of their forces deserted and joined the Sultán, and the two Viceroys were obliged to flee to Pátan. The Sultán then marched on Baroda and took possession of that city. The fort of Broach also surrendered to him, and a large amount of treasure and valuables fell into his hands.

The news of this insurrection in Gujarát having reached the

Emperor, he appointed Mirzá Khán to be Viceroy of Gujarát for the second time. Several experienced officers were also associated with him, and the troops in Málwá were directed to co-operate.

On hearing of Mirzá Khán's march, Sultán Muzaffar returned to Ahmadábád. The former Viceroy Shiháb-ad-din, who was at Pátan, also joined Mirzá Khán. In the meanwhile Sultán Muzaffar took up a position contiguous to the village of Usmánpur on the bank of the Sábarmati with a large force and many guns on the 9th of Muharam A. H. 992 (January A. D. 1584). Mirzá Khán halted his troops near Sarkhej waiting for the expected army from Málwá. It was obviously to Sultán Muzaffar's interest not to lose time, and he therefore engaged Mirzá Khán's army on the 26th January 1584, when the Imperial elephants threw the enemy's ranks into confusion, and the Sultán, giving up every thing for lost, fled to Mahmudábád, and thence to Cambay.

On that very day the forces from Málwá arrived at Barodá, where they halted, and some troops were sent from thence to take Broach, but, the gates being closed against them, they besieged the town.

At Cambay Sultán Muzaffar, having succeeded in raising a money contribution from the inhabitants, collected a hostile rabble, and accordingly Mirzá Khán, after leaving an officer in charge at Ahmadábád, proceeded to Cambay in February 1584. He at the same time sent orders to the Málwá troops to join him, which they did at Bariyá. Hearing of this, Sultán Muzaffar fled towards Baroda, whither he was pursued by Mirzá Khán, and an engagement took place, in which he was again defeated. He now fled to the mountains, but troops from Nándod overtook and killed many of the rebels. Altogether some two thousand of the enemy are said to have been slain in this campaign.

When tidings of these victories reached the Emperor, he raised Mirzá Khán to the rank of Khán Khánán (chief noble) which had been enjoyed by his father, and to other officers he gave suitable assignments for the support of their rank.

The Khán Khánán now left Nándod and came to Ahmadábád. At the place near Sarkhej, where he had gained his first victory over Muzaffar, he constructed a garden called Fateh Bág, providing it with a wall and summer houses, the remains of which still exist on the bank of the river, while the village is known by the name of Fateh Wádi (the garden of victory).

At this time Sultán Muzaffar and the officers with him suffered much privation. Broach was taken by the Imperial troops, and the Sultán with his followers fled from place to place. He went first to Idar and thence to Káthiáwár, where the Jám of Navánagar* gave him shelter. On the approach, however, of the hostile force the Jám, refusing him any further assistance, presented an elephant and several horses to the Khán Khánán.

Midst all these misfortunes Sultán Muzaffar did not lose heart. He came on to Parántij, from which place also he was expelled with the loss of several of his adherents. Muzaffar himself, however, was not apprehended until some time afterwards, as the sequel will relate.

The Khán Khánán, after having restored order throughout the country, returned to Delhi (A. H. 993, A. D. 1585), where he received many marks of imperial favour. After a short time, however, he came back to Gujarát to resume the government.

After having devoted considerable attention to the internal management of the country, the Khán Khánán's presence was again required at Court in connexion with the marriage festivities of the

---

* Navánagar was founded on Wednesday, the 8th of the light half of Shrávan, Samvat 1596 (A. D. 1540) by Jám Ráwal on his being driven out from Kachh by his nephew Khengárji. The fort was subsequently built by Mehráman Khawás in A. D. 1788.

Emperor's son prince Murád (A.D. 1586–87), and accordingly he departed, leaving one Khalij Khán as his Deputy in Gujarát.

During his absence, Mirzá Aziz Koká was transferred from Málwá to Gujarát, where he arrived in A. H. 997, A. D. 1588-89. His first business was to quell a rebellion raised by Muzaffar Sháh, who was aided by the Jám and other chiefs. The Viceroy proceeded at once to Káthiáwár, and there an engagement took place near Dhrol, in which Muzaffar and his confederates suffered a severe defeat*, and fled to Junágadh (A. D. 1591). The Imperial troops then plundered Navánagar and proceeded thence towards Junágadh. The season, however, being far advanced, and the army fatigued, Mirzá Aziz Koká returned to Ahmadábád, whither he had already sent his son with some of the troops, as he anticipated that Sultán Muzaffar might soon cause trouble in that quarter.

In A. D. 1592 the Viceroy, having equipped a fresh force, proceeded again to Káthiáwár, where several chiefs tendered their submission. Nineteen seaports including Goghá, Mangalur and Somnáth were taken possession of without a blow. Junágadh was then besieged, and the garrison, after suffering severe privations for some three months, surrendered. Here intelligence was received that Sultán Muzaffar was concealed in the neighbourhood of Okhá. An army was accordingly sent there under the command of the Viceroy's son. The chief, Savá Wádhel, was slain while bravely covering the retreat of his guest, who fled to Ráo Bhármalji of Kachh. The army was then concentrated at Morbi, and was about to cross the Ran, when the Ráo, taking warning from the fate of Navánagar and Junágadh, surrendered the unfortunate Sultán to the detachment sent for his capture. He was being escorted to the Viceroy's camp, when, after travelling

* So great was the slaughter that the place has since been known as the Bhuchar mori which is almost a synonym of massacre. The date of this battle as given by Mr. Ranchodji Amarji, late Diwán of Junágadh and author of the Twárikhe Sorath is the 8th of the bright fortnight of Aso Samvat 1648.

the whole night, he alighted from his horse at Dhrol, and, going behind a tree on some pretence, put an end to his existence by cutting his throat with a knife (A. D. 1592). His head, sent to the Emperor, was duly recognised. Thereafter the Navánagar Chief's territories were restored to him, and he was ranked as one of the Imperial vassals. Morbi was granted in Jágir to the Ráo of Kachh as a reward for his services.

With the death of Sultán Muzaffar III. ended the dynasty of the Gujarát Sultáns, established three centuries previously by the illustrious Muzaffar I. His early successors, Sultán Ahmad, Muzaffar the Clement, Mahmud Begadá and Bahádur Sháh had, in addition to the territories originally belonging to Gujarát, conquered and annexed Junágadh, Chámpáner, Málwá, Jhálod, Nágor, Sirohi, and (in the Konkan) Janjirá, Bombay, Bassein and Daman. Though not a single one of the descendants of the Sultán's family can be traced at the present day, many of the noble works they initiated still remain. Their magnificent mosques and mausoleums may, indeed, be considered as built for a purely religious purpose, but these have none the less on various occasions proved of much utility* to the general public. Moreover numerous wells, tanks and gardens in many parts of the province still attest the thoughtful regard those early Sultáns evinced for the public weal. The British Government, with a commendable desire to preserve historical and architectural remains, sets apart a sum of money every year for the restoration of ancient buildings, and it is hoped the judicious application of these funds, as well as of the revenues of lands and villages assigned to some of the institutions by the founders, will long preserve from decay and ruin those works of utility and beauty that are the most conspicuous memorials of the Gujarát Sultánat.

* It is well known that during the flood of A. D. 1875, hundreds of people, who had been made houseless, or who considered their homes unsafe found shelter in the strong stone mosques of Ahmadábád.

Chapter III.

Appointment of Prince Murád Bakht as Viceroy. Disturbances by Sultán Muzaffar's son. Death of the Emperor Akbar. Viceroys in the time of his successors. Ascendancy of the Maráthás; advent of the English to Surat, establishment of their factories.

From 1592 to 1615 A. D.

When the news of Mirzá Aziz Koká's successes and of the death of Sultán Muzaffar reached the Emperor Akbar, he sent a letter of congratulation to the victorious nobleman, and invited him to Court. The Mirzá, however, begged to be excused on the plea that it was necessary to subdue the Portuguese, now powerful in Gujarát. It would seem that he did commence operations with this end in view, but eventually with his family and attendants he went on a pilgrimage to Meccá after obtaining a free pass from the Portuguese, who had established their supremacy in the Indian Ocean (A. D. 1592). The Emperor was much displeased on receipt of this news, still, owing to the great regard he entertained for Mirzá Aziz Koká, his elder son was appointed to the rank of Commandant of a thousand horse, and the younger son to that of five hundred. The post of Viceroy of Gujarát was then conferred on the Emperor's son Prince Murád Bakht, with orders to concentrate the forces of Málwá and Gujarát and march on the Deccan, which province had hitherto successfully resisted the Emperor's army. During Murád's absence in the Deccan, a Hindu prince, Rájá Suraj Singh of Jodhpur, was deputed to act for him in Gujarát (A. D. 1594–95).

In this year the late Sultán Muzaffar's son Bahádur, who with his younger brother and two sisters had found refuge with the Parmár Zamindár of Loári, took the opportunity occasioned by the greater portion of the Gujarát troops being sent to the Deccan, to raise an insurrection. The Deputy Viceroy proceeded against him, when the prince, after a faint demonstration of fighting, fled and went into retirement. It seems that as late as A. D. 1609, this prince approached Surat, causing a panic amongst its inhabitants. The timely arrival of succour from Ahmadábád, however, compelled him to withdraw. No more mention is made in history of Sultán Muzaffar's descendants, except that in 1606 A. D. Bahádur Khán sacked and held Cambay for fourteen days.

On Wednesday the 12th of October A. D. 1605 the Emperor Akbar died at Agrá after a brilliant reign of forty-nine years. Throughout this period Hindus and Muhammadans were, for the first time during the Moslem ascendancy in India, treated impartially, and the Jezzia Vero*, unjustly levied from all adult Hindus and Pársis at the rate of Rs. 5½ per head, was abolished. Gujarát continued a dependency of the Mughal empire until A. D. 1753, and was ruled by Viceroys from the Imperial capital. Among them were the princes Sháh Jahán and Aurangzeb, who afterwards succeeded to the Delhi empire. The principal events that took place in this province between the death of Akbar and the taking of Gujarát by the Maráthás in A. D. 1753 will now be briefly mentioned.

In A. D. 1609 Malek Ambar, the Abyssinian General and minister of the infant king of Ahmadnagar in the Deccan, who had gained conspicuous successes against the Imperial forces, invaded Gujarát with a large army, and plundered the rich cities of Surat and Baroda. To prevent a repetition of such inroads in the future, a body of twenty-five thousand men was stationed on the frontier at Rámnagar (now Dharampur), some fortytwo

---

* This obnoxious impost was re-instituted in the seventeenth century by Akbar's great grandson Aurangzeb.

miles distant from Surat. This force included a contingent of one thousand men sent by the Rájá of Rájpiplá.

The year 1608 is memorable for the advent of the English to continental India, when Captain Hawkins proceeded as Envoy on a mission to Agrá. Under royal charter from Queen Elizabeth, a company with the title of "The Governor and Company of Merchants trading to the East Indies" was formed in England in 1600 A. D. After some mercantile expeditions had been despatched to the Indian Archipelego, a ship named the "Hector" under the command of Captain Hawkins, being separated from the other ships of the fleet, arrived at the mouth of the Tápti river in August 1608. The Commander was provided with letters to the address of the Emperor from James I. king of England, and was therefore allowed to bring his cargo into the city. In August 1609 Hawkins started on his mission to Agrá. Another ship which arrived in September of the same year was wrecked off the coast, and the crew, through the hostile influence of the Portuguese with the Governor of Surat, being denied refuge in that city, landed at Gandevi and Umrá. The English commander, who had been left by Captain Hawkins at Surat, was called by him to Agrá, and the Surat factory was temporarily closed in 1610.

Ever since 1573* A. D., in which year the Portuguese concluded a treaty with the Emperor Akbar, they had been regarded as undisputed masters of the Surat coast and the gulf of Cambay. They proved a source of extreme annoyance to the English, and an open rupture was soon inevitable. In A. D. 1612 a fleet of four ships, fully equipped, arrived at Surat, and under their commander Captain Best, defeated the Portuguese in a

* Before this year the Portuguese had thrice sacked and burnt the city of Surat, once in 1512, then in 1530 and again in 1531 A. D., while they were at war with the king of Gujarát.

naval engagement. The Emperor Jahángir, seeing the superiority of the English over the Portuguese, concluded a treaty with the former, giving them permission to trade and to open factories at Surat, Cambay, Goghá and Ahmadábád. It was also stipulated that an ambassador from the English Court should permanently reside at the Imperial Court of Delhi. This treaty was received by the English at Surat in February 1613, and thus their first official connexion was established with an empire which was destined ere long to fall under their sway. Surat was made the presidency seat of Western India with control over the trade in the Persian Gulf, and continued for a long time the most important city in Gujarát.

Chapter IV.

Arrival of Sir Thomas Roe as the first English Ambassador at the Delhi Court. Establishment of several factories. Building of the Sháhi Bág and Azam Khán's palace Sháh Jahán dethroned by his son Aurangzeb. Navánagar taken by the imperial troops. Additional privileges obtained by the East India Company through Dr Boughton. Bombay granted in dowry by the king of Portugal to Charles I, and by him transferred to the Company.

From 1615 to 1691 A. D.

In 1615 A. D. king James I. sent as his first Ambassador to the Imperial Court Sir Thomas Roe, who had already gained experience of diplomatic duties at the Court of Constantinople. Sir Thomas Roe reached Surat with a fleet on the 26th of September, and after a short stay proceeded to the Emperor Jahángir's camp at Ajmer, where he was received with due honours. His fearlessness, ability and courtesy soon secured him a position of intimacy with the Emperor, who, in spite of many obstacles raised by his courtiers then under the influence of the Portuguese, granted the East India Company several important privileges. Sir Thomas Roe returned to England in 1618 A. D.

In this connexion it is right to mention that Dutch merchants from Holland, arriving in Surat in 1616 A. D., were also permitted two years later to establish a factory in that city as well as at Cambay, Broach, Baroda, Ahmadábád and other places. The first attempts by the French also to start a factory at Surat date from 1620 A. D., but it was not till the expedition under M. Caron in 1668 that even moderate success attended their efforts. The weavers in France strongly resenting the import of Indian cloth, the French Government eventually sent a fleet of four ships in A. D. 1692 with orders to close the Surat factory, and a few years afterwards it was virtually abolished. The Portuguese and the Dutch also eventually abandoned their factories in disgust at the tyranny of the Governor of Surat.

In A. D. 1616 the Emperor Jahángir visited Cambay and thence went to Ahmadábád in the month of March. His dislike to the climate of this place, which in the hot season is any thing but agreeable, found strong expression in the names he gave the city. These were, amongst others, Giradábád (city of dust), Bimáristán (abode of sickness) and Jahánamábád (city of hell). During Jahángir's stay in Gujarát, Ráv Bhármal of Kachh paid him a visit in A. D. 1617, presenting the Emperor with one hundred Kachh horses, 1000 Ashrafis and 2,000 rupees. Jahángir was much pleased with the old chief's visit, and on condition of his agreeing to give free passes to persons proceeding on pilgrimage to Meccá, presented him with a male and female elephant, his own horse, a dagger, a sword with diamond mounted hilt and four rings. It is said that during Jahángir's stay of nine months in Gujarát, his favourite wife Nur Jahán (the light of the world) ruled as the lady Governor of Gujarát*.

At the time of his departure for Agrá, the Emperor appointed his son Sháh Jahán as Viceroy of Gujarát. That prince ruled by Deputies as he was mostly engaged with wars in the Deccan, where he gained some singular successes. Sháh Jahán, during a year of scarcity in Ahmadábád, ordered the Sháhi Bág to be built (1622 A. D.). It is a noble edifice situated on the bank of the Sábarmati about two miles to the north of the city. This building has been kept in good repair by the present Government, and is now the residence of the Commissioner of the Northern Division of the Presidency. It is said that Sháh Jahán never set foot within it as the gateway before the entrance had been built very low, and he refused to alight from the huge elephant on which he was riding when coming to see the building.

* The Rev. Mr. Taylor assures me that in the bazárs of Ahmadábád are still to be found coins bearing along with Jahángir's name that of his queen. The legend on these coins reads "By order of Sháh Jahángir gold gained a hundred beauties by the name of Nur Jahán Pádisháh Begam."

Another noble building built in Ahmadábád by the Mughal Viceroys, is Azam Khán's palace situated at the south-eastern corner of the Bhadar citadel. This structure dates from 1637 A. D., and is said to have been first used during the latter period of the Mughal sovereignty as a college, but shortly after the city came into the possession of the British, it was converted into a jail about 1820 A. D., probably because no other equally strong building was available. It still continues to be used for that purpose, but as the Government are now constructing a larger jail at some distance from the city, there is a probability that the present building will soon be utilized for Civil Courts and offices. It will then better deserve the name of "House of goodness and favour," still to be read in the inscription over its entrance. Azam Khán also caused a fine castle and palace to be built at Ránpur at the confluence of the Gomá and Bhádar rivers. Their ruins still look very picturesque. He also built there a fine well and a mosque. There are inscriptions on all of these denoting the years A. H. 1048, 1050, 1051, and 1053 (1640, 1642, 1643 and 1644 A. D.).

In 1622 A. D. Sháh Jahán rebelled against his father Jahángir, but this insurrection proved abortive. Ultimately, however, on the death of the latter he succeeded to the Empire of Delhi in January 1628. During his reign of thirty years there is not much to record regarding Gujarát, except that in the year 1631-32 A. D. there occured a great famine commonly known as the Satyásiá Kál (the 87th year's famine) from its having taken place in Samvat 1687. The famine was indeed so severe that the streets were blocked by the dying. For the destitute alms-houses were provided, and a sum of rupees fifty thousand was distributed. Owing to the weakness of some of the Viceroys, the Government of the province became lax, and depredations were boldly committed by Kolis and others. But

Azam Khán, who had been appointed Governor in 1635 A. D., recognising the danger resulting from such lawlessness, subdued the refractory Chunwáliá chiefs. He built forts at Azimábád, Khalilábád and Sháhpur. He also marched against the Jám of Navánagar (1640 A. D.) and compelled him to pay the full amount of tribute due. Just appreciation of one's services was not, however, always to be expected from such despotic monarchs as the Emperors of Delhi were in those days, and Azam Khán was, on the misrepresentations of envious courtiers, recalled in the year 1642 A. D. Mirzá Isá Tái Khán Governor of Sorath, who was next appointed Viceroy, signalized his term of office by introducing the Bhágvatai* system of revenue collection.

Prince Aurangzeb succeeded the Mirzá as Viceroy in 1644 A. D. During his government religious disputes took place between the Shiás and Sunnis, and also between Hindus and Muhammadans, in connexion with which the Jain temple of Chintámani in Saraspur was destroyed by his orders (A.D. 1644). Aurangzeb was recalled in 1646, and one Shaistáh Khán was appointed his successor. The last named nobleman was, in A. D. 1654, succeeded by Prince Murád Baksh, who, instigated by a Bárot named Vaitál whom the Rájá of Idar Ráv Jagannáth had disgraced on a false charge, marched against Idar, and, expelling the Ráv to the hills, took the fort (1656 A. D.). His son Punjá, however, recovered it two years afterwards with the help of his maternal grandfather, the Ráná of Udaipur. There took place, after this, a series of troubles, in which the Rávs were on some occasions expelled from Idar and on others were able to regain their territory. One instance in which one of the Rávs is said to have lost his life for want of opium is worth recording. He was Ráv Gopináth, who had succeeded in driving

* A system of revenue management under which a certain share of the produce is taken in kind by the crown.

out the Muhammadan Governor, but in A. D. 1664, a rival, Garibdás, Thakor of Ranásan, brought an army from Ahmadábád, which drove the unfortunate Ráv from his fort and obliged him to take shelter in the temple of Kulnáth Mahádev, where he remained concealed. His stock of opium having been exhausted, the Ráv took the opportunity of the visit of a Bráhman to the temple to give him a gold bracelet, and asked him to purchase for him some opium from its proceeds. He also presented him with a second bracelet for his own use. The covetous Bráhman, however, is said to have appropriated both the bracelets for himself, and never to have gone back to the chief, whose daily allowance of opium is stated to have been a pound and a quarter, and who consequently died for want of his favourite drug.*

In 1657 A. D. when the rumour spread that the Emperor Sháh Jahán was dangerously ill, prince Murád Baksh at once proclaimed himself king. In order to obtain money, the sinews of war, he caused the houses of the Governor and Kadsi Begam of Surat to be plundered, and borrowed large sums from bankers in Ahmadábad. From the sons of Sántidás Jhaveri he took on loan Rs. 550,000, from Sántidás's partner Rohidás Rs. 40,000, and from Sámal and others Rs. 88,000. The revenues of certain districts of Gujarát were set apart for payment of these and other debts. Murád Baksh, after raising a large army, marched in conjunction with his brother Aurangzeb against his father. The issue of the war that followed was that Aurangzeb, after holding his father a prisoner in the palace at Agrá, and confining his brother Murád (whom he subsequently caused to be murdered) in the fort of Gwálior, himself usurped the throne in A. D. 1658.

During Aurangzeb's reign, Gujarát was far from enjoying

* Bombay Gazetteer vol. V, p. 405.

peace. Disturbances again broke out at Idar and in the Chunwál (now a part of the Viramgám parganá). On the death of Ranmalji the Jám of Navánagar in A. D. 1661, disputes arose regarding the succession between the deceased chief's widow, who is said to have reared a spurious child, and Ranmal's brother Ráe Singh. The former was turned away, and applied to the Viceroy Kutb-ud-din for aid, and that officer accordingly marched on Navánagar, slew Ráe Singh in action and annexed his territories to Gujarát. He gave to Navánagar the name of Islámábád* (1664 A. D.). The Chunwáliás were next subdued, and new military outposts were established at Gájná and Bhilápur.

Other events which proved of far greater importance in the future also happened during the period embraced in the present chapter. In 1624 A. D. the East India Company obtained authority from the Emperor Jahángir to punish their own servants, and in 1638, at the request of Sháh Jahán, Mr. Gabriel Boughton, an English Surgeon, was sent to attend that Emperor's sick daughter. Succeeding in curing her, he, instead of asking for any personal favours, solicited and obtained extensive privileges for the East India Company, one of which was that it should be allowed to trade free of duty in Bengal besides being permitted to establish a factory at Hugli and another at Bálásor. The most valuable acquisition was made in A.D. 1661, when the king of Portugal granted in dowry to Charles II. of England who married the princess Catharine of Braganza, the important island and port of Bombay, then a mere fishing

* Ráe Singh's son Tamáchi was restored to his dominions in 1673 A. D. at the intercession of Mahárájá Jasvatsinghji of Jodhpur then Viceroy of Gujarát, on condition of serving the Viceroy when required, and of maintaining order in his territory. The Jám was not however allowed to reside in Navánagar until after the death of Aurangzeb in 1707 A. D., nor to work the pearl fisheries in the Gulf of Kachh. He resided in the interim at Khambhália.

village which the Portuguese had possessed since A. D. 1532. King Charles II., who had already by a new charter considerably extended the power of the Company, finding the grant more expensive than profitable to the crown, transferred Bombay to the East India Company in 1668 at a nominal annual rent of £. 10. Thus a most valuable seaport and island, which has, under the patronage of the East India Company and the British Crown, risen to be the second and the most enterprising city in India, was in a happy moment acquired at an altogerther trifling cost. In A. D. 1683 Bombay was made the chief seat of the Presidency, and four years later the Company's rupees were first coined there.

It may further be mentioned as regards the factors of Surat, the early presidency seat on this side of India, that though they were generally well treated by the local Governors, they had at times to suffer great privations. On the first occasion their President Sir John Child was to blame, as he rashly seized at Bombay some vessels belonging to Muhammadan merchants. On this occasion the East India Company had to pay a ransom of one lac and fifty thousand rupees before the factors were released on the 4th of April 1690. On the second occasion, some foreign pirates having plundered a Muhammadan ship, the English, Dutch and French factors were subjected to close confinement on the 27th August 1691. It being clearly proved, however, that they were innocent of any complicity in the alleged piracy, the guard over the factories was removed on the 2nd of December 1691 A. D.

Chapter V.

Rise of the Maráthás. Shiváji's grandfather Máluji and father Sháhji. Shiváji's exploits. Sack of Surat, and other events. Shiváji's death. His son taken prisoner by Aurangzeb and put to a cruel death. Kind treatment of Shiváji's grandson Sáhu. His release. Recovery of his grandfather's territories.

From 1680 to 1724 A. D.

Before coming to the period of the intimtae connexion of the Maráthás with Gujarát, it is necessary briefly to refer to the antecedent Maráthá history. We therefore turn a few years back and commence our narrative with Máluji Bhonsle, a Maráthá Sirdár who commanded a small body of Horse under the king of Ahmadnagar. He acquitted himself well in various duties entrusted to him and soon began to attain distinction. His son Sháhji made himself very conspicuous in the wars of the Ahmadnagar and Bijápur kings with the Emperor Sháh Jahán. By siding at one time with the Emperor, and at another with his rivals according to circumstances, he secured large additions to his estate.

Sháhji's son, the illustrious Shiváji, was born in May 1627. The latter enriched himself by plundering the territories of Muhammadans, and, gradually collecting a large following defeated both the army of the Emperor and that of the Bijápur king. He then on the 6th January 1664 made a rapid descent at the head of four thousand horse upon the then rich city of Surat, which he mercilessly plundered for six days*. On this occasion the English factors under their Governor Sir George Oxenden made a bold defence, and saved from plunder not only their factory but the property of several of the inhabitants. Aurangzeb,

---

* Mr. Smith, an Englishman who was taken prisoner, was an eye witness to Shiváji having ordered the hands of persons suspected to have concealed their property to be chopped off.

much pleased with this service, not only gave them a remission of one year's custom dues, equal to about rupees twenty-five thousand, but also reduced the rate of custom dues to be levied from the English factory from three and a half to two per cent. The Viceroy of Gujarát, on hearing of the attack, marched on Surat with several auxiliary chiefs, but Shiváji was much too wise to linger long in the city. Plunder was his object, and as soon as the city had been pillaged he speedily retreated to his strong fortress, taking with him booty estimated by some at a krore of rupees (£1,000,000). The Viceroy accordingly returned to Ahmadábád, first collecting, however, the arrears of land tax from the superior land-holders, and then ordering a brick wall to be built instead of the mud one that had till then surrounded the city of Surat. In 1669 A. D. Shiváji renewed the attack, and again enriched himself by plunder. On his departure he left a letter warning the inhabitants that in order to secure immunity in the future they would require to pay an annual tribute of twelve lacs of rupees.

Even after this second pillage Surat does not appear to have enjoyed rest from the Maráthás, and fresh assaults were made in 1670, 1671, 1674 and 1675 A. D. In some of these attacks Shiváji is said to have been assisted by the chief of Rámnagar, yet in A. D. 1672 he did not scruple to take advantage of a complimentary visit to that chief to take possession of his fort observing merely that he must have the key of his treasure (meaning Surat) in his own hands*. In the year 1676 A. D. the Maráthás captured the fort of Párnerá† about forty-eight miles south of Surat, and thus they, for the first time, established themselves in Southern Gujarát. The ancient town of Broach

* Bombay Gazetteer vol. VI p. 256.

† The fort, rebuilt by Shiváji, was dismantled by the British during the mutiny of 1857 A. D.

also engaged the attention of the Maráthás. In 1675 A. D. their general Hambir Ráv levied a forced contribution, and in 1686 Shiváji's son Sambháji plundered that town.

In 1679 A. D., theRáná of Udaipur, driven to rebellion by the persecutions of Aurangzeb, sent his son Bhim Singh to make a descent on Gujarát, on which occasion Wadnagar, Ahmadnagar and other towns were plundered. The chief of Idar also revolted, and recovered his ancient capital, but was again ousted from Idar, and removed to Sarván. Idar thus remained in the hands of the Viceroy for some years.

In Broach also a serious disturbance took place. Sayyid Sháhji, a religious preceptor of the Momnás, having, in consequence of certain broils, committed suicide, the Momnás assembled in great numbers, and killing its governor, took possession of the town. It was retaken by the Imperial officers with much trouble, and only after many of the insurgents had been slain (1691 A. D.)

Shiváji died on the 5th of April 1680 A. D. at the age of fifty-three years. His son Sambháji, who lacked several of the good qualities of his father, was taken prisoner by Aurangzeb in 1689 A. D. during that Emperor's long campaign in the Deccan, and having, when offered the religion of Islám, used abusive language towards the prophet, was ignominiously executed after being deprived of his eyes and tongue. The Maráthás, however, still continued their hostilities. They selected Sambháji's half brother Rájárám as their king, and with unremitting zeal carried on war accompanied by many predatory excursions, some of which are detailed below :—

In 1702 the Maráthás levied contributions from Surat and Burhánpur.

In 1705 a body of fifteen thousand Maráthás defeated the local officers in Gujarát, and laid waste the country. The

Emperor sent large bodies of troops to intercept them, and battles were fought near Ratanpur (in Rájpiplá) and near Bábá Piárá's ford on the Narbadá, in which the Maráthás were generally successful, and gained considerable booty by plundering the Mughal camps and by exacting heavy ransoms from the officers whom they had taken prisoners.

In A. D. 1707 an expedition was led by the Peshwá Báláji himself, who plundered the country as far as Batvá within four miles of Ahmadábád. The Viceroy was obliged on this occasion to pay the Peshwá a tribute of two lacs and ten thousand rupees.

In A. D. 1712 a Maráthá force again advanced towards Gujarát, but the Viceroy Sháhbut Khán marched against them, and arrested their further progress by inflicting a defeat on them at Anklesvar on the opposite bank of the Narbadá. In addition to these excursions from without, there were a number of internal commotions in Ahmadábád.

In 1709 A. D. a person whose business it was to read the Khutbáh (public prayers) was stabbed to death for having used the Shiá word Wási in his prayers agreeably to the Emperor Mahmud Sháh's orders. Three or four years later (1713-14), disturbances broke out consequent on the killing of a cow in Hindu quarters, during which the shops of Hindus were plundered and burnt. The Kolis and Káthis outside the city also grew so bold and presumptuous as to cause a stoppage to trade, and Barodá itself was a scene of plunder by Kolis for two consecutive days. Some of the Viceroys were also very tyrannical, and one of them Anopsingh Bhandári of mere caprice killed a respectable merchant named Kapurchand Bhansáli (1720 A. D.). Thus the country became a scene of anarchy and confusion.

We now return to Shiváji's decendants. The terrible fate of his son Sambháji has already been described, but Aurangzeb was pleased to treat Sambháji's child with kindness. Aurangzeb was in the habit of calling Shiváji a robber, and he therefore ironically gave the child the name of Sáhu (honest) and married him to daughters of two of his Maráthá officers. On Aurangzeb's demise in 1707 A. D., his son and successor Bahádur Sháh considered it politic to release Sáhu on his agreeing to hold himself a vassal of the Empire and to leave behind at Delhi his mother, wife and other relations as hostages for his good conduct. Thereafter Sáhu succeeded in regaining from the family of Rájárám the greater portion of his father's kingdom. To appease Rájárám's heirs, however, he allowed them to retain Kolhápur as a separate state. He also succeeded in obtaining from the local governors of the Deccan the right to levy Chauth* and Sardeshmukhi† of that province on his undertaking to protect it against plunder.

In A. D. 1719–20, during the prevailing anarchy of the Delhi Empire, Sáhu, through the intervention of Nizám-ul-mulk the Viceroy of the Deccan, sent his energetic minister Báláji Vishvanáth, and Commander-in-chief Khanderáv Dhábáde to assist Muhammad Sháh in his endeavours to gain the throne of Delhi and free himself from the control of certain Sayyids who had latterly become too powerful. This attempt, after two severe engagements, having proved successful, the Emperor, in token of his gratitude, not only confirmed the grants of Chauth and Sardeshmukhi by written Farmáns‡, but also acknowledged Sáhu's title to all the territories conquered by his illustrious grandfather Shiváji. Those of Sáhu's relations who had hitherto been kept as hostages were also restored to him.

---

* A levy of one-fourth of the revenue.

† A levy of ten per cent beyond the chauth.

‡ The Emperor's Farmán for the grant of the chauth is dated 22nd Rabi-ul-ákhir A.H. 1131, and that for Sardeshmukhi 4th Jamádi-ul-aval of the same year (1719 A.D.). They did not authorize these grants in Gujarát, but Sáhu enforced them there.

Chapter VI.

Rise of the Gáekwád's family. Dámáji's exploits and those of his son Piláji. Appointment of a new Viceroy Sirbulandkhán. Hamidkhán obtains the aid of Piláji Gáekwád and Kantháji Kadam and gives them the right to collect the chauth in Gujarát. Piláji obtains possession of Baroda. Division between Piláji and Kantháji.

From 1721 to 1724 A. D.

By the grant to Sáhu of the right to levy chauth and sardeshmukhi in certain districts, the Maráthás obtained an authoritative footing in Gujarát. In the battles which were fought for the Emperor an officer named Dámáji Gáekwád had gained considerable renown. He had many years previously left his native village, Dhávádi near Puná, to join Khanderáv Dhábáde, the Commander-in-chief*. Dhábáde having on his return from Delhi recommended him very strongly to Sáhu's favourable notice, that king was pleased to confer on him and his heirs the right to levy chauth and sardeshmukhi in Gujarát. He further appointed Dámáji as second in command of the Maráthá army, and gave him the title of Samsher Bahádur. This was the origin of the power and eminence of the present reigning family of Baroda.

Dámáji died shortly after gaining these distinctions, and was succeeded by his nephew Piláji Gáekwád in 1721 A. D. The latter, who had already risen through his own energy and talents to the rank of Commander of a Págá or body of horsemen, selected as his residence a hill belonging to the Mewási

---

* Dhábáde had for many years subsisted with his followers in Gujarát and Kháthiáwár, and exacted a tribute in those provinces. About this period he established himself in the hills round about Rájpiplá, whence he is said to have decoyed and carried off a large remittance of treasure which was being conveyed from Surat to Aurangábád.

Grant Duff's History of the Maráthás Vol. I, p. 311.

Bhils, where in 1719 A. D. he built the fort of Songadh* about forty miles east of Surat. In this year Piláji, defeating a large army sent against him by the Governor of Surat, took the Commandant a prisoner and did not release him until he paid a large ransom. Piláji also formed an alliance with the Rájá of Rájpiplá who had long shown a great aversion to Muhammadan sway. In 1723 A. D. he marched on Surat, and, by defeating Momin Khán, the Governor of that city, made more secure the levy of the chauth in that district. Piláji also won the friendship of the Patels of Pádrá, and obtained aid from them in his operations.

It has been already stated that Nizám-ul-mulk had assisted the Emperor Muhammad Shah in effecting his freedom from the control of the Sayyids. In reward for his services he was exalted to the office of Minister, and was granted the Viceroyalty not only of the Deccan but also of Málwá and Gujarát. These three provinces he ruled by deputies. Through the enmity of courtiers, however, disagreement soon sprang up between him and the Emperor, and accordingly Nizám-ul-mulk thought it safer to resign his post as Minister, and proceeded to the Deccan, where in course of time he became independent, and his descendants still rule at Haidarábád.

Soon after Nizám-ul-mulk's departure, the Emperor issued Farmáns depriving him of Málwá and Gujarát. As Viceroy of the latter was appointed a distinguished nobleman named Sirbuland Khán, who sent one Suját Khán as his deputy. That officer duly took possession of the city of Ahmadábád, but Hamid Khán determined not to surrender without a struggle the province which he was holding on behalf of his nephew Nizám-ul-mulk. Accordingly he repaired to Dohad, and there

---

* Songadh continued as the capital of Gujarát until 1766 A. D., when the seat of Government was moved to Pátan.

meeting Kantháji Kadam, one of Sáhu's officers who had recently arrived in Gujarát, invited his assistance, promising to reward him with the chauth. The offer was accepted (1724 A. D.), and Kantháji went with Hamid Khán to Kapadvanj. At this town Hamid Khán received information through his friends of Suját Khán's movements, and on a favourable opportunity attacked and slew him within a few miles of Ahmadábád. He thus regained authority in the province. Kantháji now marched through the district, collecting chauth and sardeshmukhi, and, after besieging the town of Viramgám, levied from it alone a contribution of three lacs and fifty thousand rupees. Hearing of Suját Khán's death, his brother Rustam Ali, who was in command at Surat and who had lately defeated Piláji in the neighbourhood of that town, concluded a truce with the latter, and asked his assistance against Hamid Khán. Piláji agreed, and together they crossed the river Mahi on their way to Ahmadábád. At the village of Arás a battle was fought, in which Rustam Ali was able by his superior artillery to drive back Hamid Khán. Piláji, who had in the mean time received overtures from Nizám-ul-mulk to assist his uncle, now advised Rustam Ali to charge the fugitives. While complying, Rustam Ali left his guns behind, when Piláji, seizing them treacherously, opened fire on the pursuers. Rustam Ali fought bravely, but at last despairing of success, and deeply affected by the perfidy of his ally, stabbed himself to death on reaching the village of Waso (1724 A. D.). The victory having been gained through Piláji's treachery, he was apportioned (1724 A. D.) an equal share with Kantháji in the chauth. Piláji also went to Baroda and wrested that city from Rustam Ali's widow.

Kantháji and Piláji then proceeded in conjunction to levy the chauth, but their alliance was soon broken owing to mutual jealousies. Piláji as the agent of Dhábáde the commander-in-chief considered himself the superior in Gujarát, while Kantháji as Agent of the Rájá refused to recognise Piláji's pretensions. This difference issued in a trial of arms at Cambay, in which Piláji was defeated, and had to retire to the town of Mátar about three miles distant from Kaira (1725 A. D.). Kantháji then levied a contribution of rupees one lac and eleven thousand from Cambay, of which the share to be paid by the English factory was rupees five thousand. The Resident, Mr. Daniel Innes, claimed immunity on the ground that along with other factories on the sea-coast they had obtained permission from Sáhu Rájá to trade. This plea, however, was not accepted by the Maráthás.

Hamid Khán, fearing that the contention between these two Maráthá chiefs would lead to the desertion of one or other of his allies, interposed, and effected an understanding, by which the chauth of the districts east of the Mahi was assigned to Piláji Gáekwád and that to the west to Kantháji Kadam. After this agreement was accepted, both left to spend the rainy season at their respective headquarters.

Chapter VII.

Sir-buland Khán himself marches against Hamid Khán. Affray between the two viceroys. Retaking of Baroda by the Imperial troops. Sack of Wadnagar. Resumption of Maráthá raids. Sirbuland Khán assigns to Piláji the right to levy the Chauth. The Peshwá's interference. Supersession of Sirbuland Khán and the appointment of Abhesingh of Jodhpur as Viceroy. Contest between the Peshwá on the one hand and the Gáekwád, Kantháji and Dhábáde on the other. The defeat of the three confederates. Conclusion of treaty. Treacherous murder of Piláji by Abhesingh's emissaries. Subsequent events.

From 1725 to 1733 A. D.

The Emperor of Delhi, justly offended at Hamid Khán's conduct in disobeying his orders and in giving support to the Maráthás, despatched Sirbuland Khán himself with an adequate force to crush the rebellion. Well knowing the abilities of his adversary, Hamid Khán considered it prudent to retire before the advanced division of Sirbuland Khán's army, leaving at the same time under the command of an officer, a small garrison at Ahmadábád, as he could no longer expect aid from the Maráthás. The latter, however, saw that their cause depended on the success of Hamid Khán, and accordingly they crossed the Mahi and joined him at Mahmudábád (1712 A. D.). Hamid Khán therefore returned with them to Ahmadábád, but he found its gates closed against him, the officers whom he had left there being anxious to please the new Viceroy. He accordingly encamped with his Maráthá auxiliaries near the Sháhi Bág, while the Imperial army halted at Adálaj, waiting for its artillery. The Maráthás, taking courage by the delay thus occasioned, at once attacked the enemy, and gained a victory, but their own losses were so heavy that they could not risk another battle.

Thereafter Hamid Khán and the Maráthás betook themselves to the usual desultory raids and plundering expeditions, but at Sojitrá and Kapadvanj the Maráthás were routed by Sirbuland Khán's son Khán Azád Khán (1725 A. D.), who retook Baroda, and appointed one Hasan-ud-din as its Governor. A Maráthá noble Antáji Bháskar, however, entered Gujarát by way of Idar, and besieged the town of Wadnagar at that time inhabited by rich Wadnagrá Bráhmans. These at once gave information to Sirbuland Khán, but his troops being already engaged in the pursuit of the Maráthás defeated at Kapadvanj, he could not send any assistance to Wadnagar. The inhabitants therefore purchased Antáji's retreat by collecting among themselves, and paying over, a ransom of four lacs of rupees. Antáji's success served, however, to raise the cupidity of Kantháji, who also besieged the town; but the Nágars, being unable after so short an interval to pay a second ransom, fled at night, leaving their houses open to the invaders, who did not scruple to burn down the unfortunate town. A few days afterwards, Kantháji subjected to the same fate the town of Umreth*, where also many wealthy Bráhmans are said to have resided. Piláji made a raid on Baroda, but there he was met by the Viceroy's son Khán Azád Khán. Fearing to venture a battle with him Piláji withdrew, first to Cambay and later to Sorath.

Sirbuland Khán thus remained in sole possession of Gujarát, but the Maráthás returned soon after the rainy season was over. Sirbuland Khán, failing to obtain assistance from Delhi either in money or in troops, thought it prudent, in order to save the country from devastation, again to allow Piláji the right to levy Chauth in the districts south of the Mahi (1726 A. D.). But on this occasion, the Peshvá, who bore enmity towards Piláji,

---

* Now in the Kairá district.

appeared as a competitor and sent Udáji Powár, one of his officers, to resist the collection of the levy. Piláji, however, had already gained a firm footing in the district.

The Powár, though gaining a few successes, could not succeed in driving out either Piláji or Kantháji, who continued to levy the chauth and sardeshmukhi, and Piláji also succeeded in regaining possession of Baroda.

The Peshwá Baji Ráo, however, was in negotiation with Sirbuland Khán, and, as soon as he had concluded a peace with the Nizám of Haidarábád, he sent an army under his brother Chimnáji Apá to bring pressure to bear on the Gujarát Viceroy. Chimnáji exacted a heavy contribution from Petlád, and pludered Dholká, but he agreed (1728 A. D.) on the part of his brother to secure the safety of the country if the Peshwá was given the right to levy the chauth* and sardeshmukhi†. Sirbuland Khán, regarding the Peshwá as the strongest of all the claimants, ultimately consented to the proposal, which he was the more willing to do, inasmuch as neither Piláji nor Kanthàji had been acting up to their agreements. The Peshwá promised to keep up a body of two thousand five hundred horse in order to put an end to the depredations committed by the Maráthás and other freebooters. He further undertook to prevent any Maráthás from taking part with disaffected Zamindárs and other disturbers of the public peace. These agreements were duly signed in A. D. 1729. Piláji Gáekwád had, however, during the two preceding years, possessed himself of both Baroda and Dabhoi, while Kantháji had seized Chámpáner. A part too of

* One fourth of the whole collection on the land and customs; also five per cent of the revenue of the city of Ahmadábád.

† Sardeshmukhi was ten per cent of the total revenue from land and customs with the exception of that derived from the port of Surat and the surrounding district.

the Sardeshmukhi was also assigned to Trimbak Ráv Dhábáde, who bitterly resented the Peshwá's interference with him and Piláji in Gujarát.

Sirbuland Khán's action in consenting to give tribute to the Maráthás was also highly disapproved of at Delhi, and orders were issued for his recall, Mahá Rájá Abhesingh of Jodhpur being appointed to succeed him. This was by way of reward for his having written to his brother Vakhat Singh to murder their father. Abhesingh, it is true, had written only under extreme compulsion, for, while on a pleasure excursion on the river Hughli, the Emperor gave orders that he should be thrown overboard unless he there and then wrote a letter to the above purport. No manner of excuse, however, can be given for Vakhat Singh, who, with his own hand, murdered his sleeping father in the hope of obtaining thereby the government of Nágor.

Sirbuland Khán had unquestionably done every thing in his power to settle the country. In addition to withstanding Maráthá attacks, he had marched on several tributary chiefs and refractory Kolis, had recovered their tribute and revenue with much trouble, and it was only after all his endeavours to obtain pecuniary or military assistance from Delhi had failed, that he was compelled to yield to the demands of the Maráthás, there being no other means of preventing the devastation and ruin of the country. In short, feeling himself ill requited, he determined not to leave his government without an appeal to arms.

Abhesingh, with his brother and twenty thousand men, reached Pálanpur and was joined at Siddhpur by the Bábis from Rádhanpur (1730 A. D.). Near the village of Adálaj a battle was fought between him and Sirbuland Khán, in which the Mahárájah was defeated. A second engagement also ended with the same result. At length Abhesingh entered into negotiations with his brave rival, who ultimately consented to give over the government to him on receipt of a present of a lac of rupees. He thereafter proceeded to Agrá.

The Maráthás had in the mean time been in conflict between themselves. The animosity between Báji Ráo Peshwá on the one hand and Piláji Gáekwád, Trimbak Ráo Dhábáde, and Kantháji Kadam on the other, eventually led to an open rupture, and Dhábáde had collected an army of thirty-six thousand men to attack the Deccan. The Peshwá, hearing of this, at once marched on Gujarát. As soon as his advance division crossed the Narbadá, it was met and defeated by a party under Piláji's son Dámáji. Báji Ráo, however, coming up with the main portion of his army, closed with the enemy immediately, though his force was numerically much inferior to that of the Dhábáde, who had already been joined by Piláji and Kantháji. The Peshwá's army consisted of veterans, before whom the Dhábáde's new levies fled at the very first charge. Kantháji fled, but Dhábáde continued to fight with obstinacy until a random shot from the ranks of the enemy killed him while in the act of drawing his bow. Báji Ráo thus gained a complete victory. In this battle, which took place at Bhilápur between Dabhoi and Baroda on or about the 1st of April 1731, many persons of rank fell, including one of Piláji's sons, and Pilaji himself was wounded.

Báji Ráo was, however, not able to reap the full fruits of this victory in consequence of the march towards Gujarát of the Nizám, who was in secret league with Dhábáde. A treaty was concluded (August 1731 A. D.), by which Dhábáde's infant son Yashvant Ráo was appointed to his father's post, and allowed to collect the chauth on the understanding that half the amount realized should be sent to Rájá Sáhu through the Peshwá, while Piláji Gáekwád was confirmed in the office of Dhábáde's Mutálik or Deputy, and granted the additional title of Sená Khás Khel (Commander of the special band).

Thus ended the first struggle between the Peshwá on the one hand and the Senápati Dhabáde, the Gáekwád and Kantháji on the other. Still the Emperor's purpose of freeing Gujarát from Maráthá interference was not yet accomplished, and Piláji being a thorn in the side of Abhesingh, the new Viceroy, over whom he had gained several advantages, Abhesingh determined to get rid of him by treachery. Negotiations were therefore opened, and emissaries were sent by Abhesingh on the pretext of arranging preliminaries. One day, after a protracted interview, one of the envoys, on leaving Pilaji's presence, returned at dusk saying he had forgotten something, and in the dim light stabbed Piláji to the heart (1732 A.D.), causing instantaneous death. The assassin was of course immediately killed.

Abhesingh, taking advantage of the consequent confusion, hurried his forces to Baroda, and seized that city and the fort, which were placed in charge of Sher Khán Bábi* (1732 A. D.).

The treacherous murder of Piláji Gáekwád was, however, not attended by the advantages that Abhesingh had expected. Though after capturing Baroda, he laid siege to Dabhoi, that strong fortress held out, and on the approach of the rainy season the Desái of Pádrá near Baroda instigated Kolis and Bhils to rise throughout the country, and Abhesingh was compelled to retire. Dhábáde's widow Umábái also marched on Ahmadábád in conjunction with Kantháji Kadam and Piláji's son Dámáji. They attacked the city (1733 A. D.) and though not entirely successful, made so great an impression that Abhesingh consented to pay from the treasury eighty thousand rupees in addition

* The Bábis are a celebrated family whose ancestor Bahádur Khán came from Afghahánistán upwards of three hundred years ago, and enlisted in the service of the Emperor Humáyun. The Nawábs of Junágadh, Rádhanpur and Bálásinor belong to this family.

to the usual chauth and sardeshmukhi. Piláji's brother Máhádáji Gáekwád, taking the opportunity of the abscence of Sher Khán Bábi at his estate at Bálásinor, marched on Barodá, and retook it in 1734 A. D., since which time it has remained in the Gáekwád's possession.

Piláji's son Dámáji, whom his uncle had called to his assistance, then took several important towns, and marched towards Jodhpur. This compelled his father's murderer Abhesingh to leave a deputy, Ratansing Bhandári, at Ahmadábád, while he himself proceeded to guard his native country. Ali Muhammad Khán, the author of the Mirát-i-ahmadi was at this time appointed Diwán.

It was also about this time (1733 A. D.) that Khushálchand Sheth, the ancestor of the present Nagarsheth family of Ahmadábád received an Imperial Farmán appointing him chief of the mercantile community.

Meanwhile, the tribute due to Umábái not having been paid in full, her son Jádavji Dhábáde again advanced on Gujarát; but on a treaty being concluded between him and the Viceroy he went on to Sorath to collect tribute.

Chapter VIII.

Affairs at Piram, Surat, Broach, Idar and other parts of Gujarát. Foundation of Bhávnagar and its subsequent development. Supersession of Abhesingh and appointment of Momin Khán as Viceroy. The latter makes over half of Ahmadábád to the Maráthás.

From 1729 to 1738 A. D.

While matters were thus proceeding in other quarters, one Mullán Muhammad Ali, a wealthy trader in Surat, caused disturbances in that city. At first, with a view to raise himself to the position of an independent ruler, he removed to the island of Piram near Goghá, and spent large sums in inducing merchants to settle there. Finding, however, that Piram was too remote a spot, the Mullán, in 1729 A. D., began to build a fort at the village of Athwá on the Tápti about three miles from Surat.

By intrigue first with the commandant and next with the Governor of Surat, he was the means of causing a considerable diminution in the trade of that port, his fort being situated near the entrance of the harbour. For the loss thus occasioned, the Governor Sohráb Khán made a demand on him for a lac of rupees, but the Mullán resisted the demand by force of arms and compelled Sohráb Khán to take refuge with the chief of Bhávnagar (1732 A. D.). The Governorship was then assumed by the Mullan's brother Teghbakht Khán. The latter was ordered by the Emperor to seize his brother the Mullán, which he did treacherously, making him a prisoner at an entertainment to which he had been invited. He also took possession of Athwá on behalf of the Emperor, who eventually confirmed him in A. D. 1733 in his post of Governor, which he continued to hold until 1746 A. D., nominally indeed as the Emperor's servant but practically as an independent ruler. The Maráthás, since the death of Rustam Ali, who had killed himself at Vaso as described in the foregoing pages, were, however, masters of the district nearly up to the walls of Surat. Teghbakht Khán compelled the Gáekwád to make him an annual assignment of rupees two lacs and thirty-six thousand. In Broach also the Governor declared himself independent, and was the founder of the short lived Nawábship* of that district.

During this period there was a change of rulers at Idar†. It had been held hitherto by Ráthod chiefs, who were defeated by Abhesingh's brothers Anandsingh and Ráesingh, and these took possession of Idar on the 7th of Fálgan Shud Samvat 1787 (1731 A. D.). Abhesingh was, however, promised the grant of Idar when he consented to murder his father, but, being willing to appease Anandsingh and Ráesingh, who had gone into outlawry, he willingly obtained from Delhi a fresh grant in the names of his brothers.

---

* Abdullá, the first Nawáb, received from Nizám-ul-mulk of the Deccan whose private Jágir Broach was, the title of Nek Alam Khán in or about ... ... 1736 A. D.

He was succeeded by his son Mirzá Beg in ... 1738 „

Third son (name not ascertained) who died in three months ... ... 1752 „

Mirzá Ahmad Beg, grandson of Abdullá ... ... 1754 „

His son Mázad Khán ... ... 1768 „

(deposed by the English on the 18th November)... 1772 „

† Idar was originally held by Bhils, from whom Gohá, the cave-born son of Pushpávati (widow of the last Rájá of Valabhipur) obtained it in or about A. D. 800. It was then held from 1000 to 1193 A. D. by Parihár Rajput chiefs, in whose time the Idar force was cut to pieces in the great battle of Tháneshvar. It was subsequently held by Háthi Sord a Koli and his son until about 1215 A. D., when the Ráthods known as Rávs won the fort of Idar. It was from the last of these that Idar was taken by the ancestors of the present chief (1731 A. D.). The Rávs now hold the smaller state of Pol.

In 1734 A. D., Jawánmard Khán, then governor of Viramgám, made an attempt to conquer Idar, but the Rájá sought and obtained timely aid from Ránoji Sindhiá and Malhár Ráo Holkar, so that Jawánmard Khán was able to effect his return only after agreeing to pay one lac and sixty-five thousand rupees, of which a portion was given in ready cash.

Anandsingh's rule lasted for about eleven years. In 1742 A. D. while Ráesingh was in attendance on Momin Khán, the Rehvar Chief attacked Idar, and, gaining over the Kasbátis, retook that fort after killing Anandsingh in action. Ráesingh hearing of this took leave of Momin Khán, and advanced on Idar, which he took back from the Rehvars in 1742 A. D. About a thousand Kasbátis and several of the Rehavrs were massacred on this occasion. Ráesingh placed the deceased Anandsingh's son Shivsingh, then about six years of age, on the throne and himself acted as his minister. The present Rájá Sir Kesrisinghji Jasvatsinghji, K. C. S. I., is a descendant of Shivsinghji.

During this period, Kanthájí Kadam and Piláji Gáekwád made a raid on Sirohi* (A. D. 1722-23), but they were repulsed by its Chief Bhávsinghji. So great, however, was his loss, and so deeply was he impressed with the danger he had run from having no means of escape, that Bhávsinghji removed his capital from Sihor to Wadvá on the creek not many miles from Goghá, and there he, in 1723, founded the city of Bhávnagar, with the object not only of being able to take to the sea in case his territory was invaded, but also of sharing in the rich harvest

* Sirohi had been held by Audich Bráhmans ever since its grant to them by Mul Ráj Solanki, but about the end of the sixteenth century a dispute arose between the Ráná and the Jáni divisions of these Bráhmans, in which the former asked the assistance of Kandháji, chief of Gariádhar, and the latter that of Visoji, the chief of Umrálá. Visoji, coming through a pass in the hill, surprised Kandháji and himself took possession of Sihor, which thenceforward he made his capital.

of trade then monopolised by Surat and Cambay. Goghá was then a Jágir town of the Bábi family, but subsequently fell to the share of the Peshwá when Ahmadábád was finally taken by the Maráthás in A. D. 1757. With the view of protecting the maritime trade of Bhávnagar, its far sighted founder entered into an alliance with the Sidhis of Janjirá, who were in command of the Surat castle, agreeing to give them one and a quarter per cent on the sea custom revenue of the port. When the English, in 1756 A. D., superseded the Sidhis in the command of the Surat castle, Bhávsinghji secured their assistance on the same terms. During his long reign of sixty-one years he made large additions to his territory, and, notwithstanding the fact that he had during his lifetime conferred Valá and other villages on his second son Visoji, he was able to raise Bhávnagar from being only a small chieftainship into a principality of considerable importance. His successors, continuing the policy of their illustrious ancestor and liberally encouraging trade by every means in their power, have brought not only Bhávnagar but the entire state into a very flourishing condition, and it now ranks as one of the most prosperous and wealthy states in Western India*.

In or about 1735 A. D. Dámáji Gáekwád, who was chosen by Umábái as the Dhábáde's deputy, appointed one Rang Ráo as his agent. Kantháji, naturally disappointed at this arrangement, marched with an army on Gujarát. At Anand Moghri a battle was fought between him and Rangoji, in which Kantháji was defeated and compelled to retire to Cambay. Peace was at length concluded between these two rivals by a treaty, in which it was stipulated that Dámáji should receive the chauth of the district north of the river Mahi. Kantháji then

* The Bhávnagar Gondal Railway, 201 miles in length, was the first to be constructed at State expense in Káthiáwár.

went to Sorath to levy tribute in that part of the country, and thereafter to the Deccan.

The next year, A. D. 1736, Rangoji advanced as far as Bávlá, and commenced depredations. The Deputy-Viceroy Ratansingh Bhandári therefore marched against him, on hearing of which Rangoji retired to Viramgám, where a battle took place, which ended in the defeat of Rangoji and the capture of his baggage. Rangoji himself, however, retreated into the fort, to which Ratansingh next laid siege. In the meantime some Maráthá horse from Sarnál, joined by insurgent Kolis, advanced on Kapadvanj, and captured it from the garrison. The Deputy Viceroy was, however, obliged to raise the siege of Viramgám, and proceed hurriedly to Ahmadábád on learning that Dámáji's brother PartápRáo and Deváji Tákpur were advancing towards that city. The Maráthás, however, avoided Ahmadábád, but, exacting tribute from the villages on the Vátrak river, advanced to Dholká, claiming a share of the revenue of that division, and two thousand horse were left in order to realise the amount demanded. Proceeding next to Idar and Dántá, the Maráthás plundered the latter town. Thus a large tract of country became a scene of anarchy and disorder.

The Imperial Court at Delhi, now growing dissatisfied with Abhesingh and his deputy Ratansingh's administration, appointed Momin Khán*, the governor of Cambay, to be Viceroy of Gujarát (A. D. 1737). Abhesingh none the less instructed his deputy not to resign the viceroyalty without an appeal to arms. Ratansingh accordingly prepared for war. He first marched against Sohráb Khán, who had obtained the governorship of Viramgám, and slew him in A. D. 1735. Momin Khán, seeing this, asked for and obtained the aid of Rangoji, on the condition that the Maráthás should be assigned one-half of the revenue of Gujarát, except what accrued from the city of

* Ancestor of the present Nawáb of Cambay.

Ahmadábád and the lands in its immediate neighbourhood, and also from the port of Cambay, of which he was himself the Governor. Momin Khán further invited Dámáji Gáekwád to join him. This alliance gave the finishing stroke to the tottering Mughal Empire in Gujarát, and although the Emperor of Delhi regretted having made Momin Khán's appointment, and the latter also subsequently saw that the combination he had formed would prove disastrous to the authority of the Empire, it was too late to retrace his steps. Although he received instructions from the Emperor that his appointment had been cancelled, Momin Khán marched from Cambay by regular stages, but, on reaching Kaira, halted for about a month, as the river Vátrak was then in flood by reason of heavy rains. As soon as possible, however, he advanced and besieged Ahmadábád. The siege continued for some nine months. In the meantime, one of Momin Khan's detachments had captured some guns that were being sent from Surat to Abhesingh at Ahmadábád, and soon after the Maráthás attempted to attack the city by storm. Ratansingh, however, repulsed them after a severe contest, but the day following, seeing that he would not be able to hold the city in the event of a further attack and bombardment, Ratansingh listened to Momin Khán's overtures, and, after recovering some money as a payment towards the expenses incurred, retired.

Half of the city was then according to engagement made over to the Maráthás (A. D. 1737). This half consisted of the Ráepur, Astodiá, Jamálpur, Khánjahán and Ráekhad wards. Rangoji commencing to oppress the inhabitants, most of whom were Musalmáns, the latter rose in rebellion, and drove the Maráthás out of the city for a short time in the same year. Momin Khán, however, was able to effect a reconciliation through his deputy Fidá-ud-din Khán. Some time after this, both Momin Khán and Rangoji left for the districts in order to collect the revenues that had fallen due.

Chapter IX.

Disturbances at Viramgám, Invasion of India by Nádir Sháh. Ránpur taken possession of by the Gáekwád. Disastrous flood in the Sábarmati. Bhávsing Desái obtains Pátri. Building of a fort at Borsad. Momin Khán's death. Baji Ráo Peshwá's death. The Peshwa's differences with the Gáekwád. Burning of Songhad.

From 1739 to 1744 A. D.

About this time the Kolis of the Viramgám parganá under the leadership of Kahánji chief of Chhaniár committed several excesses, and accordingly Dámáji Gáekwád marched against them. Being unable, however, to cope with the marauders, he asked for aid from Momin Khán, who responded by sending troops under the command of his deputy. The Koli chief was then subdued and his village burnt. A Koli town in Kánkrej, the Chief of which was in the habit of annoying the surrounding districts by his plundering excursions, was also sacked, the Chief not venturing a battle against the combined forces (A. D. 1739)*.

About this time, the Thákor of Wadhván attacked Ránpur, the holder of which applied to Dámáji Gáekwád for aid, which was readily granted, and Ránpur was saved. But so high a sum did Dámáji claim as the price of his assistance that the Ránpur Chief Alambhai had to part with his chief town and castle, and thus Ránpur passed into the hands of the Gáekwád, and only nine of the villages remained with the Moleslám Tálukdárs.

As might have been expected, harmony did not long prevail at Ahmadábád between Momin Khán and Rangoji. In A.D. 1739 a

---

* This period is celebrated for the invasion of India in November A.D. 1738 by Nádir Sháh, king of Persia, who ruthlessly massacred the inhabitants of Delhi and pillaged the city of its riches including Sháh Jáhán's peacock-throne of gold and jewels, which alone is said to have been worth nearly a krore of rupees. The value of the whole booty has been estimated at some eighteen krores.

serious disturbance took place, in which Momin Khán was driven from Ahmadábád, and was ultimately obliged to give Rangoji half of the Government as well as of the revenue, and also to pay up the arrears that had accumulated during the two years subsequent to the expulsion of the Maráthás by the Muhammadans.

The next year A. D. 1740*, Dámáji Gáekwád went to the Deccan with Rangoji, leaving Malhár Ráo Khuni at Ahmadábád. Expeditions were also undertaken against certain chiefs by Fidá-ud-din Khán, the Deputy of Momin Khán, who enforced tribute from Dabhorá, Atarsumbá, Mándwá, Lunávádá and other towns. A rising in the Bhil district was also suppressed.

In A. D. 1741, Bhávsing, Desai† of Viramgám, who had acquired great influence in that town, indignant at the oppression of the Maráthás, attacked and took their fort. Accordingly Rangoji and Momin Khán laid siege to Viramgám. Bhávsingh defended it gallantly, and at length a treaty was concluded, by which Bhávsingh was assigned instead of Viramgám the town of Pátri with its dependent villages, which are still in the possession of his descendants.

It was at this time that Dámáji Gáekwád, returning from the Deccan, crossed the Mahi with a large army. Having taken Bánsá after a brave defence by the Kolis, he burnt it, and then marched on Broach. This town, however, he refrained from attacking in consequence of remonstrances from the Nizám of Haidarábád whose private Jágir it was when he was Viceroy of Gujarát. Dámáji, however, appears to have obtained on this occasion a share of the custom revenues of that town, after which he returned to Songadh.

* In this year there was a disastrous flood in the Sábarmati.

† Desái is an hereditary revenue officer appointed to look after the revenue work of the district and assist the local officers in revenue administration generally.

In this year (A. D. 1741) several skirmishes took place between the troops of Momin Khán's Deputy Fidá-ud-din Khán and those of Rangoji's Deputy Malhár Ráo Khuni, but matters were at last amicably settled through the personal intervention of Rangoji and Momin Khán. Rangoji in this year built a fort at Borsad, * which he occupied as a residence.

After one more year of conflict spent in levying tribute from the Chiefs of Sihor and Navánagar, the latter of whom resisted for twenty days and was then compelled to pay the additional sum of rupees fifty thousand, Momin Khán died in February A. D. 1743. During the period of his viceroyalty his son-in-law Najum Khán acted as governor of Cambay and continued in that office until A.D. 1748, when he was poisoned by his wife's brother Muft-ákhir Khán, who, failing to retain his viceroyalty, reverted to the governorship of Cambay.

While Rangoji was most energetically promoting Maráthá interests in Gujarát, Dámáji Gáekwád's own attention was being engrossed with the affairs of the Deccan, where cordiality had never existed between him and the Peshwá. Taking therefore the opportunity afforded by the death of Báji Ráo in April 1740, he joined Raghuji Bhonsle the Chief of Berár, and sided with one Bápuji Náik a connexion of Báji Ráo who pressed his claim to the throne.

In the end, however, Báláji the son of the late Peshwá established his right to succeed, and won over both Bhonsle and Bápuji to his side. Bápuji then invaded Gujarát, and burnt Songadh, at that time the head-quarters of the Gáekwád.

His further progress was, however, arrested by the advance

* According to tradition this town is said to have been founded by a certain Ráján Nal in the fourth century after Christ.

Campbell's Bombay Gazetteer Vol. III, page 167.

of the Gáekwad's active and brave Deputy Rangoji, who gave him battle before he could cross the Mahi (A. D. 1741-42). Bapuji had in consequence to retreat towards the Deccan, after which Rangoji returned to Borsad.

After Momin Khán's death, which took place in A.D. 1743, orders were received from the Imperial Court directing the Deputy Fidá-ud-din to carry on the government in conjunction with the deceased Viceroy's son Muft-ákhir Khán. Quarrels, however, arose between them and Rangoji, and the latter, under the instigation of Anandrám, an officer who is said to have been disgraced by Momin Khán, sought to compass the death of the two Deputy-Viceroys. After Rangoji's attempts to accomplish this object had failed, open hostilities commenced, and, the Maráthás being routed in battle, Rangoji's residence at Ahmadábád was besieged. He then agreed to deliver up Anandrám, and also to surrender both Borsad and Viramgám. On this occasion Sher Khán Bábi of Bálásinor stood security for Rangoji.

Eventually, however, Rangoji contrived to escape to Borsad and the Bábi to Bálásinor, but Anandrám was put to death. In the meantime Dámáji's brother Khande Ráo joined Rangoji, and laid siege to Petlád, which ultimately surrendered to them, the Viceroy being unable to reinforce the garrison.

A serious misfortune now befell Fidá-ud-din Khán and Muftákhir Khán. One Abdul Aziz Khán, Commandant at Juner near Puná, contrived to send a forged order from the Emperor appointing him as Viceroy. Abdul Aziz Khán also appointed Jawánmard Khán Bábi as his Deputy. Thereupon the troops became clamorous for their pay, and placed the two Viceroys under arrest. They were, however, eventually released, and both departed, Fidá-ud-din for Agrá and Muft-ákhir Khán for Cambay.

After taking Petlád, Khande Ráo Gáekwád and Rangoji marched on Ahmadábád. Encamping at Vanjar about seven miles from the city, they demanded of the Viceroy their former rights and possessions. Being quite unable to cope with the Maráthás, he agreed to their demand, and accordingly one Dádu Morár was appointed Deputy-governor of the city by the two Maráthá chiefs in A. D. 1743-44.

In the latter year, Jawánmard Khán invited Abdul Aziz Khán, who had forged the order above mentioned in his interest, to join him. Abdul accordingly left Juner, and arrived safely at Surat, but, on leaving the latter city, he was followed by the Gáekwád's lieutenant Devájí Tákpur. An engagement took place at Khim Kathodrá, in which Abdul was defeated and put to flight. The Maráthás kept up a hot pursuit, and the unfortunate Abdul, while attempting to swim across the Narbadá, was overtaken and killed.

Jawánmard Khán was thus disappointed in his hope of obtaining assistance from Abdul, and the Emperor of Delhi, on receipt of a present of two lacs of rupees from one Fakhr-ud-daulá, assigned to him the viceroyalty of Gujarát. This nobleman, however, did not leave Delhi, but appointed Jawánmard Khán his deputy, and thus the latter continued in power (1744-1748). On behalf of the Maráthás, Khande Ráo Gáekwád named Rangoji as his deputy, who met Jawánmard Khán at Kaira, and, establishing friendly relations with him, sent one Krishnáji as his representative to Ahmadábád. Thus the government of Gujarát continued to be divided between the Maráthás and Muhammadans. About this time Pahárkhán Jhálori, Governor of Pálanpur, died and his uncle Muhammad Bahádur was appointed his successor.

Fakhr-ud-daulá, at this time leaving Delhi, advanced towards Ahmadábád to assume the viceroyalty, and came as far as Bálásinor, which was still governed by Jawánmard Khán's brother

Sher Khán Bábi, who received him with due honour. Jawánmard Khán, however, obtained assistance from the Maráthás, and determined to oppose him. In the first battle, which took place about six miles from Ahmadábád, the new Viceroy was so far successful as to be able to secure the suburbs of Rájpur and Behrámpur. Soon, however, affairs took a different turn. Fakhr-ud-daulá being wounded, his allies Sher Khán and the Rájá of Idar went over to the enemy, and the unfortunate Viceroy was himself taken prisoner together with two of his wives.

While this struggle was going on, Khande Ráo Gáekwád, who had proceeded to the Deccan, returned with Dámáji to Gujarát, and being dissatisfied with Rangoji's accounts, attached his property and confined him in the fort at Borsad, which, it will be remembered, had been built by Rangoji himself.

Chapter X.

Dhábáde's widow interferes and obtains the release of Rangoji, who retakes Ahmadábád and Borsad. Affairs at Surat. Dámáji, taken prisoner by the Peshwá, is released after paying a heavy ransom. Capture of Ahmadábád jointly by the Peshwá and the Gáekwád. Annihilation of the Angariá pirates.

From 1745 to 1757 A. D.

Dhábáde's widow Umábái, on hearing of Rangoji's confinement, summoned him and Khande Ráo Gáekwád to her presence. In obedience to her orders they both repaired to the Deccan. There Umábái appointed Rangoji as her Deputy in Gujarát, and this officer accordingly returned to Ahmadábád expelling therefrom Khande Rá'os agent Trimbak Ráo Pandit. He also eventually retook Borsad from Khande Ráo's adopted son Haribá. This period was, however, far from peaceful. At one time Rangoji, at another the Gáekwád's agents, obtained the ascendency, and in like manner the Muhammadan viceroys and their deputies were also frequently opposed the one to the other.

Disturbances concerning the post of Governor, arose at Surat in (A.D. 1747)* between two rival claimants Sayyid Achhan and Safdar Muhammad Khán, in which the latter was successful owing to his having secured the assistance of the Dutch and other foreign merchants, and also that of the Habshis who had commanded the castle as the Delhi Emperor's Admirals since A. D. 1670. On this occasion the head of the English factory Mr. Lambe faithfully adhered to his previous agreement to aid the cause of Sayyid Achhan. In consequence of this, however, the English factory was attacked and plundered, and Mr. Lambe, on receiving a letter of censure from the Governor of Bombay, committed suicide.

Sayyid Achhan, who eventually succeeded in 1758 A.D., had

* This was a year of famine in Gujarát.

sought aid from the Gáekwád, and had promised to pay three lacs of rupees to Dámáji's cousin Kedárji for his services. Although that chief's assistance was not required, he none the less claimed the stipulated sum. The unfortunate Sayyid was therefore compelled to assign him one-fourth of the revenue of Surat, until the demand should be paid up in full.

This period witnessed another change in the Maráthá deputies of Ahmadábád owing to the death of Dhábáde's widow Umábái. Her grandson Bábu Ráo Senápati was induced, through Khande Ráo's influence, to appoint Dámáji Gáekwád as his deputy, and the latter nominated one Raghushankar as his agent at Ahmadábád. The Gáekwád then marched on Borsad, and, in conjunction with the armies of Momin Khán II. and Jawánmard Khán, besieged that town, which they succeeded in taking after five months. They also took Rangoji prisoner in A. D. 1747. Bálájí Peshwá, however, who was still hostile to the Gáekwád, sent troops against Khande Ráo, and procured the release of Rangoji in the following year.

At Ahmadábád in the meantime, Jawánmard Khán, secretly jealous of the power of the Gáekwád, had entered into negotiations with the Peshwá, whose help he solicited in order to expel the Gáekwád's agent from that city; but the Peshwá, being then at war with the Nizám of the Deccan, was unable to comply with this request.

Events, however, soon happened which brought Dámáji into open conflict with the Peshwá. Rájá Sáhu being on his death-bed, A. D. 1749, numerous intrigues were set on foot regarding the succession. Tárábái, grandmother of the young Rájárám who had been adopted by Sáhu, and who consequently succeeded to the throne, advised him to try and shake off the Peshwá's control, but, having failed in her persuasions, she sent secret messages to Dámáji urging him to rescue the young prince and the Maráthá nation generally from the control of the Bráhmans. Dámáji, from his jealously of the Peshwá, did not hesitate to respond readily to her call.

Tárábái, on hearing of Dámáji's approach, invited Rájárám to her residence in the fort of Satárá, and there, after upbraiding him for his cowardice, made him a prisoner in A. D. 1751. She at the same time ordered the guns of the fort to be turned against the houses of the Peshwá's adherents. The latter at first treated Tárábái's conduct with contempt, but, when they heard of the Gáekwád's advance from Songadh, they recognised the gravity of the occasion, and fled from the town. Two engagements took place between them and the Gáekwád. Dámáji was victorious though his army was inferior in number. The Peshwá was at this time in the vicinity of the river Kistna, where he was assisting one of the competitors for the Haidarábád Kingdom, from whom he had received no less than fifteen lacs of rupees for the expenses of his expedition. He now hurriedly broke up his camp, and marched against Dámáji. Prior to his arrival, however, Dámáji had been compelled to retire before one of the Peshwá's generals, and, reinforcements not having arrived from Gujarát, he thought it proper to treat with the Peshwá, who craftily agreed to accept Dámáji's proposals, and induced him to encamp in his neighbourhood. The Peshwá then treacherously attacked the Gáekwád's camp while off its guard, and making a prisoner* of Dámáji, demanded from him the cession of a large portion of territory and payment of the arrears of the Peshwá's share of the chauth. Dámáji for a while made various excuses, but being sent to Puná, was there placed

* It is said that after this act of treachery Dámáji never saluted the Peshwá with his right hand, but only with the left.

Grant Duff's History of the Maráthás Vol. II, p. 36.

in confinement. Though he is said to have spent in that city more than a lac of rupees on Nazars (presents) and bribes to officers, he had at last to agree to pay the Peshwá a sum of fifteen lacs of rupees as an acquittance for all the arrears due, A. D. 1752. Dámáji also passed a bond agreeing to an equal partition of the territories then in his possession, and of any which might thereafter be conquered; also to an equal division of revenue of every kind. He further agreed to maintain ten thousand horse, and to assist the Peshwá when necessary; and also, as being the deputy of Dhábáde Senápati, to pay an annual tribute of five lacs and twenty-five thousand rupees from the Dhábáde's share of the revenue. These terms Dámáji was compelled to accept, for during his absence affairs in Gujarát had assumed a serious aspect. In A. D. 1753 the Peshwá sent his brother Raghunáth Ráo with an army to that province in order to complete the arrangements entered into with Dámáji Gáekwád, and to take possession of Ahmadábád. Dámáji himself also joined the army soon afterwards. They arrived, without being impeded on the march, as far as Ahmadábád, where Jawánmard Khán Bábi the Imperial viceroy had, during Dámáji's confinement in Puná, usurped the whole power of the city, and merely permitted the Gáekwád's agent to realise his master's dues.

The combined Maráthá army laid seige to the city, which was well defended, but at length Jawánmard Khán agreed to surrender it on condition of their supplying a lac of rupees for payment of his troops, besides presenting him with an elephant and various articles of value. It was further stipulated that Jawánmard Khán and his brothers should be allowed in Jágir, free from any claim on the part of the Maráthás, the districts of Sami, Rádhanpur with Terwárá, Pátan, Wadnagar, Tharád, Kherálu and Bijápur, also that the members of Jawánmard

Khán's family should not be disturbed in their present possessions, and that he and his army should be allowed to retire with the honours of war. These stipulations having been agreed to, Jawáumard Khán left the city in April 1753, and the province was transferred to the Peshwá and the Gáekwád, who realised the revenue in equal proportions. The garrison was, however, provided by the Peshwá, except that the Gáekwád agreed to pay annually six thousand rupees towards the expenses of management.

After appointing Shripat Ráo as his deputy to carry on the government, Raghunáth Ráo left for Limbdi, the Chief of which state consented to the payment of tribute amounting to forty thousand rupees a year, while Pálaupur was compelled to supply ten thousand rupees a year, A. D. 1753. Dámáji also, after levying tribute in the Vátrak Kanthá villages, took Kapadvanj from Sher Khán Bábi.

Shripat Ráo now entertained the design of conquering Cambay, but after two indecisive battles, returned in A. D. 1754, Momin Khán agreeing to pay an annual tribute of rupees seven thousand. About this time too an expedition was sent against the Bhils and Kolis who, had again begun to ravage the country, carrying off women and children in broad daylight.

The Peshwá's deputy Bhagvant Ráo next marched on Cambay. He was, however, entrapped by the cunning of Momin Khán, and made prisoner. The Peshwá accordingly sent another force under the governors of Jambusar and Viramgám, who for three months besieged the city, but without success. Ali Muhammad Khán Diwán, the author of the Mirát-i-Ahmadi, at length effected a reconciliation, and secured the release of Bhagvant Ráo. The latter was recalled from his post of deputy, but establishing himself at Nápád, he there carried on warfare with Momin Khán, whom he at last compelled to pay ten thousand rupees being the share of the Maráthás which he had for a time withheld.

Momin Khán was at this time hard pressed for money to pay his troops, and, in order to raise it, began to plunder several villages belonging to the Limbdi Thákor and other chiefs. He also marched on Goghá which formerly belonged to Cambay, but which had been usurped by Sher Khán Bábi and taken from him by the Peshwá in or about A. D. 1751. Momin Khán obtained easy possession of Goghá*, and putting a garrison therein, returned in A. D. 1755. He then marched on Borsad, but timely succour under Dámáji's son saved this town from capture and plunder.

Various causes were now producing discontent amongst the inhabitants of Ahmadábád. The rule of the Maráthás was felt to be most oppressive; the town-wall having tumbled down in several places in consequence of heavy rain, the inroads of robbers were becoming frequent, and the sense of general insecurity was heightened when the agent of the Maráthás was assassinated by a Rohilá. Momin Khán, recognising in this discontent his opportunity, conceived the bold idea of capturing the city. Accordingly he formed an alliance with the Rájá of Idar, and, marching by regular stages, arrived before the city gates at the end of A. D. 1755. After one or two battles in the suburbs, a portion of his forces, augmented by the Kolis who had joined him in hopes of plunder, succeeded in effecting an entrance into the city, and threw open its gates to the entire army. After a hand-to-hand fight the Maráthás were routed, and the city was taken possession of by Momin Khán, who then appointed Shambhurám Gárdi as his deputy.

---

* When the news of Momin Khán's capture of Goghá reached the Emperor at Delhi, that potentate sent him a sword of honour.

The Peshwá was much displeased when he heard the news of the capture of the city,and sent a force under Sadáshiv Rámchandra in order to retake it. These troops were joined by Khande Ráo Gáekwád and Jawánmard Khán, whom the Maráthás had called to their aid, and the combined army laid siege to Ahmadábád. Momin Khán and Shambhurám made a brave defence, and, in a night sally, even burnt some of Sadáshiv's tents. All the attempts to seduce Shambhurám, Sidhi Salim* and other officers from their allegiance failed, but at length Momin Khán's troops began to clamour for arrears of pay. Shambhurám, however, was able to raise a contribution of one lac of rupees from the residents in the city, and this for a time pacified the troops. After the siege had been protracted for a year negotiations were opened, in which Momin Khán agreed to evacuate the city on condition that he should retain undisputed possession of Cambay, without however infringing the right of the Peshwá to half its revenue; also that a lac of rupees should be supplied him for the payment of his troops. Momin Khán on his part agreed to give up all claim to the town of Noghá, and to pay an annual tribute of ten thousand rupees to the Maráthás. These terms were mutually accepted, and the city was finally surrendered to the Maráthás in April 1757.

With all the daring and enterprise shown by Momin Khán on this occasion, it is not to his credit that in the arrangements entered into no stipulation was made in favour of Shambhurám, who had so bravely and faithfully assisted him, and the unfortunate Deputy Governor, along with his sons, was sent in chains to Baroda and thence to Puná. Momin Khán's ally Ráesingh,

* Sidhi Salim's Haveli still exists in the Jamálpur division of the city. It was for a long time used as an office by the Assistant Collector of Continental Customs, and is now used as a civil jail.

the Rájá of Idar, had also to make over to the Maráthás Parántij, Bijápur and the half share of Modásá, Báyar and Harsol.

While Gujarát was passing through these troubles, the English, destined at no distant period to be the rulers not only of Gujarát but of the whole of India, were gaining renown by their exploits. The Angriás had recently become the curse of all the seaports, and were in the habit of plundering the vessels of every nation without distinction. Their piracies proceeded so far that for some time the East India Company was compelled to maintain a large fleet at a cost of four lacs of rupees in order to protect their trade. For the annihilation of these Angriás the English and the Maráthás entered into an alliance, and in February, A. D. 1756 bombarded their strong fort of Gheriá (Veziádrug) in the Ratnágiri district on the sea-coast. This was soon captured, the Angriá fleet was destroyed, and their chief Tulàji was taken prisoner. Thus the death blow was given to the ravages of these daring pirates, a fact of no small importance to vessels sailing along the coast from the Gujarát ports. The plunder amassed by the Angriás, amounting to no less than ten lacs of rupees, fell into the hands of the victors. Gheriá was retained by the Maráthás, while the English were assigned ten villages including Bánkot, in order to provide for the maintenance of the local fort, known as Fort Victoria, distant about sixty miles from Bombay.

PART IV.

From the conquest of Gujarát by the Maráthás to the present time.

FROM 1757 to 1893 A. D.

CHAPTER I.

Maráthás coin money in the Ahmadábád mint; they attack Cambay and levy tribute. Affairs at Surat. The English take command of the castle, and turn out the Habshis. Disastrous defeat of the Maráthás at Pánipat. Dámáji's return. The Bábi recovers Bálásinor. Dámáji marches on Cambay and frustrates the league of the Muhammadans to regain Gujarát. His alliance with Raghunáth Ráo against the Peshwá. Raghunáth Ráo's and Govind Ráo's defeat and capture by the Peshwá's army. Dámáji's death.

FROM 1757 to 1768 A. D.

The coining of Mughal rupees in Ahmadábád had ceased ever since the Maráthás first took possession of Ahmadábád. Accordingly Sadáshiv Rámchandra and Dámáji Gáekwád now ordered new coins bearing the representation of an elephant goad to be struck in the Ahmadábád mint, A. D. 1757. These officers then set out towards Sorath and other parts of the province in order to collect tribute, leaving their respective deputies in the city.

Sadáshiv Ráo had not forgotten the trouble given by Momin Khán, and therefore, as soon as his affairs were settled and he had despatched a force to aid the Ráo of Kachh in his contemplated attack on Tattá, he proceeded against Cambay in A. D. 1758, and, besieging that town, compelled Momin Khán to pay twenty thousand rupees, being arrears of two years' tribute. He also levied tribute from the chiefs of Umeitá, Bálásinor, Lunávádá and Pálanpur.

During this year important changes took place at Surat. Sayyid Achhan, who has been already mentioned as having been ousted by Safdar Jang, went to Puná and, obtaining from the Peshwá the appointment of Governor, returned to Surat with a body of Maráthá horse, and, with the assistance of Neknám Khán, Governor of Broach, succeeded in expelling Safdar Khán's son and successor Ali Naváz Khán. The English also, considering this a good opportunity for retaliating on the Habshis, who had plundered their factory and killed two of their clerks, obtained some men-of-war from Bombay, and, thus strengthened, captured the fort in March 1759, after which Mr. Spencer the chief factor was appointed Commandant in lieu of the Habshis. Momin Khán Nawáb of Cambay also entered into alliance with the English, and, backed by their influence, went on to Puná to have an interview with the Peshwá. On the news of the English having taken the fort of Surat reaching the Emperor at Delhi, the latter sent a Farmán, appointing the Honourable East India Company as Admirals of the Imperial fleet, and the Governor of Bombay as Commander of Surat Castle. This order reached Surat in A.D. 1760, when Mr. Spencer and other gentlemen marched out in procession with due pomp to receive the bearers of the Farmán. The yearly payment of two lacs of rupees that had been made on account of this command to the Habshis of Janjirá was now transferred to the Company in accordance with the Imperial Farmán dated 4th September A. D. 1759.

The year A. D. 1761 was full of misfortune for the Maráthás. The Peshwá's brother Raghunáth Ráo, being elated by his successes in the Deccan, had the audacity to invade the Panjáb in A. D. 1758, then recently wrested from the Mughal Empire of Delhi by Ahmadsháh Abdáli ruler of Afghánistán. Raghunáth Ráo and his auxiliaries Holkar and Sindhiá were twice defeated and put to flight. Hearing of this in the summer of A. D. 1760, Vishvás Ráo, the son of the Peshwá, with his cousin Shivadás Ráo Bháde marched to the Panjáb with a large army, consisting of fifty-five thousand horse and fifteen thousand foot, besides some Pindháris and other followers. Taking Delhi, they spent the rainy season in that city but on Abdáli's marching towards it the Maráthás advanced to Pánipat. From October 1760 till the end of the year there were continual skirmishes with various results, but, supplies falling short, the Maráthás could delay no longer, and on the 7th of January 1761 they marched out to attack Abdáli's camp. A bloody contest ensued, in which, though in the early part of the day fortune seemed to favour the Hindus, the hardy Afgháns at last proved victorious. The chief Hindu Generals, including Vishvás Ráo and Shivadás Ráo were slain, and their army was almost annihilated*. Dámáji Gáekwád was one of those who took part in this fatal campaign. He, however, after showing great gallantry in the early part of the battle, saved his life by flight.

The Maráthás having thus received a severe blow, the Emperor, who had regained his throne at Delhi, took the opportunity of enjoining the principal Muhammadan chiefs in Gujarát to unite and expel the Maráthás from that province. Accordingly Sher Khán's son Sirdár Muhámmad Khán Bábi, defeating the garrison at Bálásinor, regained that district, which has remained in the possession of his family ever since, he having subsequently agreed to pay tribute for it to the Maráthás. The Nawáb of Broach, with the aid of Momin Khán of Cambay, retook Jambusar. At this juncture Dámáji Gáekwád, in aid of their common cause, marched with an army to Cambay, and, defeating Momin Khán, plundered one of his villages.

By degrees Dámáji Gáekwád succeeded in possessing himself

* Three-fourths of the entire Maráthá army and its followers are said to have been killed either in action or in the subsequent cruel massacre of the prisoners.

of Kaira and the districts of Pátan, Bijápur, Wadnagar, Visalnagar and Kherálu, which were then held by Jawánmard Khán and other Bábis. He transferred the seat of his government from Songadh to Pátan, once the capital of the Hindu Kings of Anhilwár, A. D. 1763. He also took possession of Amreli from the Káthis, and having espoused the daughter of the Chief of Láthi, that Chief presented Dámnagar with its ten dependent villages as her dowry. Dámáji next conquered several towns in the territory of the Nawáb of Junágadh, and his army was present with Raghunáth Ráo when the latter, on a quarrel with his nephew Mádhav Ráo,* defeated the Peshwá's army before Ghod Nadi.

This action brought on Dámáji the wrath of the reigning Peshwá, who, on the pretence that the original partition of territory between him and the Gáekwád had been too favourable to the latter in consequence of his acquaintance with the resources of Gujarát, took from him six districts yielding an estimated revenue of two lacs and fifty-four thousand rupees.

This deprivation of territory was soon afterwards followed by a still greater calamity, which befell Dámáji shortly before his death. In A. D. 1768 his ally Raghunáth Ráo, having assembled a force in the Chandur range to fight against the Peshwá, Dámáji sent to his assistance some troops under the command of his son Govind Ráo. The Peshwá, however, succeeded in driving this force into the fort of Dhodap, and there compelled both Raghunáth Ráo and Govind Ráo to surrender unconditionally, whereupon they were taken as prisoners to Puná.

On this occasion, the Gáekwád was required to pay a fine of rupees twenty-three lacs and twenty-five thousand, besides another sum of rupees fifteen lacs and sixty-five thousand as

---

* Báláji Peshwá died soon after the disastrous battle of Pánipat.

arrears of tribute. The six parganás, recently taken from the Gáekwád, were to be restored to him, but the annual tribute was increased from rupees five lacs and twenty-five thousand to seven lacs and seventy-nine thousand. However, before this settlement was finally effected, Dámáji Gáekwád met with a fatal accident in some experiments which an alchemist had persuaded him to make with a view to the discovery of the philosopher's stone. Thus strangely closed the eventful career of this illustrious soldier, A. D. 1768.

Chapter II.

Govind Ráo succeeds Dámáji, but is ousted in favour of Sayáji. Fateh Singh is appointed the latter's deputy. Broach taken by the English. Raghunáth Ráo Peshwá's and Fateh Singh Gáekwád's treaties with the British. Disputes between the Peshwá and the British.

From 1769 to 1775 A. D.

Dámáji Gáekwád left four sons, Sayáji the eldest by his second wife, Govind Ráo by the first wife, and Mánáji and Fateh Singh by the third. At the time of his father's death Govind Ráo was a state prisoner in Puná. He easily secured the consent of the Peshwá to his succession by at once acceding to his demands mentioned in the preceding chapter, and by presenting in addition a Nazar (present) of twenty one lacs of rupees.

Govind Ráo's brother Sayáji was weak-minded, but his younger brother Fateh Singh, who was in Baroda at the time of his father's death, took possession of the throne on behalf of Sayáji, and in A. D. 1771 repaired to Puná, where he forcibly urged the claims of Sayáji. The Shástri of the Court having pronounced in his favour, the Peshwá cancelled Govind Ráo's nomination, and appointed Sayáji as his father's successor with Fateh Singh as his deputy. This ambitious prince further obtained from the Peshwá permission to withdraw his contingent from Puná, and to pay in lieu of it six lacs and seventy-five thousand rupees a year. Fateh Singh then offered to conclude an offensive and defensive treaty with the English, but the authorities at Bombay could not accede to his wishes in the absence of orders from the Court of Directors.

Ever since A. D. 1759, when the English acquired the command of Surat Castle, they had gained a complete ascendency over the Nawábs, who became thenceforward rulers in name only. The actual government of the city soon passed into the hands of the English, who controlled the succession of the next three Nawábs. The amount due from Broach to the Surat Nawáb on account of the latter's right to the custom revenues and on account of certain claims of the English for refund of excessive levy of custom duties, estimated in all at one lac and fifty thousand rupees, not having been paid in spite of repeated warnings, the English in A. D. 1771 sent a force against Broach. This army sustained a repulse, but the next year another expedition was despatched under the brave General Wedderburn* who was killed while reconnoitring. The town, however, was stormed and taken on the 18th of November 1772, the Nawáb fleeing for protection to the Koli Thakor of Dewán, where he shortly afterwards died. Fatehsingh tried hard to persuade the English to assign him Broach in consideration of an annual payment of six lacs of rupees and an annual abatement of sixty thousand from the Gáekwád's share in the customs revenue of Surat. Owing to its convenient situation on a navigable river he had a great desire to make it his capital, but the Company did not accede to the terms proposed. Fatehsingh then claimed a share in the management, but could not establish his right, and the British Government therefore entered into an agreement with him allowing him a three-fifth share of the revenues of the city, which the Gáekwád had enjoyed from the late Nawáb.

Mention has been already made of Fatehsingh's success in getting his brother Govind Ráo's succession to the Gáekwád's Gádi cancelled. This, however, caused great enmity between the two brothers, and Govind Ráo determined not to resign his

* Brigadier-General Wedderburn's tomb, situated on high ground close to the ramparts and near the present Civil Hospital, still exists. It bears an inscription commemorating the General's services and shows he was only thirty-two years of age when he fell.

authority without a struggle. In the meantime events favourable to his cause occurred. In November 1778, Mádhav Ráo Peshwá died of consumption at the early age of twenty-eight years. His son and successor Náráyan Ráo, was murdered, it is said, at his uncle Raghunáth Ráo's instigation. As he left no child, Raghunáth Ráo, whom Govind Ráo Gáekwád had assisted in his father's life-time, succeeded as Peshwá, and acknowledged the claim of Govind Ráo. In April 1779, however, a posthumous child was born to the late Náráyan Ráo's widow, and the majority of the ministers supported his cause. Raghunáth Ráo had therefore to flee from Puná, and arrived on the 3rd of January 1775 with a small army at Baroda. The two Gáekwád brothers Fatehsingh and Govind Ráo were now in conflict, and the latter had besieged Baroda in conjunction with his uncle Khande Ráo Gáekwád the Jágirdár of Kadi. Sindhiá and the ministers at Puná having espoused Fatehsingh's cause, Raghunáth Ráo applied to the English for help, and on the 6th of March 1775 a treaty was concluded at Surat, by which the Bombay Government agreed to assist him on condition of his granting them Bassein and Salsette. These two places the English had long desired to obtain in order to complete their possession of Bombay. Raghunáth Ráo further agreed to cede Jambusar, Olpád and the districts round Surat, and promised to induce Govind Ráo Gáekwád to relinquish his share in the revenues of Surat and Broach. The Bombay Government engaged on their part to assist him with a force of two thousand five hundred men, for whose payment a sum of one hundred and fifty thousand rupees monthly was promised. The districts of Amod, Hánsot, Balsár and a part of Aukleswar were temporarily made over as security for the payment, and jewels*

* These were duly returned to Raghunath Ráo's son Báji Ráo on his installation in A. D. 1803.

worth six lacs of rupees were also deposited with the Company.

Before the conclusion of this treaty, a detachment under Colonel Keatinge sailed from Bombay at the end of February 1775, but before its departure, the Peshwá's army, accompanied by some troops belonging to Holkar and Sindhiá numbering in all some thirty thousand men, had entered Gujarát and compelled Raghunáth Ráo and Govind Ráo to raise the siege of Baroda, and retreat beyond the Mahi. The combined armies of the Peshwá and the Gáekwád, having followed them thither, attacked and completely routed them on the plains of Adás on the 17th of February 1775. Raghunáth Ráo fled with about one thousand horse to Cambay, but the Nawáb being afraid to give him shelter, he applied to the Company's Agent Mr. Charles Malet, who, although not officially aware of the treaty between Raghunáth Ráo and the Bombay Government, assisted in conveying him to Bhávnagar. Thence he embarked for Surat, where Colonel Keatinge's detachment arrived four days later on 27th of February 1775. Govind Ráo and Khande Ráo Gáekwáds, with the defeated army, retreated to Kapadvanj, and thence to Pálanpur. In the meantime Fatehsingh reduced Khande Ráo's, possessions in and about Nadiád to complete subjection.

Colonel Keatinge with his troops now embarked for Cambay taking with him his ally Raghunáth Ráo, and landed in that town on the 17th of March. Here he received reinforcements from Madrás, after which the entire body of about two thousand five hundred men formed a junction at the village of Dharmaj with the remainder of Raghunáth Ráo's army numbering twenty thousand. The combined forces arrived at Mátar near Kaira on the 3rd of May after two skirmishes with the enemy, one on 28th of April and the other at the village of Asámli three days later. Orders were now received from Bombay to induce Raghunáth Ráo to turn towards Bombay and Puna as the rains were approaching. Hence they went to Nadiád, a town belonging to Khande Ráo Gáekwád, who had deserted Raghunáth Ráo's cause after his defeat at Adás. In order to punish his defection Raghunáth Ráo levied a contribution of sixty thousand rupees from this unfortunate town. To realize this amount houses were stripped of every thing, and their owners of their very clothes. Some also were tortured on the suspicion that they had concealed valuables. The Bháts and Bráhmans had hitherto enjoyed immunity from such exactions, but Raghunáth Ráo, though himself a high caste Bráhman, sought to subject them also to a contribution. Accordingly they determined in this extremity to resort to Trágá, the usual expedient employed by the former class to secure immunity from oppresive burdens. An interesting account of this horrible practice of self-immolation has been given by Mr. James Forbes in his "Oriental Memoirs". From this account it appears that one of the Bháts, more cool and deliberate than the rest, even took his two younger brothers and sister,each under eighteen yearsof age, to Raghunáth Ráo's Darbár premises, and there stabbed them to the heart with the object of bringing Divine displeasure on the tyrant whose conduct had compelled him to resort to such a deed. A particular sect of Bráhmans, with the same object, purchased two old Bráhman matrons from their heartless daugters, each for forty rupees*, and killed them in the centre of the market. All this, however, produced no effect on the relentless "protector of cows and Bráhmans", as the Peshwás were then wont to be called.

The army now marched towards Nápád, and on the 18th of May, after leaving that town, an engagement took place with the enemy near Adás,which resulted in a victory for Colonel Keatinge,

* This sum was not taken as a selling-price, but only to defray the expense that would be incurred in the performance of funeral rites.

though with the loss of many of his officers and men. After his arrival on the 29th of May at Broach, where the sick and wounded were left, Colonel Keatinge tried to surprise the Marathá army which was encamped at the Bábá Piárá pass on the other bank of the Narbadá. The Maráthás, however, on learning of this stratagem, threw their guns and heavy baggage into the river, and fleeing in great confusion, abandoned Gujarát, 10th June 1775.

At the express request of Raghunáth Ráo the orders for the march back to Bombay on account of the rains were countermanded, and the troops under Colonel Keatinge moved to Dabhoi, a town nineteen miles to the south-east of Baroda, while Raghunáth Ráo's troops formed a camp for the monsoon months in the neighbourhood of Bhilupur.

CHAPTER III.

Defeat of the Maráthá fleet by Commodore Moor. Treaty between Fatehsingh, Raghunáth Ráo and the British. Defeat of the English at Talegáon near Puná. Capture of Dabhoi by the English Offensive and defensive treaty between Fatehsingh and the British Government Capture of Ahmadábád on behalf of the Gáekwád by General Goddard. Birth of Sehjánand Swámi; his beneficial influence as a religious teacher.

FROM 1775 to 1780 A. D.

Simultaneously with the campaign against the ministerial party in Gujarát, their fleet was also engaged on the sea by Commodore John Moor, and their largest ship, the "Shamsher Jang" was blown up in action.

Colonel Keatinge proposed to the Bombay Government to be allowed to reduce Baroda as soon as the monsoon was over, and preparations were made to supply him with additional troops and ammunition.

Fatehsingh Gáekwád, with whom communications had in the meantime been opened by Colonel Keatinge, now earnestly desired to conclude a treaty, and Colonel Keatinge, being of opinion that it would be more advantageous to all concerned to accede to his terms, persuaded Raghunáth Ráo to agree. At length a treaty was drawn up on the 8th of July 1775, in which Fatehsingh Gáekwád bound himself to pay Raghunáth Ráo an annual tribute of eight lacs of rupees and to serve him with three thousand horse. The Gáekwád conferred on the East India Company his share of the revenues of Broach, and granted them in perpetuity the revenues of Chikhli, Variáv and Koral, of the estimated value of three lacs of rupees, while Khande Ráo Gáekwád's possessions were continued to him. The sum of three lacs of rupees annually paid to Govind Ráo since the time of his father Dámáji, was discontinued, but in lieu of it Raghunáth Ráo undertook to grant him as soon as possible a Jágir in the Deccan worth ten lacs of rupees. In addition to these terms Fatehsingh bound himself to pay Raghunáth Ráo the sum of twenty-six lacs of rupees, of which ten lacs were advanced before the 30th of August under pressure from Colonel Keatinge. It is not certain whether the remainder was ever paid.

Thus through the intervention of the East India Company matters were amicably settled between Raghunáth Ráo and Fatehsingh, though not without loss of life on both sides, especially at Adás, where in a narrow passage the English were at one time hemmed in. Their services were, however, well appreciated, and in addition to what was assigned them by Fatehsingh, Raghunáth Ráo presented them with the Parganás of Hansot and Amod of the then estimated value of two lacs and seventy-seven thousand rupees. The total revenue of the territory acquired by the English in this war has been reckoned at twenty-four lacs and fifteen thousand rupees.

The proceedings of the Bombay Government were, however, disapproved of by the Governor-General's Council at Calcutta, and after much discussion a second treaty was concluded at Purandhar in A. D. 1776 through Colonel Upton the representative of the Calcutta Government, by which the one entered into with Raghunáth Ráo, whom the Supreme Government held to be implicated in the murder of his nephew Náráyan Ráo Peshwá, was annulled. By this new treaty all claims on the part of the Peshwá to the revenue of Broach and its neighbourhood, amounting to about three lacs of rupees, were abandoned in favour of the English, who were also to be reimbursed in the sum of rupees twelve lacs for the expenses of the war. It was stipulated that the 'territories ceded by Fatehsingh should be restored to him, if it could be proved that he had no authority to alienate them. The army of Raghunáth Ráo was to be disbanded within a month, and that Chief was to reside at Kopergáon on the Godávari river as a pensioner on a personal monthly allowance of twenty-five thousand rupees from the Peshwá's Government, while in addition an establishment of one hundred horse and two hundred domestics was to be allowed him.

The Bombay Government were bitterly disappointed on hearing of this treaty, and they attributed the condemnation of their proceedings to a jealous assumption of authority on the part of the Calcutta Government. Raghunáth Ráo also expressed a determination to carry on the war himself rather than submit to such humiliating conditions. He sent renewed overtures to the Calcutta Government, offering greater concessions than he had agreed to at Surat, promising even a tenth part of the revenue derived from the whole of the Maráthá territory, but the Calcutta Council would not accept his terms. Raghunáth Ráo then appealed to the Court of Directors, and even sent a Bráhman named Hanumant Ráo and a Pársi named Maniár as agents to England, and fixed his own residence at Surat, keeping his army meanwhile in the neighbourhood. However, before receipt of this appeal or even of the intelligence of the conclusion of the new treaty, the Court of Directors had sent a despatch, received in Bombay in August 1776, approving of the Surat treaty. This greatly encouraged the Bombay Council, although it recognised that eventually the Supreme Government would be supported in an affair of such gravity.

While matters were in this unsatisfactory state, war broke out between England and France. The Peshwá, ever jealous of the rise of the English, eagerly grasped the opportunity of entering into an alliance with the French, and the latter agreed through an adventurer, named St. Lubin, to supply the

Peshwá with a body of two thousand and five hundred Europeans, and to raise and discipline ten thousand native infantry. Warren Hastings, the Governor General, in whose hands fortunately the destinies of India were then placed, saw the danger to be apprehended from this combination, and, with his wonted promptitude, determined to anticipate the French. He accordingly prepared to send an army to Bombay to aid the cause of Raghunáth Ráo, who was to be appointed Regent for the then infant Peshwá.

This force crossed the Jamná in May 1778, but its subsequent progress was much impeded by the Chiefs of the intervening territories except Bhopál. Before its arrival the Bombay Government had sent two thousand five hundred men under Colonel Egerton to commence hostilities against the Peshwá. Unhappily this expedition ended in failure, as on the 13th of January 1779, the little force was completely hemmed in at Wargaun by the Marathá army of fifty thousand men under Mahádáji Sindhiá, to whom they made an unconditional surrender, and agreed to restore to the Peshwá all his territories taken since 1773.

In the meantime, the army from Bengal had arrived at Surat on the 26th of February 1779 under the command of Colonel Goddard. That officer had orders from the Governor General to enter into a treaty with Náná Fadnávis on the basis of the Purandhar treaty, and further to stipulate that the French should be forbidden the Maráthá dominions. Náná Fadnavis, with a view to gain time, delayed his reply till October. He then demanded the surrender of Raghunáth Ráo and the relinquishment of Salsette. With these demands the English could not, consistently with their honour, comply. At the same time rumours were afloat that the Nizám and Haidar Ali of Mysore, were conspiring with the French to attack the

English at all their settlements. Accordingly the English General determined to renew the war by assailing the Peshwá's possessions in Gujarát, and with this object an alliance with Fatehsingh Gáekwád was concluded. On the 1st of January 1780 the General moved his army from Surat, while a detachment under Mr. Boddam, a member of Council, took the Peshwá's districts in the neighbourhood of that city. The battery from Broach having joined him, General Goddard appeared before Dabhoi on the 18th of January 1780. The garrison opened fire, but secretly abandoned the fort during the night of the 19th, and Mr. James Forbes, subsequently well known as the author of the Oriental Memoirs, was left in charge. On the 26th of the same month, Fatehsingh met the General, and signed the offensive and defensive treaty proposed to him. It stipulated that the Peshwá's districts north of the Mahi should be given to the Gáekwád, and that in consideration for this the latter should cede to the English his share of the city of Broach, the Surat Athávisi south of the Tápti, as also Sinor and his villages in the Broach district. The Gáekwád further agreed to assist the General with a body of three thousand horse. General Goddard now marched on Ahmadábád, and arrived before it on the 10th of February 1780. The place was found to be strongly garrisoned by about six thousand Arabs and two thousand cavalry. The Peshwa's Subá, who was in charge of the city, was summoned to surrender, but on his sending an evasive reply, and on the following day firing upon some of the men of General Goddard's force, the latter opened a battery, and succeeded in effecting a breach at the south-west corner of the strong wall near the Khán Jahán gate. No offer of submission having been tendered, a storming party was formed under the command of Colonel Hartley, who advanced to the breach on the morning of the 13th. The garrison offered a stubborn resistance, and did not yield until three hundred of their number had fallen.

The General now entered, and found that the Subá and his party had fled by the Khánpur gate. The inhabitants were apprehensive that the city would be given up to plunder, and, according to one account, a deputation headed by Nathu Shá Nagar Sheth, Muhámmad Sále Kázi and Mirzá Amu the Bádsháhi Diwán, waited on the General, who issued a proclamation to the people, desiring them to remain at peace and follow their usual occupations. The proclamation is dated 5th Safar A. H. 1194 (13th of February 1780). The English loss in killed and wounded in the storming of the city is reported to have been one hundred and six*.

After leaving a detachment of British troops to garrison the place, the city was made over to Fatehsingh Gáekwád according to agreement, and the latter assigned to the British his share in the districts south of the Tápti.

The year 1780 is noteworthy for the birth of the religious reformer Sahajánand Swámi, whose followers in Gujarát now number fully two hundred thousand. By his influence as a religious teacher the Swámi was helpful in reducing to order the Káthis and other turbulent tribes. A translation of his Shikshá Patri (the Epistle Instructions) by the late Ráo Sáheb Bhogilál Pránvalabhdás, (the first and one of the most popular Head Masters of the Government English School, afterwards Superintendent of Schools in Káthiáwár, and eventually Director of Vernacular Instruction at Baroda), will be found as Appendix E to Mr. Briggs' Cities of Gujaráshtra.

---

* That part of the city wall where the assault took place, is still pitted with shot.

There is a tomb in the Protestant Cemetery near the Khán Jahán gate, the inscription on which runs thus:—

"Erected by order of General Goddard to the memory of Captain Thomas Gough, who died of the wounds received in the assault of Ahmadábád on the 13th of February 1780."

Chapter IV.

Arrival of Sindhiá and Holkar before Baroda. Their retreat and overtures. Sindhiá's defeats in Gujarát. Forts of Párnerá and Bagwádá taken by the British. Events in the Deccan and other parts. Treaty of Sálbai. Salsette given to the English and Broach to Sindhiá. Fatehsingh's death. Affairs at Cambay.

From 1780 to 1789 A. D.

Soon after the taking of Ahmadábád by General Goddard, information was received of the approach of Mahádáji Sindhiá and Tukáji Holkar, who, with fifteen thousand horse, crossed the Narbadá on the 20th of February 1780 and proceeded towards Baroda, in the vicinity of which they halted. However, on General Goddard's marching against that town, they moved in the direction of Pávághad, then in the possession of Sindhiá. The latter released two European officers, Mr. Farmer and Lieutenant Stewart who had been given to him as hostages at the time of the disastrous defeat of the English at Wárgáon. He also sent Vakils professing friendship for the British Government, and attempted to induce the General to become a party to a treaty requiring Raghunáth Ráo's retirement to Jhánsi as a pensioner. General Goddard rejected these negotiations, and Sindhiá then tried to form an alliance with Govind Ráo Gáekwád. Thereupon, the General determined to engage him in action, and on the 3rd of April, and again on the 19th, surprised and routed Sindhiá's army. On the 8th of May a portion of the English troops left for the Konkan, their services being urgently required there, but General Goddard with the remainder of his army stayed on in Gujarát, being unwilling that his ally Fatehsingh should be placed at the mercy of the enemy. Under urgent orders from the Bombay Government, a second detachment was sent to engage a Maráthá officer named Ganeshpanth, who, quitting the Konkan, had plundered the

Athávisi, and was advancing to the very walls of the city. Lieutenant Welsh, the officer commanding this detachment, fell upon Ganeshpanth's camp on the morning of the 23rd of April, and captured his baggage and guns. Ganesh himself was mortally wounded, and his men took to flight. Lieutenant Welsh next wrested from the Peshwa's officers the forts of Párnerá, Bagwádá and Indarghad, and eventually tranquillity was restored in the newly acquired districts. Sindhiá's forces near Sinor on the Narbadá were also attacked and routed by another party under Major Forbes. General Goddard then posted his troops for the rainy season at convenient stations in Broach and its neighbourhood.

In this year there were wars in the Konkan and the Deccan also, but these do not enter into the history of Gujarát. It suffices to say that the British army won several successes, and a detachment from Bengal took the forts of Gwálior and Lahári. General Goddard, having received orders to attack Bassein, moved out from Surat on the 10th of October 1780, after leaving a sufficient force with Fatehsingh Gáekwád for the protection of Gujarát. The Bassein fort built by the Portuguese was very strong. It was, however, besieged, and the artillery succeeded in effecting a breach. Náná Fadnávis sent large reinforcements to aid the garrison, but the troops, judiciously posted at a convenient point under Colonel Hartley, the officer who had commanded at the storming of Ahmadábád, prevented their junction. The Maráthás then attempted to destroy Colonel Hartley's force, and marched in a body to attack him. A brilliant action took place on the 12th of December, in which the Maráthá General Rámchandra Ganesh fell bravely fighting, and a Portuguese officer named Signor Noronha in the Peshwá's army was wounded, after which the Maráthás were completely routed.

Bassein had surrendered to the British the previous day (11th December 1780), and immediately afterwards General

Goddard marched to assist Colonel Hartley. The whole British force was thus united. Affairs in the Deccan, however, took at this time a serious turn, all the Maráthás, except the Gáekwád Fatehsingh to whom the English had rendered such great assistance, having allied themselves with the Nizám of Hydarábád and Haidar Ali* of Mysore against the English. On Haidar's gaining some successes, the Government of India strove to alienate the Maráthás from the confederacy, and the Governor General accordingly opened negotiations through Sindhiá with the Peshwá, but the latter, who was waiting to see what turn events might take, declined to listen to any overtures unless Haidar Ally became a party to it.

Under these circumstances General Goddard considered that an advance movement so as to threaten Puná was more likely to facilitate negotiations with the Peshwá than operations round about Bassein and in the Konkan, the forts in which were well nigh impregnable. He accordingly made a rash demonstration of moving on Puná, but was met by a large army under Haripanth Fadke, Holkar and other chiefs, and had to retire with heavy loss to Pánwel, which he reached on the 23rd of April 1781.

The British arms, however, obtained several successes over Haidar, and this induced Sindhiá in October 1781 to make overtures for peace. A treaty of several articles was at length concluded at Sálbai near Gwálior on the 17th of May 1782 between Mr. David Anderson, whom the Governor General Warren Hastings had deputed to Sindhiá's camp, and Mahádáji Sindhiá, who acted on behalf of the Peshwá Náná Fadnavis and other

* Haidar Ali, a soldier of fortune, had usurped Mysore from its Hindu Rájá, in whose service he was, about the middle of the 18th century A. C. His successor was the atrocious Tipu Sultán, who fell on the 4th of May 1799, when the English took by storm the town and fort of Seringapatam.

Maráthá chiefs. By that treaty the English, though retaining Salsette, Elephantá, Karanjá, Hog Island and Broach, gave up Bassein and other territory acquired since the treaty of Purandhar. Raghunáth Ráo was to be granted by the Peshwá a pension of twenty-five thousand rupees per mensem, and was to reside with Sindhiá. The possessions of Fatehsingh were to remain the same as before the war, and no claim was to be made on him by the Peshwá on account of arrears of tribute during the period of the late hostilities. Haidar Ali was to surrender his conquests from the English and their allies, and no factory of any European nation was to be allowed in the Maráthá dominions,save only those already estabiished by the Portuguese in the Maráthá territories. Thus it was that the Peshwá regained along with other advantages his share in the revenue of Gujarat. To Sindhiá the English assigned the district of Broach in consequence of his humane conduct towards the army that had surrendered at Wargáon in 1779 and his kind treatment of hostages then left with him. This treaty was ratified at Calcutta on the 6th of June 1782,and, after Haidar Ali'sdeath,by Náná Fadnavis on behalf of the Peshwá on the 20th of December following. Raghunáth Ráo died shortly after the conclusion of the treaty*. Thus ended what is known as the first Maráthá war.

Fatehsingh Gáekwád thereafter ruled in peace till his death by a fall from the upper storey of his palace on the 21st of December 1789.

The city of Surat was visited in A. D. 1782 by a severe storm, which destroyed many of its houses and owing to this and other causes the trade of this once prosperous port suffered a serious decline. The city had hardly recovered from the

* Raghunath Ráo's eldest son Báji Ráo succeeded as Peshwá on the 4th of December 1796 on the death of Mádhow Ráo Náráen.

damage caused by the storm, when the famine of 1790 occurred, adding greatly to the distress of the country. The revenues during this period were shared by the Nawábs, the Maráthás and the English in the proportions that had been agreed upon.

Cambay was still under the vigorous, though somewhat oppressive, administration of Momin Khán. Raghunáth Ráo's flight to Cambay in 1772 has been already mentioned, but as Momin Khán was the ally of Fateh Singh he refused to give shelter to Raghunáth Ráo, who was at that time hostile to the Gáekwád. Accordingly when two years later Raghunáth Ráo returned to Cambay with an English force, he tried to induce the English General to strip the Nawáb of his territories. Sir Charles Malet, the Resident, succeeded, however, in effecting their reconciliation. Momin Khán also co-operated with the ruling Gáekwád to suppress the Káthi incursions into Gujarát, though not until he had learned that by secretly encouraging the Káthis he had been causing the ruin of his own subjects. After the capture of Ahmadábád in 1780, the Gáekwád remitted to Momin Khán the Peshwá's share, to which he became entitled by General Goddard's success at Ahmadábád, and Momin Khán on his part made over to the English the charge of the Custom House gate at Cambay. By the treaty of Sálbai, however, the Peshwá regained his share, and the charge of the Custom House gate was restored to the Nawáb in A. D. 1783.

Chapter V.

Accession of Mánáji Gáekwád. Acknowledgement of Govind Ráo's claim. Wars in the Deccan and against the Pindáris. Battle of Kadi with Malhár Ráo. Expulsion of the Peshwá's Subá Abá Shelukar from Ahmadábád. Surat taken by the British. The Peshwá's share of the revenues of Gujarát leased to the Gáekwád.

From 1789 to 1800 A. D.

On Fatehsingh's death his brother Govind Ráo, who had long been his rival, was the only rightful successor to the regency. However his younger brother Mánáji, who happened to be at that time in Baroda, immediately took charge of the Government and of the person of Sayáji. By offering to present to the Peshwá a Nazar (present) of thirty lacs, thirteen thousand rupees, and by promising to pay the large amount of arrears of the annual tribute, some thirty-four lacs, he succeeded in obtaining the Peshwá's confirmation of his investiture. The unfortunate Govind Ráo's claims, though strongly represented, were not then favoured. Mahádáji Sindhiá, however, who then exercised great influence over the Peshwá, interfered and procured the reversal of Mánáji's confirmation. Mánáji then appealed to the Bombay Government, who recommended a compromise in the interests both of the country and of the rival claimants. The dispute was, however, set at rest by the death of Mánáji in A. D. 1793. None the less Náná Fadnávis refused to allow Govind Ráo to leave Puná until he had sent a present of elephants, horses and jewels, worth about a lac of rupees. Náná further insisted on Govind Ráo agreeing to the stipulations entered into by the deceased Mánáji, and in addition ceding to the Peshwá the Gáekwád's share in the districts south of the Tápti together with his portion of the Surat Customs. The British Government, however, objected to the dismemberment of the

Gáekwád's territory as being contrary to the treaty of Sálbai, and thus managed to save that state, whose friend and protector they had been since their first connexion with Fatehsingh, from ruinous loss and destruction. Govind Ráo accordingly left Puná to assume the regency on the 19th of December 1793.

The period subsequent to the treaty of Sálbai was one of constant wars which the English found themselves compelled to undertake against Sindhiá, Holkar, Haidar and his son Tipu. It was marked by reverses as well as successes, in which the English displayed great courage and finally effected the overthrow of their enemies. The Pindáris, who, by their plundering excursions and regularly organised raids in which they are said to have been assisted by Sindhiá and Holkar, had long proved a scourge to the whole of India, were also suppressed. The details of these wars, however, can scarcely be entitled to record in a history of Gujarát, and accordingly we pass them by.

Govind Ráo, after all the pecuniary sacrifices he had made in favour of the Peshwá, was still unable to take undisputed possession of Barodá.* His own illegitimate son Kanhoji having obtained aid from Dharampur and Broach, the latter then under Sindhiá, had entered Baroda, and sought to secure it for himself. He was, however, treacherously surrendered by his own men, and subsequently he fled to Sankhedá and Bahádurpur. On these places being ravaged, he was joined by Malhár Ráo, son of Khande Ráo Gáekwád who has frequently been mentioned in

* An interesting prophecy of a Bráhman, who is said to have foretold the difficulties Govind Ráo would have to contend with and his eventual success, is published in the Indian Antiquary for November 1887, Vol. XVI. pp. 317 to 320. All the prophecies having been realised, the Bráhman, Chinte Máhá Dev Gole was granted in Inám the village of Ayaná in the Nawsári Táluká of the estimated revenue of five thousand rupees.

the foregoing pages, and three battles, were fought near Malhár Ráo's Jagir town of Kadi, in which Govind Ráo's men were on each occasion repulsed. Harmony did not, however, long prevail between Malhár Ráo and Kanhoji. The latter eventually submitted to his father, by whom he was kept in confinement. Malhár Ráo then purchased peace in A. D. 1794 by paying a fine of five lacs and fifty thousand rupees. His annual Peshkash (tribute) was, however, reduced from one lac and twenty thousand to one lac and fifteen thousand rupees.

The Gáekwád next attempted to regain from the Nawáb of Cambay the six villages that had been granted to the latter on condition of his keeping the Káthis in check, which service was being performed in a very unsatisfactory manner. The villages were indeed re-annexed to Baroda in A. D. 1792, but were later restored again to Cambay.

Another event of importance was the Gáekwad's expedition against Abá Shelukar, the deputy-governor of the Peshwá's share of Gujarát. This officer ravaged the district of Gondal in Samvat 1850, A.D. 1794 at the instigation of Mehráman Khawás of Nawánagar. Shelukar was very rapacious, and imposed new and heavy taxes, from which even the poorest classes were not exempted. Unable to witness the distress caused by this burden of taxation, Lálá Harakhchand, a rich and patriotic banker of Ahmadábád, himself paid a hundred thousand rupees with the object of relieving the people from the additional imposition. Shelukar also built a spacious building* in the Bhadar mostly by forced labour.

---

* This edifice known as the Adálat, was for many years used as the residence of the District Judge, his court-house and those of his Assistant and Sub-judges with record-room and other offices. It was pulled down in 1862, the terrace over the magnificent court-hall having been pronounced unsafe.

Many are the stories still current regarding his oppression, which is kept in memory by songs sung by women during the Navrátri holidays. It seems that he even plundered a band of wealthy Gosains passing through the Baroda territory, and ventured to attack the Gáekwád's Haveli* at Ahmadábád. Accordingly Govind Ráo Gáekwád reported matters to the Peshwá and prepared for war. Shelukar belonged to Náná Fadnavis's party, and the Peshwá was therefore not well disposed towards him. Accordingly he gave orders to the Gáekwád to expel him by force, and further expressed his willingness to farm out his share to the Gáekwád. Bábáji, the Commander of the Gáekwádi troops, at once marched rapidly on Ahmadábád, and gained two victories over Shelukar's army before Batwá. The capital was then besieged and taken; Shelukar was made prisoner and sent to Barodá, A. D. 1798–99, whence he was removed to Borsad, and, confined in the fort for several years. His ultimate release was an act of grace on the part of the British Government. Besides being tyrannical Shelukar was notoriously profligate. It is said that when he entered Ahmadábád to take charge of his government, there were in his procession courtesans dancing on platforms borne on the heads of porters. When news of the enemy having entered the city was brought him while a Nautch-dance was proceeding, he merely exclaimed "Never mind, let them come", and repeated these words even when informed of the arrival of the enemy at the Three Gates facing the Bhadar citadel. Regarding his folly a popular refrain runs :—

"હાથમાં દંડો, બગલમાં મોઈ;
હવેલી લેતાં, ગુજરાત ખોઈ.

"Háthmán dando, bagalman moi;
Haveli letán Gujarát khoi".

---

* This Maráthá citadel is situated in the southern part of the city, and was, until lately, used as an arsenal by the British Government.

With stick in his hand for the game of tip-cat,
In taking the Haveli he lost Gujarát.

After Shelukar's expulsion from Ahmadábád, the Peshwá, according to promise, leased his share of the revenues of Gujarát to the Gáekwád for a term of five years at five lacs of rupees per annum. Though pecuniarily not very profitable in the state of the revenue at that time, this agreement, which was finally agreed to in October 1800, was of great advantage to the Gáekwád as it at once put an end to interference on the part of the Peshwá and to the confusion hitherto consequent on double government.

While matters were thus progressing in Ahmadábád, Nizám-ud-din, the Nawáb of Surat, died in the month of January 1799. The reader will recollect that the English had taken the command of the Surat Castle from the Habshis in A. D. 1759. Ever since that year the Nawábs had been appointed by the English instead of by the Delhi Emperor, from whose Court even the Agent for the Nawáb had been recalled in A. D. 1764. The three Nawábs between 1759 and 1799 were,

1.	Miá Achhan	1759 to 1763	A. D.
2.	Háfiz-ud-din	1763 to 1790	„
3.	Nizám-ud-din	1790 to 1799	„

During the rule of these Nawábs the usual anarchy prevailed, and the revenues greatly sufferred owing to the decay of the spice trade with Java and the loss of the trade with the Persian Gulf. The city had also suffered severely by the cyclone of 1782 and the famine already mentioned. The authority of the Nawáb became so inconsiderable that he was quite unable in 1795 to check a serious faction-fight, which broke out in the city between the Hindus and the Muhammadans and continued for several days. The districts too had become so unsafe that in 1788 a European traveller, Hove, required a guard of no less than sixteen horsemen to proceed from Surat to Broach. On his way back he found the police-station at Khim held by a marauder chief whose depredations the authorities were powerless to prevent.

A disturbance possessing somewhat of a humourous element took place in the city in A. D. 1799. The Nawáb having imposed a tax on grain and tobacco, the price of these daily necessaries had greatly risen. Accordingly some four or five hundred Musalmáni women of the poorer classes went in a body to the residence of the English chief, on whose devoted head they poured forth execrations and curses. When given to understand that the chief had nothing to do with the imposition of the tax, they assailed the Nawáb's Bakhshi (Paymaster), who happened at the time to be passing in his palanquin, and detained him for some two hours by the voluble expression of their grievances. On the Bakhshi representing their case to the Nawáb, the latter sent them out twenty rupees, which they stoutly refused to accept. On the following day they again in a body assailed the Bakhshi with their clamours for relief. This story affords sufficient evidence of a disaffection, wide spread and deeply felt.

With a view to terminate the existing misrule and confusion, the English took the opportunity, presented by the death of Nawáb Nizám-ud-din and his infant son, to assume the sole government of the city of Surat, and instructions to that effect were sent by the Governor General to Mr. Jonathan Duncan, the Governor of Bombay. That eminent officer forthwith proceeded to Surat, and opened negotiations with the Nawáb's brother Násir-ud-din. The latter, after several interviews, was persuaded to agree to resign to the Honourable East India Company the entire Government of Surat on condition of his being allowed to retain the title of Nawáb, and assigned an annual pension of one lac of rupees in addition to one-fifth* of the surplus net revenue of the city.

The English were accordingly put in possession of the towns of Surat and Rânder with their dependencies, and greatly to the satisfaction of thei inhabitants, a proclamation announcing the assumption of the sole government was issued by Mr. Duncan on the 15th May, 1800. The arrears of pay to the troops, amounting to one hundred and nineteen thousand, nine hundred and seventy-seven rupees, were at once met by the Honourable East India Company, who also guaranteed the payment of the Nawâb's private debts, amounting to sixty-seven thousand, six hundred and seventy rupees, out of the pension due during the first twelve months.

* The fluctuating one-fifth allowance was commuted in A. D. 1818 into a fixed annual payment of fifty thousand rupees. In 1842 the Nawâb Mir Afz-ud-din, son and successor of Nâsir-ud-din, died without male issue, and the office of Nawâb thereby became extinct, but a pension of rupees forty-four hundred a month was settled on his son-in-law Jafar Ali Khân and two granddaughters. In this year the fleet was also re-called to Bombay, and the flag of Delhi was removed from the Castle tower. In 1857 the annual allowance was raised to one lac of rupees, with the stipulation that it should be enjoyed till the death of the last survivor of the three grantees.

Chapter VI.

The death of Govind Ráo. Anand Rao's succession. Disputes between Kanhoji and the Minister Rávji. Both apply to the British for assistance. The Minister's application complied with. Malhár Ráo joins Kanhoji. Battle of Kadi and surrender of Malhár Ráo. Appointment of Major Walker as Resident at Baroda. Attack on and surrender of Sankhedá and Bahádarpur. Revolt of Arabs and their expulsion. Cession of territory to the British.

From 1800 to 1802 A. D.

Govind Ráo Gáekwád died in September 1800, a month before the conclusion of the agreement for the farming out of the revenues of Ahmadábád. Of his eleven sons the eldest, Anand Ráo, was acknowledged by the principal officers as successor. He was, however, a weak prince, and his half-brother Kanhoji, whom his father had placed in confinement, not only effected his release, but, by gaining his brother's confidence, usurped the post of minister, and with it gained the entire control of the Government. However, in A. D. 1801 he was deposed by Rávji Apáji, a Parbhu minister of the late Govind Ráo, and both parties applied to the Bombay Government for help, offering the cession of considerable territory. The terms proposed by Rávji were accepted by the treaty of Baroda, dated 25th July 1802 and, pending instructions from the Government of India, the Governor of Bombay, Mr. Jonathan Duncan, sent a small force of sixteen hundred men under the command of Major Alexander Walker to oppose Kanhoji, whose cause was now espoused by Malhár Ráo Gáekwád, the Jágirdár of Kadi. Major Walker's detachment joined the Gáekwádi force under Rávji's brother Bábáji, and marched on Kadi, where Malhár Ráo, pretending to negotiate, made a treacherous attack on the 17th of March 1802. He was, however, repulsed after some loss on the part of the British. At this time it became evident that Malhár Ráo had seduced from their allegiance many of the Gáekwád's men, and Major Walker's position thus became very critical. Reinforcements, however, arrived from Bombay *via* Cambay under the command of Sir William Clarke, and] the entrenchments before Kadi were gallantly carried on the 30th of April, on which occasion the British lost in killed and wounded one hundred and sixty-three men. Malhár Ráo now surrendered, and Kadi was made over to the Gáekwád. Immediately afterwards Malhár Ráo was removed to Nadiád, from the revenues of which district the liberal annual allowance of one lac and twenty-five thousand rupees was assigned to him for his maintenance with the promise of an increase on the condition of his giving no further trouble.

Major Walker was at this time appointed Political Resident at the Gáekwád's Court, 11th July 1802, and the command of the detachment devolved on Colonel Woodington, Sir William Clarke having returned to Bombay after the taking of Kadi.

A detachment was now sent against Sankhedá, which was held by Ganpat Ráo, a relative of the Gáekwád. On the fort surrendering in the same month, Ganpat Ráo, and with him Morár Ráo, another illegitimate son of Govind Ráo, who had joined cause with Málhár Ráo, escaped to Dhár.

Major Walker then turned his attention towards the Gáekwád's finances. These were in so deplorable a state that it became necessary to consider the propriety of effecting a reduction in the mercenary force. The Arabs, who were all-powerful at Baroda, taking alarm, advanced exorbitant claims for arrears. They confined Anand Ráo himself, but allowed Kanhoji to escape. At this juncture Malhár Ráo fled to Bhuj* from Nadiád

* At Bhuj Malhár Ráo entered into a confederacy with certain chiefs of Káthiáwár, and, at the head of five thousand men and some troops from Junágadh, attaked Amreli without success. After two other equally unsuccessful attempts, he was taken prisoner by Bábáji in 1803, and sent to Bombay, where he ended his days in confinement.

on the 4th of December 1802, and serious disturbances were apprehended. Major Walker tried to bring the Arabs to terms without resorting to force, but, having failed in this, he again obtained help from Bombay. Colonel Woodington invested Baroda on the 18th. The siege continued for ten days, during which the Arabs, under cover of the walls and houses, caused considerable loss to the assailants, but at length, seeing that the walls would be breached and that further resistance would be unavailing, they surrendered, and agreed to quit the country so soon as such arrears as might be found justly due were paid. These amounted to seventeen lacs and fifty thousand rupees, which sum was duly handed over. A number of the Arabs, however, under Jamádár Abud forthwith joined Kanhoji, who had fled to Rájpiplá and was marching thence to Baroda.

Major Holmes (afterwards Major-General Sir George Holmes, K. C. B.) was sent in pursuit of Kanhoji on the 1st of January 1803. After a month of unsuccessful search, the English force, on the 6th of February, entered a ravine near the village of Sávali, where Kanhoji had secretly taken up a strong position. He at once opened fire on the British troops with deadly effect. The Arabs also charged sword in hand, and overpowered the advance guard. Major Holmes, however, dismounted from his horse, and placing himself at the head of the Grenadiers, charged with his whole force, and soon drove the enemy before him. On this occasion Major Holmes met in personal encounter an Arab of giant height, whom he laid dead at his feet with a single stroke of his sword. Later, Kanhoji made another stand at Kapadvanj, where, however, his force was utterly dispersed. He then fled to Ujjain.*

---

* In 1808 Kanhoji surrendered himself to the British Government. He was allowed his liberty, and granted a liberal pension, but shortly afterwards, being a party to a conspiracy against Baroda, he was removed to Madras as a State prisoner.

For the eminent services they had rendered, and for the maintenance of a force, three thousand strong, for the protection of the Gáekwád's territories, the Honourable East India Company received cession of the undermentioned territory and revenue by the subsidiary treaty of A. D. 1802, concluded on the 6th June, and confirmed by the Mahárájá on the 29th July of that year.

Jaydád, (for payment of Subsidy).			Revenue. Rupees.
Parganá of Dholká	...	...	4,50,000
" " Nadiád	...	...	1,75,000
" " Mátar	...	...	1,30,000
" " Mahundhá	...	...	1,10,000
" " Bijápur	...	...	1,30,000
Tapá of Kadi	...	...	25,000
Customs of Khim Kathodrá	...	...	50,000
Annual orders on Káthiáwár.	...	...	1,00,000
			11,70,000

Inám (present).			
Parganá of Chorási ...	...	90,000	
Chauth of Surat ...	...	50,000	
Parganá of Chikhli ...	...	76,000	
Killádári of Khedá* ...	...	42,000	
			2,58,000
		Total...	14,28,000

The revenues of the Petlád, Baroda, Koral, Sinor and Ahmadábád Parganás were pledged to the Honourable Company for repayment of the amount advanced to meet the arrears due to the Arab mercenaries.

* Khedá (Kaira) was made the headquarters of the district north of the Mahi in 1803, and soon became a place of much importance owing to a large body of troops (infantry, cavalry and artillery) being stationed there until 1830. The large English church and the ruins of barracks, officers' bungalows &c., indicate the former extent of the original cantonment.

Chapter VII.

The events at Puná. The Peshwá, defeated by Holkar, takes refuge at Bombay. Treaty of Bassein. General Wellesley's march on Puná. The Peshwá's restoration. Confederacy against the British. Victories at Assaye and other places. Treaties with Sindhiá and Bhonsle. Affairs at Baroda. Mulkgiri expeditions and their evils. Permanent settlements of tribute effected by the Resident, Colonel Walker; his humane efforts to prevent female infanticide.

From 1802 to 1807 A. D.

While the English were thus gaining power in Gujarát, the authority of the Peshwá, after the death on the 13th of March 1800 of his celebrated Minister Náná Fadnavis, one of the ablest and wisest statesmen of his time, declined more and more. Báji Ráo Peshwá had become entirely dependent on Sindhiá, between whom and Yashvant Ráo Holkar great jealousy existed. Vithobá, a brother of the latter, having been taken prisoner in a raid, was, notwithstanding the most abject entreaties, put to a cruel death, being trampled under the feet of an elephant, 1st April 1801. The Peshwá is said to have witnessed the execution from a balcony, and to have manifested delight at hearing the screams of the unhappy victim. To avenge his brother's death Yashvant Ráo Holkar marched on Puná, defeated the Peshwá's army on the 25th of October, and gained possession of the city. Báji Ráo fled, and eventually took refuge with the British in Bombay, where he was received by the Governor Mr. Jonathan Duncan on the 6th of December. A treaty was then concluded at Bassein on the 31st of the same month by which the Peshwá agreed to subsidize the British army for the protection of his territory, and to cede districts of the value of twenty-six lacs of rupees per annum. He further ratified the arrangement agreed on between the Gáekwád and the English, and relinquished his claims on the Chauth of Surat and the districts of Chorási and Chikhli. The Peshwá further agreed not to harbour any Europeans hostile to the English.

A large British force, collected from different places, marched on Puná with all possible speed under the command of the illustrious General Arthur Wellesley. Holkar in the meantime did all in his power to oppress the people of Puná during his short règime, and, though two influential Sardárs raised large sums from the inhabitants with the object of saving them from plunder, these very Sardárs, with other persons known to possess property, were subjected to the most cruel tortures. On hearing that a British army had approached to chastise him, he even threatened to burn down the city of Puná. To prevent this catastrophe the British General, who with heavy artillery had rapidly advanced through a country devastated by the enemy's troops, made a forced march of sixty miles in thirty-two hours. Holkar, however, well aware of the power of the British, did not then consider it prudent to measure his strength with them, and the General, on his arrival before Puná on the 20th of April 1802, found that Holkar had fled some hours previously, accompanied by Amrat Ráo who had been proclaimed as temporary Peshwá. Amrat Ráo had been adopted by the late Raghunáth Ráo before the birth of Báji Ráo, and he was therefore a ready tool in the hands of Holkar.

Báji Ráo was then escorted to his capital from Bassein by a body of troops, two thousand three hundred strong, of whom one thousand two hundred were European infantry, and was re-seated on his Masnad on the 13th of May 1802. The above events have been mentioned here as the treaty of Bassein proved to have considerable bearing on the affairs of Gujarát.

While omitting reference to much that transpired in other parts of India subsequent to the restoration of the Peshwá, it is necessary to mention that the treaty of Bassein involved the

English in a war with Sindhiá and Rághoji Bhonsle of Berár, both of whom naturally disliked the interference of the English, and, in secret league with the ungrateful Báji Ráo, united to defeat the purpose of the treaty. This led to a tedious and hazardous campaign in the territories of those chiefs, in the course of which, some brilliant battles were fought and victories gained by the British arms, particularly at Assaye, Delhi and Agrá. Eventually both Sindhiá and Bhonsle were compelled in December 1803 to enter into treaties, similar to those entered into by the Peshwá at Bassein, and promising not to enter into any alliance with the French or with other European powers. Both these chiefs were also required to cede a large portion of their territory between the Jamná and the Ganges, and also to the northward of the Rajput principalities of Jaypur, Jodhpur and Gohad. It was during this war that the English took Broach by storm on the 29th of August 1803. Páwágadh was also taken on the 17th of September, but was restored to Sindhiá on the conclusion of the treaty. Sindhiá also agreed to relinquish all his claims against the Gáekwád, the ally of the British. These events all took place within the memorable five months between August and December 1803.

At this period Sindhiá conceived the desire of effecting a footing in Gujarát on the plea that ever since Govind Ráo's time, the Gáekwád had owed him a large sum of money. Sindhiá's object was, however, frustrated through the interposition of the British Government, who induced Sindhiá's agent, Sheth Prabhudás of Broach, to pay the money on the Resident's guarantee, and thus Baroda was freed from the interference of an enemy. Fatehsingh, one of the sons of Govind Ráo, had been made over by his father to the temple of Khandobá near Puná. He was now seized by one of Holkar's officers, to whom a ransom of fifty thousand rupees had to be paid, after which Fatehsingh was brought to Barodá in August 1803 for political reasons. A conspiracy was then formed on the part of certain Patháns and Anand Ráo's favourite wife Takhtbai to seize the person of the Resident and of the Minister Sitárám, brother of the former Minister Rávji Apáji, but this conspiracy was opportunely discovered and thwarted.

These internal troubles being ended, the Resident Colonel Walker, to whom not only Baroda but the whole of Káthiáwár owes a deep debt of gratitude, set himself earnestly to do away with certain expeditions, called the Mulkgiri (circuit of the country), which were annually undertaken against that peninsula to realize tribute. These occasioned great expense to the Gáekwád and caused much injury to the country. The reader will recollect that the Muhammadan rulers, and after them the Maráthás, had secured the right to levy tribute from chiefs in Káthiáwár. The tribute, however, could not be collected without the presence of a large military force, and often fell in arrears. To the original demands were frequently added other charges such as Gám Verá (village tax), Nálband Verá (charge for horse-shoeing), and the Ghás Dáná (grass and grain charges). Every year there was a tendency on the part of the officer commanding the expedition to realize a larger sum than his predecessor had collected. If the chief refused to pay and prepared to fight, the Maráthá army systematically destroyed the crops, pillaged and burnt villages, and did an incalculable amount of injury. The chiefs also, whenever they found a favourable occasion, retaliated by attacking and plundering inoffensive villages belonging to either the Gáekwád or the Peshwá.

Colonel Walker determined to put an end to these disorders, and, embracing the opportunity afforded by applications* from

* The applications had commenced as early as 1804, and were fully considered before they were accepted. The whole of the correspondence with Government was duly published in Part I of Colonel Walker's able Reports of Proceedings in Káthiáwár, No. 39, new Series.

several of the minor chiefs to be taken under British protection, placed himself at the head of an English force and joined Bábáji's Mulkgiri expedition in August 1807. At the same time he invited the chiefs in Káthiáwár to send their agents to his camp at Gutu in Morvi. With these, after a thorough enquiry he made permanent settlements, fixing the amount of tribute to be paid by each through the British Government, who were to remit the same to the Gáekwád. Even this reasonable arrangement, which at once freed the country from annual devastation and plunder,was not accepted by some of the chiefs, though it was manifestly to their own advantage and to the benefit of their subjects. The more powerful chiefs had selfish motives in withholding their consent, as they conjectured that such a settlement would put an end to their opportunities of oppressing their less powerful neighbours. Even while the negotiations were pending, the Jám of Navánagar had the audacity to take from the Ráná of Porbandar the fort of Kandorná in November 1807 by bribing the officer in charge. On the Ráná's appeal Colonel Walker at once marched on Kandorná on the 5th December 1807, retook it by force of arms, and restored it to its rightful owner. It even became necessary to make a demonstration against Navánagar itself before the Jám was induced to give his assent. The turbulent town of Máliá had also to be subdued. In short this permanent settlement of the tribute has proved an unmixed blessing, bringing in its train peace and contentment to all parties concerned. The Mulkgiri expeditions, with their many and great evils, have become a thing of the past, and the Gáekwád now receives his tribute* practically undiminished by the cost of its collection. Similar arrangements were made later regarding the tribute which Junágadh had forced from some of the chiefs under the designation

* The Gáekwád's tribute amounts to about nine lacs of rupees in Káthiáwár and three lacs in the Mahi Kánthá.

of Zor-Talbi (forcible levy). Permanent settlements were also effected with the Mahi Kánthá and other chiefs, greatly to their relief and advantage.

Peace and quiet having been secured to the country by Colonel Walker's permanent settlement of the tribute payable by the several chiefs, that sagacious and energetic officer turned his attention to the suppression of the barbarous and inhuman practice of female infanticide, which had for centuries prevailed in Kachh and Káthiáwár, particularly among the Jádejá Rajputs, and from them had extended to other Rajput tribes also. Colonel Walker had to make very strenuous efforts to persuade the prejudiced chiefs that this custom was not only unnatural and cruel in the extreme, but was contrary to the teaching of their own religion, and it was not until December 1807 that they were induced to pass agreements engaging to prohibit the practice of female infanticide within their territories. Though it took many years and much additional labour on the part of future political officers to effect the suppression of this criminal custom, the initiative taken by Colonel Walker so early as 1805 was the means of saving the lives of thousands of helpless female children, who would otherwise have been destroyed immediately after birth by their merciless parents.

In connexion with this subject it may perhaps not be out of place to mention that besides the Rajputs, the Levá and Kadwá Kunbis of Northern Gujarát, a thrifty and respectable class of agriculturists, were also more or less under the thraldom of this baneful practice, inasmuch as they could not well afford the expensive amounts demanded as dowries by the aristocratic families in this community, whose sons they were proud to seek in alliance for their daughters. The expenses of marriage feasts and incidental expenses were also enormous. The depression thus brought on this useful class of cultivators attracted the attention of Mr. E. G. Fawcett, Collector of Ahmadábád in 1848, when that officer induced some of the inhabitants of his district to enter into agreements* to marry their daughters into families of equal rank, to limit the amount of dowries and marriage expenses, and to pay a penalty for infringement of any of the clauses of the covenants. Under orders from Government, the Collector of Kaira, Mr. John Webb, also induced his ryots the next year to enter into similar agreements, and the system worked to the benefit of the people concerned until its legality was questioned in a court of law in 1852, subsequent to which the agreements became a dead letter, and the former state of things revived. In 1870, taking the opportunity afforded by the passing of Act X of that year for the prevention of female infanticide, Mr. A. A. Borradaile, then Collector of Ahmadábád, again took up the subject, and at the request of Sheth Bechardás Ambaidás,† a leading and philanthropic citizen of Ahmadábád belonging to the Kadwá Kunbi community, induced Government to pass certain rules under the act. This had the desired effect for some time in so far at least as the Kadwá Kunbis were concerned. They were not quite suited to the circumstances of the Lewás, and caused some discontent in that community. Gradually, in consequence of the usual objection to the interference of Government in social matters, the difficulty of proving the existence of the practice of female infanticide, and the assurance that both the Lewá and Kadwá Kunbis had made binding arrangements among themselves, which would tend to remove the motive for crime, Government were pleased to place the rules in abeyance.

* Vide comprehensive report by the late Mr. H. R. Cooke, I. C. S., published as Selection Number CXLVII of the Records of the Government of Bombay, New Series.

† This gentleman was rewarded by the Government of India for his philanthropy by the grant of the title of Ráo Bahádur and a gold medal.

The experience of some twelve years and the statistics collected proved that the rules and the arrangements made by the people themselves did not work well. Mr. G. F. Sheppard, the popular Collector of Kaira and subsequently Commissioner of the Northern Division, then took up the subject, and his exertions, combined with the co-operation of many of the more aristocratic families of Gujarát, resulted in the promulgation of formal rules, which have had the force of law from 1st February 1888.* These rules, if duly enforced, and backed by the increasing intelligence and education of the people will, it is hoped, eventually remove the possibility of a recurrence of the hateful crime of female infanticide.

In the year 1889 similar rules were enacted for the Kadwá Kunbis at the instance of Mr. H. E. M. James, then Collector of Ahmadábád, and accepted by them.

* For a detailed account of Mr. Sheppard's work, see Indian Magazine for August 1889, Volume XX, No. 224, page 386.

Chapter VIII.

The renewal of the Gáekwád's lease of the Peshwá's share in the revenue. Disputes as to settlements of accounts. Deputation of GangádharShástri to Puná. The Shástri's treacherous murder. Surrender of the suspected murderer Trimbakji Dánglié. His confinement and escape.

From 1804 to 1816 A. D.

The farming of the Peshwá's share of the revenue of Gujarát to the Gáekwád for the term of five years from October 1800 has already been mentioned. Previous however to the expiry of this period, the Peshwá had ceded to the Honourable East India Company by the treaty of Bassein the districts of Dhandhuká, Ránpur and Goghá, together with his rights in Cambay. A fresh agreement was therefore concluded on the 2nd of October 1804, renewing for ten years the lease on condition of the payment of four lacs and a half of rupees per annum. Some time, however, prior to the expiry of this last agreement, the two Governments sought to settle their accounts, which had been in arrears for several years. According to the Peshwá, his claim on the Gáekwád amounted to a krore of rupees, but inasmuch as the embarrassment in the Gáekwád's finances had for the most part arisen in consequence of the adhesion of that state to the cause of Báji Ráo's father Raghunáth Ráo, the Peshwá remitted the sum of sixty lacs of rupees. The Gáekwád, however, urged counter claims on the Peshwá for loss caused by the cesion of Broach to the British in A. D. 1775, for expenses incurred in the expedition against Shelukar, and for the cost of the management of the country, towards which the Peshwá had contributed nothing from the time when his share was first farmed out to the Gáekwád. These matters formed the subject of many and prolonged discussions between the Peshwá and the Gáekwád's agent Bápu Mairál, and the latter was sent back to Baroda before any satisfactory conclusion was arrived at. Another agent Gangádhar Shástri was therefore deputed to the Peshwá's Court in A. D. 1814 under the guarantee of the British Government for his safety. The object of this deputation was two-fold; first the settlement of the accounts, and secondly the renewal of the lease. The Peshwá refused to see the Shástri on his arrival, on the plea that the latter had once, when a Kárkun, behaved insolently towards him. As, however, the Peshwá had previously given his consent, and as the Shástri was a respectable and honest man, the objection was over-ruled by the British Government. Dissensions then commenced between him and the Peshwá's confidant Trimbakji Dánglià, a notoriously bad character. It is almost needless to state that as regards the claims for arrears no satisfactory settlement was found possible, and the Peshwá refused altogether to renew the lease. He appointed Trimbakji as Sirsubá of his share of Gujarát. The latter forthwith got ready his troops, and sent forward his agents, who commenced a systematic plan of insurrection and intrigue, which threatened to throw the whole country into disorder. Accordingly Gangádhar Shástri, with the consent of the Resident at Puná, determined to return to Gujarát, leaving to the British the settlement of the disputed claims.

This step alarmed both the Peshwá and Trimbakji, and the latter, in order to gain over the Shástri, assured him that the Peshwá, being much pleased with his address and talents, also with his devotion to the cause of his master, was desirous of appointing him his own Minister. To inspire further confidence, the Peshwá proposed to give his sister-in-law in marriage to the Shástri's son. The Shástri, believing in the sincerity of the Peshwás intentions, consented to the marriage, but when the preparations had been far advanced, and considerable expense had already been incurred in view of the final ceremony, the Shástri, fearing lest his acceptance of the alliance would be construed as infidelity by his own prince the Gáekwád, withdrew from his agreement. He further ordered his wife to desist from visiting the Peshwá's palace. This roused the Peshwá's anger. He, however, refrained from giving open expression to his feelings, while Trimbakji pretended to treat the Shástri with more kindness than ever. Accordingly, when the Peshwá went on a pilgrimage to Pandharpur, the over confidant Shástri accompanied him, though advised against this step by Bápu Mairál the Gáekwád's banker. The result was that on the 14th of May 1815, after dining with the Peshwá, he was invited by Trimbakji to be present that night at a religious ceremony in some temple. The Shástri, suspecting no evil, went according to his promise, made obeisance to the idol, and paid his respects to the Peshwá, who had seated himself at a window. He was returning to his house almost unattended, when, within three hundred yards of the temple, a number of assassins fell upon him, and cut down the unfortunate man. Among Hindus the taking the life of a Bráhman, even for the most heinous offence, is regarded as the worst of crimes, and this murder of a high-caste Bráhman of exalted position, committed in such a sacred place as Pandharpur, was viewed with the utmost abhorrence, and popular indignation against Trimbakji, who was universally suspected of the crime, rose to a very high pitch. As might have been expected, both the Peshwá and Trimbakji denied any complicity in this foul murder, but Divine vengence was soon to overtake them. The Resident at Puná called for an immediate investigation, yet the Peshwá remained inactive, even though Bápu Mairál openly accused Trimbakji of the murder. Accordingly the Resident himself instituted the most minute inquiry, in the course of which Trimbakji's guilt was clearly established. The Peshwá was then called upon to deliver up the culprit. For a time he evaded compliance, but on the troops collecting round Puná, he at last, on the 25th September 1815, surrendered his favourite to the British Government. Two agents of Sitárám Rávji the Gáekwád's Minister, who was jealous of the ascendency of the Shástri, were also seized and sent to the Gáekwád, who confined them in hill forts. Sitárám himself, being delivered up to the British by the Gáekwád with some reluctance, was kept in custody. Trimbakji was confined in the fort of Thána, whence he escaped on the night of the 12th of September 1816 and remained concealed among the Bhils and Rámusis. His further actions will be narrated in the next chapter.

Chapter IX

Peshwá's intrigues against the English. Fresh treaty. The Pindári war. Battle of Kirkee. The Peshwá's defeat and flight. His further reverses and surrender. Fresh treaty with the Gáekwád.

From 1817 to 1818 A. D.

From his retreat Trimbakji held secret communications with the Peshwá, and by his commands raised an army from among the hill tribes. The Resident the Honourable Mountstuart Elphinstone obtained complete information of all that was being done, and, though the Peshwá and his Ministers denied that they were raising any troops or that there were any insurgents in the country, the British Government kept itself in readiness for any emergency that might arise.

The Peshwá's intrigues against the English could not, however, remain long disguised. None the less, on the 13th of May 1817 he entered into an agreement binding himself not to hold any communication with any power save the British, he further admitted Trimbakji's guilt in the murder of Gangádhar Shástri, and promised his surrender. He also withdrew all his demands on the Gáekwád, and agreed to cede to the British territory* estimated to yield a revenue of thirty-four lacs of rupees in lieu of furnishing the contingent of three thousand foot and five thousand horse agreed upon in the treaty of Bassein. This humiliation was but the natural result of his own foolish intrigues against the power that had sheltered his father, and by which he had himself been reinstated on the masnad usurped by Holkar.

The fresh treaty secured very great advantages to the Gáekwád also, inasmuch as by it the Peshwá granted in perpetuity a renewal of the lease of his share in the revenues of Gujarát

---

* This territory included the Konkan, Dhárwár and Ahmadnagar. The Peshwá also relinquished his share of the tribute in Káthiáwár.

for four lacs and a half of rupees. The Gáekwád was henceforward virtually recognised as independent of the Peshwá, and with the exception of four lacs a year in consideration of all past claims, he was freed from the necessity of paying either an annual tribute or the Nazaráná on succession.

The present opportunity was taken to induce Fatehsingh to increase the British subsidy, and to give over with certain reservations his tenure of Ahmadábád into the hands of the British. Certain exchanges of territory were also effected between the British and the Gáekwád by a treaty dated 6th November 1817 with a view to consolidate the possessions of each. By this arrangement the Gáekwád obtained Dabhoi, Bahádarpur and Sávli in lieu of his share of the Ahmadábád district except the Daskroi. The partition was favourable to the Gáekwád, inasmuch as in the city of Ahmadábád* there were certain vexatious imposts, the realizations from which amounted to nearly one-third of the Gáekwád's dues from the city, which the English out of sympathy for the inhabitants soon consented to abandon. Later on other territorial exchanges, convenient to both Governments, took place. Beyt and Okhámandal, which were taken after a severe contest with the ever turbulent Vághers in Samvat 1875 (A. D. 1818-19), were given over to the Gáekwád on his undertaking to pay the balance of compensation due by the pirate chiefs and the expenses of management since the conquest of Okhámandal. These places are held sacred by the Hindus, and for the same reason Siddhpur was relinquished in exchange for the Peshwá's share of Petlád, which was subsequently given to the Gáekwád in exchange for Umreth.

* Ahmadábád was taken possession of by the British on the 30th November 1817. The first Collector was Mr. Andrew Dunlop, and the first Judge Mr. Edmond Ironside.

The British now found themselves able to place in the field an army of one hundred and twenty thousand men for the suppression of the Pindáris,* who had become a scourge to all parts of India, Gujarát included. Only after considerable trouble and an organized war were these marauders destroyed (November 1817). The Peshwá still nourished his resentment against the English, and at Baroda he succeeded in raising a strong hostile party, headed by the late Minister Sitárám and the Ráni Takhtbai. The Resident at Puná, the Honourable Mountstuart Elphinstone, was aware of these machinations, but the Peshwá succeeded in deceiving the Governor General's Agent Sir John Malcolm, who, relying on his candour, permitted him to raise troops against the Pindáris. Having, under this plea, collected a considerable force, he conspired to take the life of the Resident, and to kindle disaffection among the native troops at Puná. Providence, however, over-ruled his plans, and one Yashvant Ráo, who had received fifty thousand rupees in order to assasinate the Resident, not only refused to carry out his agreement, but even warned Mr. Elphinstone of the vile conspiracy. At the Dasará festival on the 19th of October 1817 the opportunity was taken of a grand display to show the British sepoys their insignificance as compared with the Maráthá army, and each sebsequent day's proceedings served only to render more critical the position of the Puná Residency. On the night of the 28th of October, the Peshwá had made all his preparations for attacking the Residency, but fortunately he wavered at the last moment, and waited to receive tidings that the native portion of the small force with the British had been won over to

* The Pindáris were not a separate race or tribe, but an agglomeration of lawless men of all faiths. At first they were heard of only as free-booters, but they had of late become so powerful that even the Maráthás found themselves obliged to treat with them.

his side. The following morning the Resident, no longer able to conceal his suspicions, sent a message to the Peshwá relative to his threatening attitude, but he received only an evasive reply. In the meantime, a regiment of Europeans under Major Wilson, who, on hearing of the crisis, had made extraordinary exertions to reach Puná, safely arrived, after which, on the 18th of November 1817, the British left their old cantonment, which was very badly situated, and removed to Kirki. The Maráthás, elated by this measure, which they construed into flight, forthwith plundered the abandoned cantonment.

Even so late as the 5th of November, the Peshwá attempted to distract the attention of the English by negotiations, and requested that the newly arrived reinforcements should be sent back to Bombay. Mr. Elphinstone, however, proved more than a match for him in diplomacy, and demanded that the removal of troops should commence on the side of the Peshwá. Up to this time Mr. Elphinstone and his party had remained on at the Residency, but they now joined the army at Kirki. Towards this spot marched the vast Maráthá army, twelve times as numerous as the British troops, which latter numbered only two thousand native soldiers and eight hundred Europeans. On the morning of November 6th, Mr. Elphinstone boldly commenced battle, and so vigorously was the attack carried on under the gallant Colonel Burr, that before night fell that officer had succeeded in utterly defeating the Maráthá force, which lost five hundred in killed. At the very outset of the contest the Peshwá had gloomy forbodings owing to the accidental breaking of the pole on which was borne aloft the Jadi Patká or national standard. Seated in the temple of Párvati, which overlooks the plain, the Peshwá witnessed the discomfiture of his army, and, while the battle was yet raging, he gave orders for the plundering and burning of the Residency, including Mr. Elphinstone's valuable library, and the demolition of the graves of all Europeans. He also caused to be hanged two European officers, brothers, who while travelling had fallen into his hands.

The battle of Kirki ended in the victory of the English who expected a second engagement before their reinforcements could arrive on the 10th, but the Peshwá would not venture on another battle, and fled from Puná on the 17th, on which day the British took possession of the city. The strictest order was maintained, and no plundering was allowed. The pursuit of Báji Ráo and his army was undertaken as soon as possible, which led to a short campaign and a series of exploits, of which the battle of Koregáon on the river Bhimá was the most conspicuous. Three hundred Irregular Horse and a battalion of five hundred men, with two six-pounders, manned by twenty-four Europeans, found themselves, after a wearisome night-march, face to face with twenty-five thousand horse and a large number of Arab mercenaries, commanded by the Peshwá in person. The British position was at once attacked (1st January 1818), and, though the soldiers and officers were hard pressed both from fatigue and from their inferiority in numbers, the little band under Captain Francis Staunton kept the Peshwá's army at bay the whole day. Probably fearing reinforcements for the English troops, the Peshwá abandoned Koregáon during the night. In a second engagement, which took place at Assáye, the Peshwá's brave Commander Bápu Gokhlá fell, sword in hand. Fort after fort was then taken including Shiváji's stronghold of Ráigadh, whither Báji Ráo had recently sent his wife, and where his valuables were stored. The lady, on her capture by the English, was removed to Puná under safe and honourable escort. Báji Ráo fled from place to place, and at last made overtures for peace, but was told that he had, by his treacherous conduct, forfeited all claims to consideration, and that no terms short of unconditional surrender would be accepted. He obtained mercy, however, at the hands of Sir John Malcolm the Governor-General's Agent, notwithstanding that he had previously duped that officer into allowing him to augment his force under the plea of suppressing the Pindáris. Sir John acceeded to Báji Ráo's request to be allowed a pension of eight lacs of rupees per annum, and to select a holy place for his residence. The Governor-General, who was highly displeased with Báji Ráo for the treacherous course he had pursued ever since the treaty of Bassein, and for his cold-blooded murder of the two British officers, was not disposed to allow him such a liberal pension. However, inasmuch as the pledge of a high officer was involved, and as Báji Ráo had the wisdom to surrender in person on the 3rd of June 1818, the full allowance was sanctioned, and permission accorded him to reside at Bithur on the bank of the Ganges. Thus ended the rule of the Peshwá, and thereafter his rights and possessions in Gujarát, as indeed in all other parts of India, were transferred to the East India Company.

It only remains to mention that Trimbakji Dángliá, the murderer of Gangádhar Shástri, was not delivered up by the Peshwá. He was, however, captured by a party of Irregular Horse in Khándesh, and subsequently confined for life in the fort of Chunárgadh in Bengal. The following chapter is reserved for a brief résumé of the chief events that transpired at this period in the more distant parts of Gujarát.

Chapter X.

Insurrection at Mándvi and Bodhán by a Bohrá fanatic. Death of Dhanjishá Behremand Khán. The fanatic slain in action, and Mándvi restored to its chief. Affairs in Kachh, Bhávnagar, Junágadh, Pálanpur and Rádhanpur.

From 1804 to 1813 A. D.

In A. D. 1810 a Bohrá fanatic, named Abdul Rehmán, proclaiming himself to be the Imám Máhdi, collected a number of followers, consisting chiefly of Bohrá cultivators, and advanced against Mándvi. This little state was at that time under the rule of a Hindu Chief. Abdul took the Rájá prisoner and killed his minister. He then proceeded to Bodhán, whence he sent letters on the 10th and 15th of January to Mr. Crowe, the British Chief at Surat, calling on that officer to supply three hundred rupees, and to embrace the Muhammadan faith. Impressed by such boldness, numbers of the lower classes of Muhammadans in Surat joined the pretender, while others raised the cry of "Din, Din" and assailed the Hindu inhabitants of the city. Mr. Crowe accordingly sent detachments of infantry and cavalry to suppress the fanatical uprising, which they succeeded in doing, Abdul and some two hundred of his followers being slain in a severe engagement. Mándvi was then taken by the English troops and restored to its Chief* (22nd January 1810). It was in this revolt that Dhanjishá Barjorji, on whom the Emperor of Delhi had conferred the title of Behremand Khán (fortunate officer), volunteered to accompany the detachment in the capacity of native agent. He was, according to Mr. Crowe, among the first to cross the river, and, while endeavouring to talk over the infatuated Abdul, was killed. The

---

* Owing to failure of male heirs, Mándvi lapsed to the British in 1839, and is now a sub-division of the Surat Collectorate.

British Government generously granted Dhanjishá's widow a pension of three thousand rupees a year. Ardesir, the celebrated Kotwál of Surat, was the son of this distinguished officer.

The important state of Kachh was at this period in a state of utter disorder and confusion owing to the rapacity of two rival ministers, Fateh Muhammad and Hansráj, and also to the imbecility of Ráo Ráidhan II (1778-1803) and the intemperate habits of his successor Ráo Bhármal II (1814-1819). Violent depredations and piracies were being committed by the turbulent characters in Kachh on subjects under British protection, to prevent which it became necessary to send a force against that state, which took the fortress of Anjár on the 25th December 1815 and the seaport of Tuná. The troops then moved towards Bhuj. At Lákand envoys met the British agent Captain Mac Murdo on the 3rd of January 1816, and on the 14th it was agreed that compensation should be paid for the losses in Káthiáwár and for the military expenses, that piracies should be repressed, that no foreigners other than the British should be allowed to dwell in Kachh, and that the Company's Agent should reside at Bhuj; further that the Company should establish order at Vághad, and cause certain territories to be restored by the refractory chiefs. The Ráo, in return, promised to hand over to the British the fort of Anjár and twenty-three villages, and to pay annually two lacs of koris, equal to fifty-two thousand seven hundred and twenty rupees. In the hope, however, of reviving the prosperity of the State, this tribute was subsequently remitted together with the heavy charges of the expedition, amounting to rupees eight lacs thirteen thousand eight hundred and seventy six. The British army having brought Vághad and other places under complete control, Captain Mac Murdo was appointed the first Resident at Bhuj and Collector of Anjár.

Jám Jasáji of Nawánagar was also somewhat refractory. He

not only refused to grant an appanage to his brother Satáji, and involved himself in broils with the Ráo of Kachh, but refused to surrender to the British Government an Arab who had shot a British Officer at Gop and had fled for protection to the Jám's fort of Modhpur. A joint army of the British and the Gáekwád forces accordingly marched against Nawánagar, and, the artillery having done much execution, the Jám eventually came to reason and executed a treaty on the 23rd of February 1812, agreeing to deliver up the murderer and his accomplices, to destroy the fort of Modhpur, to settle the claims of Kachh, to grant certain villages in appanage to his brother, and to pay a succession duty of 25000 rupees to the Gáekwád.

Bhávnagar under its able chief Vakhatsingji appears to have maintained its prosperous condition. In A. D. 1810 the Collector of Kaira, Mr. Byram Rolls, succeeded in inducing the chief to pay an enhanced assessment in regard to his villages in the Dhandhuká, Ránpur and Goghá parganás. In 1813-14 in consequence of the chief having put to death certain persons for killing a cow, he was deprived of civil and criminal jurisdiction* in the hundred and sixteen villages of the parganás above mentioned. This seems to have been the only occasion on which he fell under the displeasure of the paramount power.

In this state, the Khumán Káthis of Kundlá gave much trouble between 1820 and 1829 A. D. They plundered and burnt several villages and lifted cattle, but Vajesingji pursued them in person on several occasions and eventually succeeded, with the aid of Captain Barnwell, the Political Agent, in bringing them to order, when they were compelled to surrender several villages to the Bhávnagar Darbár in compensation for its losses.

---

* In A. D. 1866 Government were pleased to restore complete jurisdiction to the Thákor.

At Junághad an Arab Jamádár named Omar Mukhásan, who had been tyranizing over the Nawáb, was expelled by the British in 1816, for which service the Nawáb remitted the Zor Talbi dues (forcible levy) hitherto raised in the parganás of Dhandhuká, Dholerá, Ránpur and Goghá.

In 1820 during the course of an enquiry instituted by Captain Barnwell, as Political Agent into the tributes levied in Káthiáwár, the Gáekwád agreed to make no demand on the chiefs except through the British Government. Thus the constant differences between the chiefs and the Gáekwád ceased immediately, and the supreme power in Káthiáwár became vested in the British.

Their connexion with Pálanpur* dates from A. D. 1809, when arrangements similar to those obtaining in Káthiáwár were made for the payment of the Gáekwád's annual tribute of fifty thousand Bábásháhi Rupees.

In A. D. 1813, Firoz Khán Diwán, the ruling chief of Pálanpur, was murdered by his own officers, and his brother Samsher Khán was raised to the chieftainship. Firoz Khán's son Fateh Khán then applied to the Gáekwád and the English for help, and a force was sent against Pálanpur. A reconciliation, however, was soon effected between the uncle and nephew. The former gave his daughter in marriage to the latter, and

* Malek Yusaf Jhálori, who wrested Pálanpur from its ancient Hindu Rájá about A. D. 1373, claims to have been the governor of Vihári. His successors are said to have assumed the title of Diwán when they conquered and held temporary possession of Tharád (the chiefs of which district were known by that appellation) in the beginning of the eighteenth century. Sher Muhammad Khánji, the present Diwán was recently appointed by Her Imperial Majesty Queen Victoria, a Knight Commander of the Indian Empire, and the ceremony of investiture was performed at Ahmadábád by His Excellency Lord Harris on the 28th of November 1893.

continued to manage the affairs of the state. Disagreements, however, sprang up between them, and they were both summoned to appear before a British Officer at Siddhpur. The inquiry showed that Samsher Khán had mismanaged the state and increased its debts. Foreseeing that the decision would not be favourable to him, he craftily persuaded Fateh Khán to return to Pálanpur without leave. As a punishment for Fateh Khán's conduct, a British force was sent against Pálanpur in October 1817, when the town was assaulted and taken. On this Fateh Khán at once submitted, and Captain Miles was appointed Political Superintendent with complete control over the State finances. Suitable arrangements were also made for the liquidation of the state debts.

A treaty was concluded with the Nawáb of Radhanpur on the 16th of December 1813. Marauders from Sindh having made frequent incursions into this state, the Nawáb applied for the aid of British troops. These were sent in A.D. 1819, and soon succeeded in ridding the country of free-booters. In A. D. 1822 an annual tribute of seventeen thousand rupees was imposed on the Chief by the British Government, but it was wholly remitted in 1825 in consideration of the inability of the state to meet this charge.

Chapter XI.

Events at Baroda. Deaths of Fatehsingh and Anand Ráo. Succession of Sayáji and the new treaty with him. Sayáji's failure to pay certain debts guaranteed by the British Government. Sequestration of certain districts. Dismissal of the Diwán Venirám and establishment of friendly relations. Raising of the Gujarát Irregular Horse. Death of Sayáji.

From 1818 to 1847 A. D.

It is now necessary to revert to affairs at Baroda. The overthrow of the Peshwá secured great advantages to the Gáekwád, one of which was the remission of the annual tribute of four lacs of rupees. The British Government, as successor of the Peshwá, was indeed entitled to this tribute, but it was remitted in consideration of Fatehsing Gáekwád having aided the British army with a body of two thousand horse under the able General Kamál-ud-din during the war with Holkar, which had broken out on cessation of hostilities with the Peshwá.

Fatehsingh died on the 23rd of June 1818 at the early age of twenty-eight years. His younger brother Sayáji, then only nineteen years of age, was appointed Regent though Fatehsing's widow Rádhábai* and Anand Ráo's wife Takhtbái were

---

* Rádhábai was allowed to adopt Govind Ráo of the Gáekwád family as her son, on the express stipulation that he should have no claim to the Barodá Gádi, but that he should inherit Fatehsingh's private property only. Govind Ráo, however, was tempted to raise a dispute which eventually resulted in an affray between his men and those of Sayáji on the 22nd of July 1829. Govind Ráo was compelled to take refuge in a house near the Residency. Here he was blockaded for about six months by the Gáekwád's men, when the Governor, Sir John Malcolm, settled the dispute, A. D. 1830, and Govind Ráo was sent first to Surat on a fixed allowance, and thence to Ahmadábád as a state prisoner. From 1835 till 1857 he remained in Ahmadábád, but in the latter year was handed over to the Gáekwád's Government on his being detected in secret correspondence with British troops during the mutiny.

not in favour of his nomination, inasmuch as in him they saw abilities to rule independently of themselves. Anand Ráo also died on the 2nd of October 1819, and, as Takhtbái was not his legitimate wife, his children by her were passed over, and Sayáji was thus confirmed in the succession.

Though the Gáekwád was much indebted to the British Government for the preservation of his principality, and though very much had been done for its improvement during Colonel Alexander Walker's administration, Sayáji Ráo appears to have largely forgotten his debt of obligations during the years of peace that followed. Feeling his position secure against all enemies, he often ventured to set at defiance the advice both of the Resident and of the British Government.

As early as A. D. 1820 the Government of the Right Honourable Mountstuart Elphinstone took into consideration the expediency of relaxing that absolute direction of the internal affairs of the Gáekwád's Government which had become necessary during the imbecility of Anand Ráo. In that year, the Governor visited Baroda, and certain fresh stipulations were entered into, the chief of which were the following three:—

1. That with reference to the internal management of his state, the Gáekwád should have plenary powers, but that the guarantee extended to certain bankers, ministers and others should be maintained, and the Resident should be made acquainted with the estimated expenditure of the year, should have access to accounts, and should be consulted regarding any extraordinary outlay.

2. That all foreign affairs should remain under the exclusive management of the British Government.

3. That the Gáekwád should choose his own Minister after consultation with the Resident, and that the latter should retain the power of advice.

Sayáji, however, failed to pay regularly the instalments* guaranteed to the bankers, and seized every opportunity of augmenting his private treasury by appropriating thereto state moneys. He oppressed those of his citizens who held British guarantees, and paid no heed to the remonstrances of successive Governors. Accordingly in A. D. 1828 the Bombay Government under Sir John Malcolm found it necessary to sequestrate certain districts†, yielding an annual gross revenue of rupees twenty-seven lacs. By previous treaties the Gáekwád was bound to maintain a force of three thousand horse in addition to the English subsidy, but he having, in spite of repeated warnings, failed to keep even two thousand in an efficient state, a further sequestration of territory, yielding an annual revenue of fifteen lacs of rupees, was made in A. D. 1830.

Differences, however, continuing between the Gáekwád and Mr. Williams, the Resident, the latter was directed, 1st December 1830, to reside at Ahmadábád, exercising from that city control over Baroda as Political Commissioner for Gujarát. The subsidized force was also incorporated with the Northern Division of the army, and its headquarters fixed at Ahmadábád. This change, however, did not prove much to Sayáji's advantage, for in February 1831 some of his relatives in Baroda were found to have entered into a conspiracy to seize him and to proclaim his son Ganpat Ráo as king. The conspiracy, being discovered in time, failed, and several of those who were party to it suffered execution.

---

* These debts even then amounted to no less than one hundred and seven lacs of rupees.

† Those districts were :—

1. Petlád, 2. Bahiyál, 3. Kadi, 4. Dabhoi (Bahádarpur), 5. Sinor 6. Amroli, 7. Songadh. Further the tributes received from Káthiáwár, Mahi Kánthá and Rewá Kánthá were attached. Vide Notification dated 28th March 1828.

Lord Clare, the new Governor of Bombay, visited Baroda in November 1831 and March 1832, on which occasions the banker-creditors of the Gáekwád having agreed to release the Bombay Government from its guarantees, and Sayáji having consented to deposit ten lacs of rupees for payment of the Gáekwád's Contigent in the event of his monthly payments falling short, the sequestrated districts were restored in April 1832. Thus amicable relations were again restored, at least for the time, and at the end of 1835 Mr. Williams, though still holding office as Political Commissioner in Gujarát, again took up his residence in Baroda.

The Minister Venirám Aditrám did not, however, allow perfect concord to prevail, and, acting under his advice, Sayáji failed to carry out several of his engagements. The Minister even caused the hands of a Garásiá named Punjá Joráji, a British subject, to be cut off for the sole reason that he had been pressing his Garás demands. He also attached the estate of the Desái of Navsári, Mancherji Kharsedji, who enjoyed a British guarantee. A Vániá broker, named Valabhdás Mánekchand, was driven to commit suicide in consequence of the oppression to which he was subjected, and, as Sayáji turned a deaf ear to the remonstrances alike of the Political Commissioner and of the Bombay Government, the latter, as a warning, sequestrated the district of Navsári in February 1838, and threatened to depose Sayáji in favour of his son. The sequestration of Petlád followed in November, and in February 1839 the Government of Indiá caused it to be publicly notified that by his conduct the Gáekwád had forfeited all claim to that town.

These decisive measures, together with the deposition of the Rájá of Satárá for similar contumacy, eventually brought Sayáji to a more reasonable frame of mind, and accordingly on the 28th of November 1839, he went to the Residency, begged forgiveness for all his past contumacy and entered into fresh agreements. The obnoxious Minister Venirám was dismissed on the same day, and the Mahárájá promised that he would not have any further communication with him.

On the 26th of January 1841 the Governor, Sir James Carnac, came to Baroda. A fresh agreement, satisfactory to all, was then entered into, and the sequestrated districts of Petlád and Navsári were restored on the Gáekwád agreeing not to molest any person who had complained against him. The deposit of rupees ten lacs already mentioned was also refunded to him. The maintenance of the body of Irregular Cavalry, commonly known in Ahmadábád as the Risálá, or the Gujarát Irregular Horse, which had been raised in March 1839 as a punishment to the Gáekwád, and had since been a charge on the revenues of Petlád, was, however, continued, and Sayáji agreed to pay annually for its support three lacs of rupees. This body consisted of six hundred and eighty horsemen with a complement of officers. Opportunity was also taken of this new agreement to do away with the practice of requiring British officers at Baroda to take part in the religious processions of the Dasará, and those in honour of Ganpati. The Gáekwád also promised to prohibit throughout his dominions the practice of Sati (self immolation of widows), and on the 13th of April 1840 issued a notification making abetment of Sati a penal offence. This noble example was soon followed by the chiefs of Rewá Kánthá.

In short the treaty of 1840 established those friendly feelings which still exist between the two Governments, and which have contributed so largly to the happiness of their subjects. After the conclusion of these agreements Sayáji ruled in peace for seven years. He died on the 19th of December 1847, beloved by his people. Though for a time he had placed himself in opposition to the views of the British Government, most of his contentions admitted of reasonable explanation, and the good sense and justice of the British Government, coupled with Sayáji's return to submission, secured to him all that he could reasonably have expected. His high moral character is still held in remembrance. In Petlád the story is told that on one occasion, seeing a beautiful girl pass along the road near the palace, one of his sons exclaimed, "Lo, how lovely she is!", when Sayáji quietly replied, "Yes, and so is our———", naming one of his own daughters, thus giving the prince to understand that the unknown girl should be regarded as a sister.

CHAPTER XII.

Reign of Ganpat Ráo. Colonel Outram's Khatpat Report and dismissal of the Native Agent. Control of Baroda transferred to the Supreme Government. Commencement of the B. B. & C. I. Railway. Death of Ganpat Ráo, and succession of Khande Ráo. The Bengal Mutiny. Khande Ráo's administrative and other reforms. Disturbance at Okhámandal. Khande Ráo's death.

FROM 1847 to 1870 A. D.

Sayáji Ráo left eight sons of whom five were legitimate. Ganpat Ráo, the eldest, succeeded to the throne at the age of thirty years. He ruled peaceably and maintained friendly relations with the British Government especially during the time of the acting Resident Colonel French. This excellent officer fostered the Mahárájá's literary tastes, and by presenting him with model steam-engines and an electric telegraph apparatus induced him to become acquainted with their working. Under his advice, the Mahárájá for the first time visited Bombay. He connected the Baroda Camp with the city by a made road, overshaded with trees on either side, and built a Dharamshálá at Tankáriá Bandar. Designs also for a tramway were taken in hand. The Mahárájá issued a regulation prohibting female infanticide among the Levá Kunbis in his dominion, and devoted half the proceeds from the Mohsal (fines) in the Mahi Kánthá to form a fund for checking this crime. He also took steps to prevent the sale of children by poor parents.

While Colonel French thus availed himself of his position to induce GanpatRáo to adopt measures tending to the welfare of his subjects, Colonel Outram, the Resident, undertook, with no little courage, the task of stamping out the corrupt practices then rampant in the State. He wrote his celebrated Khatpat Report dated April 1852, and procured the dismissal both of the Resident's Native agent and of the Gáekwád's minister. Consequent on the detection and exposure by this energetic Resident of several long standing intrigues, the control of Baroda affairs was temporarily transferred from the Government of Bombay to the Supreme Government in A.D. 1854. This control was, however, restored to the Bombay Government in 1860 under orders from the Home Government.

The construction of the first portion of the Bombay, Baroda and Central India Railway was commenced during this period. The State, however, had no part in this great undertaking. The requisite land was granted on condition that private owners should receive payment in full, and that the Gáekwád should be compensated* in full for the loss of transit duties, the amount of the latter being determined from year to year.

After a short but peaceful reign of nine years, Ganpat Ráo died on the 19th of November 1856, leaving no male issue. His younger brother Khande Ráo accordingly succeeded him. It was only a few months after the accession of this prince that the mutiny broke out in the Bengal army, and extended more or less to other parts of India, though happily in only a slight degree to Gujarát. At this time Khande Ráo, to the credit of his judgment be it said, rightly identified his interests with those of the British Government. The troops of his contingent were kept in an efficient state, and being judiciously distributed in various portions of his dominions, contributed in a great measure towards preserving the public tranquillity.

For his loyalty and unswerving attachment Khande Ráo was

---

* In 1877, when the British Government determined to extend the Railway to Rajputáná, this claim to indemnity was withdrawn during the administration of Sir T. Mádhav Ráo in consideration of the vast advantages the Railway had secured to the Gáekwád, and the consequent increase in Custom duties.

amply rewarded by the British Government, who were pleased to remit, with retrospective effect from the date of his accession, the annual payment made by the Gáekwád of the sum of three lacs of rupees towards the maintenance of the Gujarát Irregular Horse, which, as mentioned in the foregoing pages, had been stationed at Ahmadábád ever since 1839. Khande Ráo was also presented with the Morchál, a royal emblem consisting of a fan of peacock feathers, and was further empowered to adopt a son. In the Sanad dated 11th December 1862 conferring this right on the Gáekwád, he is styled "His Highness the Mahárájá of Baroda".

Khande Ráo now turned his energies towards the introduction of reforms in his standing army. He also took in hand several public works, the most notable of which was a Railway from Miágám to Dabhoi, a distance of twenty miles, on the very narrow gauge of two feet six inches, constructed in 1872-73 at a cost of upwards of four lacs of rupees. For some time it was used as a kind of tramway, but eventually the management was given over to the Bombay, Baroda and Central India Railway Company, and Dabhoi has now become the junction of three important lines, which will be mentioned further on.

Being much devoted to manly exercises and the chase, Khande Ráo caused a palace to be erected at Makarpurá near his deer park. While in Bombay, he endowed several educational institutionsand made the princely gift of two lacs of rupees towards the building of the Sailor's Home, and one lac and eighty thousand rupees towards a statue of Queen Victoria. In private life he was rather over-liberal, and, in order to meet his lavish expenditure, had to impose heavy taxes on his subjects. He is said to have spent a lac of rupees on a chadar, or sheet, richly bedecked with jewels, to be sent to Mediná to be placed on the tomb of the prophet. Owing however, to his death, it does not appear to have been sent. He was the first to cause the Civil and Criminal Procedure Codes and other laws to be codified according to the regulations of the British Government. He also tried to introduce several reforms both in the Revenue and Judicial Departments, and designed public works on an extensive scale. His ministers were, however, comparatively uneducated men, and owing to the absence of co-operation on their part, and also to his want of perseverance in the projects he took in hand, Khande Ráo failed to accomplish much that he had desired to see done. Still, the beginning made by him served to point the way to more solid reforms, and to greater achievements under future administrations.

In addition to the excited state of the country caused by the mutiny in other parts of India, the little province of Okhámandal, bordering on the Ran of Kachh, which at his request had been made over to the Gáekwád by the British Government owing to the reputed sanctity of the temples at Bet and Dwárká, became a source of considerable trouble. In February 1858, on the pretence that their allowances were not regularly paid, the Wághers inhabiting that province rose in arms against the Gáekwád, and took possessionof Bet from the Sibandi. A British detachment under Lieutenant Barton, however, soon repulsed them, and restored Bet to the Gáekwád. A few months later, however, on hearing of the mutiny, they again rose in arms, regained both Bet and Dwárká, and expelled the Gáekwad's officers from Okhámandal. Khande Ráo Gáekwád, seeing that his own Sibandi was disaffected, wisely placed the military affairs of this troublesome little province in the hands of the British, and a campaign ensued, in which Bet was retaken on the 6th, and Dwárká on the 31st of October 1859. The war, however, did not come to an end until 18th December 1859, when the Wághers were dislodged by Colonel Homer from their strong position on a hill. Some of those taken prisoners on that occasion escaped, and continued to give trouble till 1868, when their chief Mulu Mánek was surprised and killed by the Porbander Sibandi. Since 1859 a British officer has been appointed to the command of the local battalion at Okhámandal, but the collection of revenue and the conduct of administration remain with the Gáekwád's officers.

His Highness Khande Ráo Maharájá, after enjoying for more than ten years the honours conferred on him by the paramount power, breathed his last on the 28th of November 1870.

CHAPTER XIII

Malhár Ráo's accession. His antecedents. His misrule. Appointment of a Commission of inquiry and its decision. Mr. Dádábhái Naurozji's appointment as Diwán. Direct control again assumed by the Supreme Government. Malhár Ráo's attempt to poison the Resident Colonel Phayre, his arrest and trial.

FROM 1870 to 1875 A. D.

Khande Ráo left no male issue, and was consequently succeeded by his younger brother Malhár Ráo. The short reign of the latter was fraught with evil, and would have brought to a close the rule of the Gáekwád, had it not been for the moderation of the British Government and the right of adoption accorded to Khande Ráo in recognition of his loyal conduct during the mutiny. Prior to his accession to the throne, Malhár Ráo had been suspected of complicity in an attempted risfng of the Kolis of Bijápur and other places during the mutiny, whose object was to plunder Ahmadábád and to depose Khande Ráo. Happily the plot did not succeed, and although the ringleaders, Magan Bhukhan, Potdár of Shivrám Kadus' Págá, and Jethá Modi, were blown from guns, and others were suitably punished, no steps were taken against Mulhár Ráo, who was then considered too weak to be dangerous. In 1863 he tried to take Khande Ráo's life by sorcery or poison, and was on that occasion confined in the fort at Pádrá as a state prisoner. In 1867 a fresh conspiracy was discovered, and one of the persons concerned in the plot was trodden to death under the feet of an elephant. This cruel mode of punishment was, however, abolished that same year at the instance of Sir Bartle Frere, then Governor of Bombay.

Malhár Ráo, thus suddenly elevated from a prison to the throne, showed at first a disposition to rule with clemency, but he soon set himself to take vengeance on his deceased brother's ministers and advisers. Releasing those who were suffering imprisonment for conspiring against Khande Ráo's life, he cast the minister Bháu Shindé into prison, where, after being subjected to great indignities, he died on the 18th of May 1872 by poison, suspected to have been administered by Malhár Ráo's orders. His family was also stripped of its wealth. Several other instances of oppression and misrule occured. To put a check to the growing evil, the Government thought it proper to appoint as Resident Colonel R. Phayre, C. B. This officer having exposed some of Malhár Ráo's misdeeds, a Commission was appointed by Government to inquire into the allegations against him. The Commission, after a patient inquiry extending from the 10th of November to 24th December 1873, held the charge of mismanagement to be substantiated. It was also proved that several people had been grossly ill-treated, and that many women of respectable position had been forcibly dishonoured in Malhár Ráo's seraglio.

Under these circumstances the Viceroy, unwilling to take extreme measures, gave Malhár Ráo two years' time to reform his administration, and warned him that failure to do so would issue in his deposal. Malhár Ráo was also asked to dismiss certain obnoxious officers, and to appoint a minister to be selected by the Bombay Government.

The Gáekwád, however, did not set himself heartily to effect the reforms suggested, and contented himself with appointing (4th August 1874) as minister Mr. Dádábhái Naurozji, a distinguished and highly educated Pársi gentleman of Bombay. With the assistance of several intelligent and experinced officers of the Bombay Government, Mr. Dádábhái applied himself rigorously to his task, but Colonel Phayre, the Resident, seems to have doubted Mr. Dádábhái's capabilities, and also whether Malhár Ráo would accord him the requisite powers. Mr. Dádábhái* appears thus to have been considerably hampered, and the relations between the Gáekwád and the Resident became more strained. The Viceroy, however, on learning of these differences, was of opinion that a change of Resident would remove from the Gáekwád all cause of complaint, and accordingly on the 25th November 1874 he appointed Colonel Sir Lewis Pelly Special Commissioner and Agent to the Governor General for Baroda, which was thus a second time placed under the control of the Supreme Government.

Matters, however, came to a crisis at the close of 1874 by the discovery of arsenic in the sharbat of pomelo-juice prepared for Colonel Phayre by his servant. Subsequent inquiries having aroused suspicion that Malhár Ráo was a party to this attempt at poisoning, the Viceroy determined to suspend him from power and to put him on his trial before a commission composed of independent and unbiassed gentlemen†. Orders were therefore issued to Sir Lewis Pelly to arrest Malhár Ráo, which was effected in so judicious a manner that no disturbance or hostile demonstration was attempted. Mr. Dádábhái had, in the meantime, resigned, and the management of the Baroda affairs was at once assumed by Sir Lewis Pelly.

---

* Mr. Sorábji Jahángirji's short sketch of the Representative Men of India shows that the Government of India had, in a short despatch to the Home Government, mentioned Mr. Dádábhái as "being honestly desirous of reforming the administration", and Sir L. Pelly has given him full credit for the purging of corruption in the Civil and Criminal administrations. Mr. Dádábhái was subsequently chosen as additional member of the Council of the Governor of Bombay for making Laws and Regulations. At the General Election of 1892, he was returned as a Member of Parliament for the borough of Finsbury.

† The members of this Commission were:—

1. Sir Richard Couch, Chief Justice of the High Court of Calcutta. } President.
2. Sir Richard Meade.
3. P. H. Melvill, Esquire.
4. The Mahárájá Sindhiá.
5. The Mahárájá of Jaypur.
6. Sir Dinkar Ráo, Minister of H. H. Jiájiráv, Mahárájá of Gwálior.

Chapter XIV.

Decision of the Commission. Deposition of Malhár Ráo. The adoption of Sayáji Ráo as the heir of Khande Ráo. Sir T. Mádhav Ráo's appointment as Administrator. His measures of reform. Sayáji Ráo's investiture with powers of Government. His beneficent rule.

From 1875 to 1892 A. D.

The Commission after an inquiry extending from the 23rd of February to 31st of March 1875 gave their decision. The three English members were of opinion that Malhár Ráo was guilty of the fourth charge, namely of attempting to poison Colonel Phayre by means of persons instigated thereto, but the native members held that Malhár Ráo's guilt had been established regarding only one or more of the minor counts, inasmuch as either by his agents or in person, he had held communications with the Resident's employees, and had bribed them to obtain private official information and to effect the removal of Colonel Phayre.

The Government of India, in view of this difference of opinion, were unwilling to proceed to harsh measures in the punishment of Malhár Ráo, and accordingly on the 15th of April 1875 they suggested to the Secretary of State for India to depose him, to invite Sir T. Mádhav Ráo, who had successfully managed the Trávankor State, to carry on the administration of Baroda, and to ask Her Highness Jamnábái, the widow of Khande Ráo, to adopt a son for the succession to the throne.

Her Majesty's Government refused to admit that the case was proved, but ultimately ordered Malhár Ráo's deposition, because, as stated in the Government of India's Notification dated 19th April 1875, "Having regard to all the circumstances relative to the affairs of Baroda from the accession of His Highness Malhár Ráo, his notorious misconduct, his gross mis-management and his evident incapacity to carry on reforms, the step was imperatively called forth". He was accordingly deported to Madrás on the 22nd of April 1875 under the surveillance of a European medical officer. Six days after this, an attempt was made to seat Malhár Ráo's son by Lakshmibái on the throne. The city gates were closed by the insurgents; the Agent, however, quietly despatched a military force, which immediately put down the disturbance. After this Lakshmibái and her son were also sent to Madrás to reside with the exiled Malhár Ráo. Lakshmibái is said to have been the wife of a poor labourer residing in British territory, but Malhár Ráo caused her to be taken to his harem. The injured husband complained to the Resident Colonel Phayre, but, while inquiry was proceeding, Malhár Ráo went through the form of marriage with her at Navsári on the 7th of May 1874. The Resident, in accordance with orders from Government, absented himself from the festivities. On the 16th of December Lakshmibái gave birth to a son, whom, however, the Government rightly refused to acknowledge as the Gáekwád's heir.

The British Government had no desire to annex Baroda to their vast Empire. They therefore caused inquiry to be made as to whether there was amongst the Gáekwád's connexions any one who might after suitable training succeed to the throne. It was reported that in the village of Kauláne, Taluká Málegáon, in the district of Khándesh, were three brothers, descended from Zingoji Gáekwád the brother of Dámáji I. The second, named Gopál Ráo, then only thirteen years old, was, by reason of his tender age and natural ability, adopted by Khande Ráo's widow Jamnábái, at the suggestion of the paramount British Power, and seated on the throne on the 27th of May 1875 under the name of Sayáji Ráo III. Thus this young scion of a noble Maráthá family, by a sudden turn in the wheel of fortune, became at once the Rájá of an important kingdom.

The British Government, with its wonted solicitude for the welfare of the native principalities which it has pleased Providence to place under their guardianship, took immediate steps to provide for the education of the young prince. Mr. F. A. H. Elliot, C. S. I., of the Indian Civil Service, was appointed his tutor, and the prince soon proved himself a promising pupil, not only at his books, but also in wrestling, riding and other manly sports. Sayáji Ráo was further carefully instructed in the work of administration, and has already shown himself to be a worthy and benevolent ruler. During his minority the administration of the state was entrusted, 10th May 1875, to Sir T. Mádhav Ráo, who came from the Madras Presidency, having served as Diwán of Trávankor for fourteen years, during which time he had succeeded in introducing several beneficial reforms. In Baroda this excellent minister gathered round him a number of the ablest and most intelligent native officers,* including some who had been formerly engaged by Mr. Dádábhái. He also obtained the services of several other officers of experience from the British Government, and thus inaugurated a wise and vigorous administration, which has secured lasting benefits alike to the state and to the people. The cheif features of the

---

* Khán Bahádur Kázi Sháhbuddin C. I. E. Revenue Commissioner.
Khán Bahádur Pestanji Jahángir C. I. E., Settlement officer and Military Secretary.
Ráo Bahádur Venáyakráo Janárdhan, Náib Diwán.
Khán Bahádur Kharsedji Rastamji, Chief Justice.
Mr. Janárdhan Sakhárám Gádgil, B. A. L. L. B.
Ráo Bahádur Lakshman Jagannáth.
Diwán Bahádur Manibhái Jasbhái.

programme laid down by Sir T. Mádhav Ráo for the government of the province, entrusted to his care, were as follow* :—

(a). To maintain public order and tranquillity with firmness and moderation.

(b). To redress the accumulated complaints of the Sardárs, bankers, ryots and others, arising out of past maladministration.

(c). To establish a suitable organization for dispensing justice in both its branches.

(d). To provide a police having regard to the extent of the country and the density and character of the population.

(e). To provide for the execution of necessary or useful public works.

(f). To promote popular education.

(g). To provide suitable medical agencies for the benefit of the people.

(h). To reduce the burden of taxation where it was excessive, to readjust taxes where they required modification, and to abolish such taxes as were objectionable.

(i). To enforce economy in the expenditure, to restrain waste, to reduce extravagance and to prevent losses arising from corruption and malversation. And, pre-eminently to keep the expenditure well below the receipts, so that a surplus might become available as a provision for adverse seasons, and for administrative improvements.

---

* From the Report on the Administration of the Baroda State for 1875-76, para. 25, page 20.

(j). To strengthen the executive establishments, so that the Government might make its power felt through-out these dominions.

To narrate in detail the many able measures undertaken by Sir T. Mádhav Ráo during his prosperous administration of six years would fill a large volume. Suffice it to say that a carefully devised revenue system was drawn up, the excessive land assessments were reduced,and anomalous and needlessly vexatious taxes were abolished. Regular Courts of Justice, presided over by officers of known probity and experience, were established, the Police Department was put on a sound footing, and the Central Jail was also placed under an efficient and experienced officer, whose services were lent by the British Government. Medical and educational institutions were founded, railway communication was largely extended, and public works were undertaken on an extensive scale. The revenues have been so judiciously financed that after defraying all the cost of these liberal reforms, also the expenses in connexion with the marriages of His Highness Sayáji Ráo, 6th January 1880, and of his sister Tárábái, 21st December 1879, and the erection of a palace* for the Gáekwád, the Administration has been able to reserve a crore and a half of rupees.

On the 28th of December 1881, His Higness, having attained his majority, was formally invested by Sir James Fergusson, then Governor of Bombay, with the powers of Government. Great preparations were made to celebrate the joyful event, and an exhibition was held of native arts and manufactures of the Baroda territory. In the following year Sayáji Ráo undertook a tour in the Kadi division with the object of becoming practically acquainted with the condition of the people.

* The foundation stone of the Lakhshmi Vilás palace was laid by the Governor of Bombay, Sir Richard Temple, on the 12th January 1880.

This tour extended from 23rd November 1882 to 20th January 1883. He then proceeded to Calcutta on a visit to His Excellency the Viceroy, and returned to Baroda on the 23rd of March 1883 after visiting Agrá, Gwalior, Ajmer and other places. In the cold weather he again visited various districts in his territory. One important result of this tour was the solution of the long vexed problem as to a suitable water-supply for the city of Baroda. His Highness, after having visited the Munwál tank near Sávli, caused several places to be examined, and plans submitted. At length sanction was accorded to the scheme* of supplying water from the Surya lake at Ajwá, a distance of about fourteen miles from Baroda, at an estimated cost of twenty five lacs of rupees, exclusive of establishment and compensation for land. The first sod of this useful work was turned by Lady Watson, wife of General (now Sir John) Watson, K. C. B., V. C., Agent to the Governor-General, on the 8th of January 1885. The work has since been completed, being opened to the public on the 29th of March 1892, so that the inhabitants of Baroda, numbering about 112000 souls according to the latest census returns, are now blessed with a plentiful supply of water. Baroda also boasts of several important lines of railway. All of these, except the lines from Miágám to Bahádarpur, Baroda to Chándod *via* Dabhoi, and Mehsáná to Vadnagar, have been constructed after Sayáji Ráo's succession. His Highness has also abolished many objectionable cesses and imposts, and has made vast improvements in the currency of the state by substituting machine-made silver and copper coins for the old hand-made Bábáshai rupees and pice. These were easily counterfeited, and

* Mr. Jagannáth Sadáshivji, one of the state engineers, has the credit of discovering this source of water supply.

often afforded the money-changers an opportunity for exacting heavy charges in their transactions with the ignorant ryots.

Sayáji Ráo has taken special interest in education, and the number of schools in his territories has remarkably increased, being now nearly three times as many as they were when he assumed the reins of Government. In addition to these, a flourishing Arts College and a Techinal School have been established. In short the past twenty years of peace have been years of steady progress for Baroda, and Sayáji Ráo's rule has proved of great benefit to his subjects.

Chapter XV.

Refractory conduct of Ráv Bhármal of Kachh. His deposition and appointment of the Council of Regency. Ráv Desal formally installed on the throne. Khumán outlawry in Káthiáwár. Affairs in the Mahi Kánthá, Rewá Kánthá &c.

From 1818 to 1838 A. D.

Having in the preceding chapters narrated the history of Baroda from the downfall of the Peshwá to the present time, we now turn to the history of other parts of Gujarát. The period from 1818 to 1892 has been marked by great advances, and the province has enjoyed, in common with the rest of India under the benign rule of the British Government, a degree of peace and prosperity unknown in earlier times. There have, indeed, been occasions when the employment of military force became necessary, but these have been few and far between. In the early part of the present century Ráv Bhármal of Kachh proved somewhat refractory. Unmindful of the kindness shown to him by the British Government in remitting his annual tribute of two lacs of rupees together with the expense of the military expedition to Kachh he resumed his turbulent courses. At the end of 1818 he murdered his cousin Ládhubá, and commenced raising troops with the view of attacking Anjár. He also marched on Wághad, while its chief, who held a British guarantee, was in attendance at Captain Mac Murdo's camp. Unable to tolerate the continuance of such conduct, the British Government declared war against the Ráv, and on the 25th March 1819, the walls of Bhuj were escaladed. The Ráv surrendered on the following day. The British Government, unwilling to annex his territory, raised his infant son to the throne on the 19th April 1819 under the title of Mahá Rájá Mirzá Ráv Shri Desalji, and with the concurrence of the Jádejá Rajputs, appointed a Council of Regency to conduct the administration of the State during the prince's minority. The British Resident was, at the request of the Jádejás, appointed President of the new Council. A fresh treaty was concluded in October 1819, and a British force was stationed at Kachh for the protection of the country.

In A. D. 1822 a further act of grace was extended to the Kachh State by the British Government, when they relinquished the fort and district of Anjár for an annual payment of eighty-eight thousand rupees. Even this payment was, in consideration of the poverty of the State, discontinued in 1832, and all arrears were at the same time written off by order of the Honourable the Court of Directors.

Notwithstanding these favours, the ex-Ráv entered into a conspiracy against the Government, on the detection of which he was removed from Kachh. In the meantime, through the kindness of the Bombay Government, the young Ráo Desalji had been receiving a sound and thorough education. His first tutor was the Revnd. Mr. Grey. On the 8th of July 1834 the prince was installed on the throne amidst public rejoicings. The new Ráv, acting on the advice of his benefactors, prohibited the practice of female infanticide, and abolished the slave trade in his dominions. Ráv Desalji remained a faithful ally of the British Government during the whole of his reign, and, as an expression of his gratitude towards the British, supplied at his own expense camels for the first Afghán war of 1839.

Káthiáwár as well as Kachh enjoyed a long period of peace. For a time the Khumán outlaws gave some trouble, but, as has already been stated, they were eventually put down in 1829.

The Mahi Kánthá, always famous for the predatory habits and turbulent character of its inhabitants, also gave much trouble, which was, however, for the most part, confined within the limits of that province. The history of this part of the country, particularly that of Idar, given in Part II of this volume, shows that during the Muhammadan period Idar had always been a thorn in the side of the Ahmadábad Sultáns, who were obliged to make several expeditions against that State. During the Maráthá sway also, although the Gáekwád was acknowledged as the supreme power in Gujarát, the Mahi Kánthá chiefs, from the natural advantages possessed by their country, were able to defy the Gáekwád's army for long periods. For example, the village of Amaliárá is stated in Mr. A. K. Forbes' Rás Málá to have stood a siege of six months against a force seven thousand strong, though it had no fort or wall, but only a thorn hedge (probably the prickly pear) on one side and a narrow strip of jungle on the other. The village was eventually carried by assault, but a number of the Kolis rallied with such vigour that the besiegers fled precipitately, leaving their guns behind. On another occasion the inhabitants of Lohár, numbering about one thousand, enticed a Gáekwádi force of ten thousand men into a defile, whence they were able to extricate themselves only after much loss of life.

The first intervention of the British in the Mahi Kánthá dates from A. D. 1813, when Major Ballantyne,* Assistant Resident in charge of the province, following the example of Colonel Walker, effected a settlement of the Gáekwád's tribute, but the settlement appears at that time to have been merely nominal.

In 1818 the Peshwá's possessions having, by conquest, fallen to the English, the latter came into closer connexion with the Mahi Kánthá chiefs. The Gáekwád, unable to maintain order among them, passed an agreement on the 3rd of April 1820, making over the management of the Mahi Kánthá to the British

* This is the same Major Ballantyne, whose large Haveli (mansion) stands in the Three Gates Ward of Ahmadábád.

Government, who undertook to collect, without charge, the tribute due to the Gáekwád. In 1821, the Governor of Bombay, Mountstuart Elphinstone, visited this part of the country, and established the present Political Agency with the view of securing the tranquillity of the district, and providing for the peaceful collection of the Gáekwád's tribute. With this end in view the requisite agreements and securities were taken from the several chiefs.

In 1828 Mr. W. P. Willoughby was appointed Political Agent for the Mahi Kánthá, Panch Maháls and Rájpiplá, but he soon afterwards went on leave, and the Mahi Kánthá was placed under the Resident at Baroda with an Assistant at Sádrá to superintend the Gáekwád's contingent. More or less disorder, however, continued, and in 1833 the chief of Rupál seized a rich merchant, brother to the Minister of Idar, and refused to release him until a sum due to him by the Idar Chief Gambhirsingji, then deceased, was paid. The minister, unable to meet this demand, engaged Surajmal, son of the chief of Mandeti, a daring youth who had already gained notoriety as an outlaw, to procure his brother's release, and promised to pay him a handsome reward. Surajmal collected a band of mercenaries, and attacked and took Rupál, but, the minister failing to pay him the stipulated reward, he made good the amount by plundering some of the Idar villages. Several villages were also burnt. At this time the practice of Sati had become very general throughout the Mahi Kánthá. On the death of the Idar Chief Gambhirsingji on the 12th of August 1833 after a reign of forty-two years, seven of his Ránis, two concubines, one personal servant and four slave-girls immolated themselves in the presence of the assembled multitude. Only one Ráni with her infant son* was permitted to escape this

* This child, named Juwánsingh, succeeded his father, and subsequently obtained the honour of a seat in the Legislative Council of the Government of Bombay and the decoration of K. C. S. I.

painful death. Although the victims comported themselves in such a manner as to indicate their devotion to their deceased lord, the words uttered by the eldest of the Ránis, who was sixty years of age, evidenced their true feelings. Addressing the ministers assembled at the funeral pyre, she scornfully said that she had all along determined to follow her husband, but that it was strange that not a word of dissuasion had been addressed either to her or to the younger queens by any of the ministers. She then tauntingly bade them go and live on the plunder they were thus securing to themselves by the destruction of their chief's family. The sad spectacle was rendered the more pitiable as one of the Ránis, a girl of twenty, had been married to the chief only a single year. The slightest entreaties would perhaps have availed to prevent the sacrifice of at least some of these ladies.

Moved by this melancholy event, Mr. Erskine, who was then Political Agent, determined at all hazards to prevent a repitition of Sati in the Mahi Kánthá. Accordingly on the death of Karansingh, the Rájá of Ahmadnagar, in 1835, he moved his camp to that town. The Rajputs, however, collected a band of Bhils and Kolis, and even sought aid from Surajmal, the outlaw. Mr. Erskine had stationed guards at all the gates in order to prevent the widows of the Rájá being carried out to the funeral pyre. A new gate was, however, opened in the course of the night, and, in spite of the cries of the unhappy females, they were burnt along with their husband's corpse. During this painful occurrence one British officer is reported to have lost his life, being struck by an arrow when the Bhils were opposing the advance of the guard. It then became necessary to attack the city which had thus defied British authority. Intelligence was, however, received that Surajmal was marching to its assistance with one thousand Makránis, whereupon Mr.

Erskine, postponing the assault, applied for reinforcements to the General Officer Commanding the Northern Division. After the arrival of fresh troops, the fort of Ahmadnagar was stormed and taken on the 3rd of March 1835. Several other forts were also destroyed, but the outlaws evaded capture, and Surajmal continued to raid the Idar territory. He went so far as to make a bold assault on the town of Siddhpur belonging to H. H. the Gáekwád. An Atit (ascetic), named Rájbhárthi, had gone into outlawry because his claim to a monastery in Siddhpur had been disallowed. This man, joining Surajmal, persuaded him to espouse his cause on the promise of his mercenaries being adequately paid. Surajmal and the Atit went together to Siddhpur accompanied by some horsemen, who seized one of the principal merchants, named Lakhu Sheth, and took him with them as a hostage. Surajmal compelled the Sheth to supply bills on his firm, which were duly cashed, and thus the rebels for some time found an easy means of subsistence.

At length to put down this state of lawlessness Government considered it prudent again to constitute the Mahi Kánthá into a separate Agency, and appointed as Political Agent Captain, afterwards Sir, James Outram, who had early distinguished himself in restoring order and tranquillity in the Dángs and Khandeish. That officer so vigorously hunted down the leading outlaws that they were soon reduced to extremities. The Bombay Government were at that time of opinion that the principal outlaws had been compelled to have recourse to their life of rebellion by reason of family dissensions or unredressed grievances, and they therefore considered that, although none of the insurgents had been apprehended, they had been sufficiently punished by the dispersion of their followers, and by the taking and burning of their forts and villages. Believing therefore that the time had arrived when lenient measures could be taken with advantage, the Government, in consideration of the sufferings of the outlaws, proclaimed a general amnesty on the 7th of February 1836, and, on promise of their lands being restored to them on submission, invited the Chiefs in outlawry to return to their homes. A guarantee was also given that all their grievances would be fully inquired into and equitably redressed.

So depressed had the chiefs become by their wanderings and privations that they immediately availed themselves of the amnesty, and surrendered one after another. The British Government faithfully restored them their estates, which had been held in attachment during their outlawry, and received pledges from them to suppress the iniquitous custom of Sati, and to refrain from employing foreign mercenaries. In company with the Siddhpur merchant Lakhu Seth, Surajmal also submitted on the 7th of March 1836. He was granted two of his father's villages, and was appointed Captain of the garrison of Ilorá by the Idar Darbár, who took his troops into their pay. Rájbhárthi, the Atit of Siddhpur, surrendered to the Gáekwád's Government, and was by them kept in confinement for some months, but was subsequently placed in charge of the monastery in that town on his presenting a Nazáráná (present).

In short, by the conciliatory measures so wisely adopted by Government, and carried out with much tact and judgment by Captain Outram, tranquillity was restored in the Mahi Kánthá before the end of the year 1836. Captain Outram further restored the fair at Sámláji on the border between the Mahi Kánthá and Mewár, which, though of long standing, had fallen into disuse consequent on the disorders of the eighteenth and early part of the present century. This restoration, which took place in 1838, gave a welcome impetus to trade. He also established a system of border administration, and, with a view to the employment of the turbulent classes in the Mahi Kánthá, he formed a Bhil corps, which has since been amalgamated in the Ahmadábád Armed Police, and has done useful service.

About this time a military force had to be despatched against the widow of the Thakor of Amliárá, who, displeased at the succession to the Gádi of a posthumous son of another widow in preference to her own adopted son, betook herself to the hills along with the Thákors of Sáthambá, Rupál, and other chiefs. Their men were, however, soon dispersed, and both the widow and her son were taken prisoners. The chief of Rupál was subsequently arrested, and ended his days in the jail at Ahmadábád.

As regards the Rewá Kánthá, an agreement was concluded with the Gáekwád in A. D. 1820, by which the control of its tributary chiefs was vested in the British Government. Previous to this arrangement the Gáekwád had from time to time harassed the Rájpiplá chief, and had considerably enhanced the tribute to be paid by him. Pending the settlement of a dispute regarding the succession between the two rival claimants Rámsingh and Narsingh, Sayáji Ráo assumed the control of the Government in A. D. 1813. Though he retained possession of Rájpiplá for seven years, he was unable to effect a settlement, and disorder increased on all sides. At length the final decision of the matter was entrusted to Mr. J. P. Willoughby, the Assistant Resident at Baroda, and that officer, after a thorough enquiry, upheld Narsingh's claim. Narsingh himself, however, being blind, his son Vehrisálji was installed at Rájpiplá on the 15th of November 1821, after having entered into an engagement binding himself and his successors to act in conformity with the advice of the British Government.

Mr. Willoughby, by judicious arrangements for the collection of Revenue and by reducing to order the unruly Bhils, restored complete peace to the State in the four years of his administration, and the control over the Chief was thereafter relaxed. The Gáekwád's tribute was fixed at 65,000 Baroda Rupees. Since then it has occasionally become necessary to resume the management owing to the Chief's incapacity to administer its affairs efficiently, and at the present time the State is under the control of a British administrator of marked abitity.

Another event of importance in the Rewá Kánthá was the settlement of the Gáekwád's tribute from the Chief of Sánkhedá Mehwás in A. D. 1823. Two years later the control of the Panch Mahâls was transferred by Sindhiá to the British, and in 1838 the separate Politial Agency of the Rewá Kánthá was established. The same year witnessed a rising of the Náikrás in the Panch Mahâls, which, however, was put down by British troops, assisted by the Gáekwád, Sindhiá, and the chiefs of Báriá and Chhotá Udaipur.

Chapter XVI.

Affairs at Ahmadábád, Surat, Broach, Kairá and other places.

From 1818 to 1856 A. D.

The city of Ahmadábád was in a grievously dilapidated condition at the time of its transfer to the Honourable East India Company in November 1817. Only four years previously there had been heavy flood in the Sábarmati, and in 1819 occurred a severe shock of earthquake, which caused an incalculable amount of mischief not only in the city, but throughout the entire province and even in Kachh. Besides heavy loss in property and human life, it had an extraordinary effect on some of the springs of water. Mr. Briggs in his "Cities of Gujaráshtra", page 198, states that during his journey from Cambay to Ahmadábád in 1847, old Kunbis declared to him that they now required ten cubits less of rope than they had been obliged to employ previously in order to reach the surface of the water.

The ruined mosques and other buildings in the city gave shelter to thieves and robbers, and trade had come to a standstill in consequence of heavy town-duties and other imposts amounting in some cases to twenty-five per cent on the value of the goods taxed. Soon however, order was restored by the British Government, and an impetus was given to trade and manufactures by the immediate reduction of the town-duties to two and a half per cent, and the city soon again became prosperous.

At the end of 1824 the Kolis of the village of Dudhál near Kaira showed more than their usual refractory spirit, and repulsed a party of Native Infantry, the commandant of which, Lieutenant Ellis, was killed while storming the village. It was not until the beginning of 1825 that a wing of the 8th Native

Infantry and a squadron of dragoons were able effectully to restore order.

The next year an impostor named Govinddás Rámdás, who had persuaded his ignorant followers to believe that he was gifted with supernatural powers, attacked the town of Thásrá on the night of the 17th of March 1825 with about five hundred armed men with the object of turning out the local officer stationed by the British Government, but he did not succeed.

As regards Surat, the year 1837 is conspicuous for the great fire which took place in that city on the 24th of April. It continued for three days, and destroyed no less than nine thousand, three hundred seventy three houses of the estimated value of forty-six lacs, eighty-six thousand and five hundred rupees. There was also considerable loss of life and property.

On the 29th of August 1844 a riot took place at Surat in consequence of the imposition of a new duty on salt. It was suppressed by the District Magistrate, and a body of troops and artillery was despatched from Bombay to prevent further disturbances. Accordingly when the Salt Act was formally introduced on the 14th of Septembor following, perfect tranquillity prevailed.

In 1848 the people of Surat again resisted Government measures, the grievance complained of on this occasion being the introduction of the Bengal standard of weights and measures. The shops in the city were closed for several days, and placards were posted up threatening any who dared open their shops with expulsion from the community, and intimating that a sum of fifty thousand rupees had been subscribed "to contend the point at law as far as England". No breach of the peace was, however, committed. On the 5th of April a deputation waited on the District Magistrate, who gave them time to represent the matter officially to Government. The latter, on learning of the great unpopularity of the proposed change, decided on the 7th idem that the attempt to introduce new weights and measures should be abandoned.

This year, 1848, is further conspicuous as regards the city of Ahmadábád for the building of Sheth Hathisingh's Jain temple outside the Delhi gate on the road to the Cantonment. To the temple is attached a splendid mansion, which is often used, with the owner's permission, on occasions of public Darbárs and gatherings. The cost of the temple and of the mansion and other buildings attached has been estimated at a million rupees in addition to the large expense attending the consecration ceremonies, to witness which guests of the highest position, including the eldest son of Sir Jamsedji Jijibhái, Bart., Mr. Náná Shankar Sheth and others had arrived from Bombay and more distant cities. This speaks of the enormous wealth the bankers and merchants of Ahmadábád had been able to secure, under the benign sway of Britain, by free trade and by the commerce in opium with China. Hathisingh's father was not supposed to possess more than forty thousand rupees, but the son's property was estimated, when he died shortly before the completion of the temple he had so devoutly commenced, at eighty lacs of rupees. Another of the city merchants, Sheth Maganbhái Karamchand, also by his thrift amassed immense wealth, and, in spite of the prejudice then existing against the education of females, was the first to endow a vernacular school for girls, A. D. 1851. For this token of his public spirit, Sheth Maganbhái was rewarded with the title of Ráo Bahádur, an honour then for the first time conferred on a citizen of Ahmadábád.

An English school was established by Government at Surat

in 1842, and at Ahmadábád in November 1845, and the year 1848 witnessed the establishment of the Gujarát Vernacular Society at the last named city under the auspices of the lamented Mr. A. K. Forbes, Major Fulljames, Captain R. Wallace, Doctor G. Seaward and other philanthropic gentlemen.

The subsequent period (A. D. 1849 to 1856) was also one of profound peace and of steady progress for Gujarát. It was during this time that the surveys were commenced, A. D. 1853, for a railroad from Bombay to Gujarát, since which date railways have been opened through the length and breadth of the province, and have proved very beneficial to the country. Telegraphic communications were also established, and the education of the people steadily advanced.

Chapter XVII.

The Mutiny year, 1857. Its effect in Gujarát. Muhammadan riot at Broach. The arrival of Tátiá Topi, and his flight from the Panch Maháls. His betrayal and execution. End of the mutiny. Transfer of the Government of India to the Crown.

From 1857 to 1859 A. D.

The year 1857 was one of much disquiet throughout Gujarát. Designing persons put in circulation several false rumours, such as that the cartridges served out to the native troops had been intentionally greased with the fat of swine. Disaffection accordingly spread widely through the army, and some of the native regiments in Bengal mutinied and massacred their officers. The pensioned Emperor of Delhi, the infamous Nánà, adopted son of the late Peshwá Báji Ráo, the Begam of Bhopál, the Ráni of Jhánsi and others eagerly seized the opportunity to encourage the misguided sepoys in their suspicions, and, placing themselves at their head, caused much mischief for a time. The occurrences in Upper India do not, however, appertain to this History, and must therefore be omitted. Suffice it to say that so far as regards Gujarát the whole province was mercifully spared the ravages caused by the rebellion in several other parts of India. The refractory spirit that so widely prevailed in some districts did not affect the majority of the people of Gujarát, or the troops employed in that province. The authorities were also on the alert, and any slight symptoms that appeared were immediately checked by the Civil and Military officers, who proved themselves equal to the occasion. Among these we may mention Brigadier-General Sir R. Shakespear, Resident at Baroda, Brigadier-General F. Roberts, commanding Northern Division of the army, Major Buckle, Political Agent in the Rewá Kánthá, also Mr. Alexander Gray and Mr.

John William Hadow, then Collectors and District Magistrates of Kaira and Ahmadábád respectively, and Mr. L. R. Ashburner, then First Assistant Collector and Magistrate of Kaira, but invested with full military powers.

As stated above, Gujarat was much quieter than most other parts of India. Still there was some little commotion arising from the rumours of disaffection elsewhere, and accordingly traders and others resorted to their old expedient of burying their money and jewellery. Some of the native officers of the Gujarát Irregular Horse were indeed found to be faithless and in intrigue with the arsenal guard, but a severe example was made of them, and of the mutineers of the 2nd Grenadier Regiment, N. I. An irregular force* of about two thousand infantry and one hundred and fifty horse was also enlisted under Hussain Khán Batangi, a trusted Muhammadan gentleman, and this tended in some measure to keep the country quiet. In Kaira also an auxiliary police force was raised by Mr. Ashburner and Captain Thatcher, and some of the disaffected and ignorant Thákordás (minor Chiefs or landlords), who showed symptoms of disaffection, were tried by Mr. Ashburner, and transported to the Andamans. As soon, however, as the necessity for harsher measures was past, most of these men were, on representations submitted by the ever just and able Collector and Magistrate the late Mr. Alexander Gray, pardoned by Government, and sent back to their homes, where they have since remained peaceful and contented proprietors.

At Broach a riot took place, but enquiry proved that it had no connexion with the mutiny. The disturbance arose between Musalmáns and Pársis out of reports circulated by a Moulvi's son

---

* This force was commonly called the Hookah Paltan from the men carrying their hookahs with them.

to the effect that a Pársi, of no position or character, named Bezan Gándá (the mad) had defiled a mosque. A number of the cultivating Bohrás of surrounding villages, well known for their turbulent disposition, assembled on the 15th of May 1857 at the Báwá Rehn Dargáh about a mile from the city, where the District Magistrate Mr. C. J. Davies and the Superintendent of Police went to expostulate with them, leaving the Police drawn up near the city. The infatuated mob, however, would not listen to the advice of these officers, and went to the city, which they entered, and in conjunction with some of the Musalmáns of the city commenced to assail the Pársis. The latter were quite unprepared, some being busy in their homes, others in the market, while some were out holiday making. The Police, who consisted mostly of Musalmáns with a Muhammadan Inspector at their head, failed to check the progress of the riot, and, before the military could be called out, the rioters had slain both Bezan and a Pársi high priest, the latter of whom was killed while officiating before the altar in a fire temple. Twenty prisoners were lodged in the jail, but no immediate inquiry into their guilt was instituted, in consequence of rumoured risings in connexion with mutinies in different parts. The military force was, however, augmented by the arrival of troops from Baroda. On the 13th of June Government sent from Surat Mr. Alexander Rogers*, an energetic officer of the Civil Service, with instructions to report fully on the disturbance. As a result of his inquiry, several offenders were committed for trial to the Sessions Court, in which on the 23rd

---

* Mr. Rogers is still remembered in these parts as an excellent Revenue and Judicial Officer. By his knowledge and ability he distinguished himself in the service, and was appointed Settlement Officer of the Revenue Survey, then for the first time introduced into Gujarát. The assessments fixed by him were reasonable and moderate. He rose to be Commissioner of the Northern Division, and later on Member of Council,

August forty-seven of the accused were convicted by Mr. A. K. Forbes, then Session Judge. Two of these were sentenced to be hanged, eleven to be transported beyond the sea for the term of their lives, and the rest to various terms of imprisonment. Although this riot does not appear to have had any connexion with the rebellion in Upper India, advantage of it seems to have been taken by some of the chief mutineers to send emissaries to induce the Musalmán population of the district to revolt. A close watch was, however, kept on all suspected characters, and in September Government was able to station a company of Europeans at Broach, so that all danger of mutiny was averted. In the month of August the Chief of Rájpiplá sent information that in his capital of Nándod a certain Sayyid, named Murád Ali, was trying to organize a disturbance, and had succeeded in gaining over the Militia and troops. Mr. Rogers, with his wonted energy, at once started for Nándod with a detachment of two hundred native and fifty European soldiers, and the Sayyid forthwith fled. Thus, through Mr. Roger's promptitude, this attempted rising in the hilly country of Rájpiplá was crushed at the very outset.

Unbroken peace appears to have prevailed at Surat, though in the words of Mr. Campbell, the able compiler of the Bombay Gazetteer*, the Musalmáns of that city "were ready at a moment's notice to rise" The quiet is attributed to the beneficial exercise† of his influence amongst the people by Shaikh Sáheb Sayyid Hussain Idrus, the head of one of the chief Musalmán families in Surat. In reward for this service, the Government increased Sayyid Idrus's annual allowance by rupees five hundred, and conferred on him the decoration of the Companionof the Star of India.

---

* Page 275 of Vol. VII (Baroda).

† Page 157 of Vol. II. (Surat and Broach).

289 Affairs in the Panch Maha'ls.

The district of the Panch Mahâls was the only part of Gujarât in which the brunt of the rebellion of 1857 was felt to any perceptible degree. Hearing exaggerated reports of the temporary success of the rebellion in the north, the refractory characters in Dohad, headed by Táredárkhán, a leading Kanogá* and Inámdár of Abhor, and Chunilál Desái, assembled to the number of five hundred, and on the 6th of July laid siege to the fort of Dohad, in which the Mámlatdár and other officers lived, and which contained the public offices also. The Mámlatdár immediately sent secret information to the Political Agent Captain Buckle by a confidential person, and that officer at once came up with detachments and guns from Baroda, distant about ninety miles. Hearing of this, and disappointed at not finding the mutineers near, the Kanogás, the Desái and others fled, 11th of July. Captain Buckle arrested several persons implicated in this conspiracy, and inflicted exemplary punishments on them. Some were blown from guns, some were transported, and others sentenced to long terms of imprisonment. Táredárkhán and other leading Kanogás, however, fled, and nothing has been heard of them ever since. It is scarcely necessary to add that the lands and estates of the misguide Kanogás and Desái were sequestrated.

After this Tátyá Topi, the Commander of Náná's forces, on his defeat on at Gwálior in 1858 at the close of the mutiny, came to the Deccan, where, in consequence of the hot pursuit by columns under Generals Somerset and Mitchell, and a field force under Colonel Parke, his march soon assumed the nature of a flight, On Tátyá's arrival at the town of Chhotá-Udaipur on the 30th of November 1858 with the remnant of the mutinous Bengal regiments, the Rájá's troops cordially received him, and he was enabled to occupy the town. Here he hoped to recruit

---

* An hereditary officer of the Customs Department.

his men and develop his intrigues with some of the Baroda Sardárs, and the smaller chiefs of Kaira and Rewá Kánthá, who, he thought, were disaffected. But as soon as it was known that Tátyá had crossed the Narbadá, troops were put in motion from Kairá, Ahmadábád and Disá. Captain Thatcher held Sankhedá with the Kaira auxiliary Police force and two of the Gáekwád's guns. Godhrá and Dohad, in the latter of which town symptoms of rebellion had already appeared as stated above, were also held by detachments under military officers. Thus, none of the mischievous characters was able to gain many adherents, nor would the mutineers venture an attack on these places, which, from their reputed wealth, would otherwise have attracted their attention. In the meantime, Colonel Parke, with the 72nd Highlanders mounted on camels, fell upon Tátyá on the 1st of December 1858, and defeated him with great slaughter. Tátyá fled precipitately, and his army broke into two divisions. One of these, however, doubled back, and was able to plunder Colonel Parke's baggage, which had fallen considerably in the rear, while the other under Firoz Sháh looted Báryá, Jhálod, Limbdi and other villages. Accordingly General Somerset at once took up the pursuit, and drove the rebel army from the Panch Mahále. On the 20th of February 1859 Firoz Sháh made overtures of surrender, and a few days later a force of fifteen hundred infantry and three hundred cavalry laid down their arms before General Mitchell. Tátyá, however, continued his flight until he was betrayed by one Máusingh, Chief of Narwár, situated forty-four miles south of Gwálior, who caused him to be seized by a detachment of British troops on the 7th of April 1859. After his capture Tátyá was tried by a Court-Martial and condemned to be hanged, which sentence was executed at Siprá on the 18th April 1859. Thus was extinguished the last spark of the great rebellion. It may be mentioned that Náná, the chief of the rebels and the murderer of innocent women and children at Cawnpore, fled with the scattered remains of his army to the jungles of the Terái at the foot of the Nepál hills, where many of the fugitives fell a prey to the pestilential climate, which proved to them as fatal as the sword they had dreaded and sought to avoid. Náná is supposed to have been one of the victims. Thus ended the formidable rebellion, in which about a hundred and fifty thousand native troops had taken part. Most of the Indian princes, however, and all the more peaceful of the inhabitants, fully confiding in the strength of Britain, and foreseeing that the result could not but end in disaster to the refractory, remained loyal to the British Government, the benefits derived from which only the self-interested had, for the time, forgotton.

One great result of the mutiny was that Parliament came to the decision that the British dominion in India had grown too large to be governed by a body of merchants, and that it was expedient that that vast empire should be ruled by the Crown itself. An Act (Statute 21 and 22 Victoriá, Chapter 106) for the better government of India was accordingly passed,* and Her Majesty the Queen issued a proclamation assuming the supreme control.† On 1st November 1858, this proclamation was read in all the cities and towns of India amidst public rejoicings. By it all existing dignities, rights, usages and treaties were confirmed, and the people were assured that the British Government had neither the right nor desire to interfere with their religion. An amnesty was granted to all mutineers with

* This Act received the royal assent on the 2nd of August 1858.

† Her Majesty Qmeen Victoriá assumed the title of Empress of India on the 1st January 1877, on which date an Imperial Darbár was held in honour of that event at Delhi, when many princes, chiefs and nobles attended and were granted suitable titles. An increase was also made to the number of salutes assigned to several of the princes.

the exception of those only who had been implicated in murders. The right of adoption was also granted to several princes and chiefs.

It is worthy of record here, in connexion with the story of the mutiny, that the Almighty having granted victory to the British arms, and thus freed the country from a crushing calamity, Lord Canning, the Governor-General, publicly proclaimed peace on the 8th of July 1859, and fixed the 18th of that month as a day of general thanksgiving and humble expression of gratitude to God for the many and great mercies vouchsafed by Him. It need not be stated that all classes of the people in Gujarát, as indeed all over India, heartily joined in praise to the Great Controller of all events for His signal deliverance of the Government and country.

CHAPTER XVIII.

Rising of the Náekrás in the Panch Mahâls in 1858, their surrender. Fresh rising in 1868. Execution of the ringleaders. Transfer of the Panch Mahâls to the British Government in exchange for territory near Gwâlior given to Sindhiá.

FROM 1858 to 1868 A. D.

Since the mutiny two local risings have taken place in the Panch Mahâls. In 1858 the Náekrás of Sankhedá rose in rebellion, and under their leaders Rupá aud Keval, plundered the *Thànà* (outpost) at Nárukot, and attacked a detachment of the 8th Regiment N. I., then under Captain Bates at Jámbughodá. Though repulsed with loss, they were joined by some armed Viláyatis of Tátyá Topi's broken band, and, occupying the country between Chámpáner and Nárukot, kept plundering the villages as far as Godhrá. A field force had to be employed against them and frequent skirmishes ensued. On one occasion they put to flight a company of Husain Khán's Irregular levy under a native Subedár, who had been rash enough to neglect the ordinary precautions. A Bhil corps was then raised, having its headquarters at Dohad, and the Náekrá leaders at length surrendered in 1859. The year 1858 is further noteworthy as the year in which the disarming of the people took place throughout India. Owing to military arrangements that had been effected, no considerable opposition was made, and the people of Gujarát quietly surrendered their arms. Some of the more respectable members of the community were, however, granted licenses to keep weapons for purposes of sport or for defence of their crops. As regards the Gáekwád's territory, His Highness Khande Ráo gave his cordial support to the measure.

In 1868 the Panch Mahâls District was a scene of considerable disturbance. One Joriá, a Náekrá of Wádak near

Jambughodá, most blasphemously calling himself Parameshwar pretended that he could work miracles, and thus gained a following of superstitious and bigoted persons, the most prominent of whom was Rupsing, a proprietor of Dándiápurá. They assumed a joint rule at Wádak, and collected revenue by imposing religious fines and transit duties. The native officials at first made light of their pretensions, and did not even report the matter to the Agent Mr. Propert. At length, however, .these despised Náekrás became so daring that on the 2nd of February they went to the outpost at Rájgadh with several armed men. Leaving these outside, Joria and Rupsingh went inside, and seated themselves near the native commandant. In the course of the conversation, which turned on Joriá's supernatural powers, one of the officials, holding out his closed hand, asked him to tell what was in it. Rupsing's son Galáliá angrily replied "Death", and immediately, drawing his sword, cut the unfortunate man in two. On this the Makráni guard at once took to flight, and the Náekrás plundered the place. Rupsingh then advanced on the chief station Jámbughodá, where the Police fired a volley at the insurgents. As none fell, the Police were panic-sticken under a conviction of Joriá's miraculous power, and fled precipitately leaving two of their number dead. The Náekrás then pillaged Jámbughodá, and tore up the Government records. They then went to Jetpur, at that time the residence of the Chhotá-Udaipur Chief, who also fled in dismay. Here, however, two of Joriá's followers were killed, and thus the confidence of his men that they were bullet-proof was somewhat shaken.

The Agent to the Governor, Mr. W.H. Propert, the Superintendent of Police, Captain Segrave, and his Assistant, Lieutenant Westmacott, who were then about eighty miles distant, as soon as they heard of the sack of Rájgadh, sent expresses to Ahmadábád and Baroda, and themselves started with about twenty men of the Bhil corps by cross roads to Jámbughodá. On the road these officers heard of the capture of the latter place, and accordingly they halted at Hálol, distant from it twenty-five miles. Here two hundred men of the 26th N. I., under the command of two European officers arrived from Baroda on the 11th of February 1868. The able and energetic Commissioner of the Northern Division, Mr. A. Rogers, also joined the troops. A company of infantry from Ahmadábád was also expected. Hence, leaving a few men at Hálol, the force proceeded to Sivrájpur, a detachment being also sent to Rájgadh to join the Political Agent of the RewáKánthá. So assured was the conviction of the wild Náekrás in the supernatural powers of their spiritual leader Joriá, that over a district of many miles the Náekrá inhabitants fully believed that the British sovereignty had come to an end, and that the day of their own supremacy had dawned. Leaving some men at Sivrájpur, the force advanced to Jámbughodá on the 15th. This emboldened the Náekrás to attack Sivrájpur, but before long they were obliged to retire to Wádak with the loss of some of their men.

The British force then marched from Jámbughodá to Wádak under the command of Captain Macleod with the Police Commissioner Mr. Rogers and the Agent Mr. Propert, and found the Náekrás scattered on the sides of the hill. As the troops approached, one man in bright yellow and red was observed moving about with his followers, of whom some were armed with bows and arrows, while others were dancing in religious frenzy. The cavalry made a dash to cut off their retreat to the hill, but, two attempts to strike the man in red and yellow having failed, the troopers believed he possessed a charmed life, and fell back. This proceeding emboldened the Náekrás, who discharged their arrows with such effect that an officer of the Puná horse was killed on the spot, and Captain Macleod himself had a narrow escape. The Náekrás continued to advance until they reached a water-course, where a shot from each of the three district officers laid their magician leader and two of his devoted followers dead on the field, 16th February 1868. It was not, however, until nine more of the insurgents had fallen that the Náekrás fled, and from that day their rebellion was at an end. The man in red and yellow was found not to be Joriá, but one whom the latter had decked in his own clothes. A diligent search was made for Joriá, Rupsingh, Galáliá, and Joriá's minister. They were all apprehended within a month, and, after being duly convicted, were sentenced to be hanged. Ever since then, the Panch Mahâls have remained quiet.

In connexion with the Panch Maháls it may be mentioned that that district, including the hill fort of Páwágad and the once famous city of Chámpáner, belonged to Sindhiá. In consequence of the great difficulty of managing this hill country from Gwálior, Sindhiá in 1853 entrusted its control for ten years to the British Government. This proved to be a very fortunate occurrence, for, had it been under Sindhiá's rule during the mutiny of 1857, the wild inhabitants of that district would in all probability have made common cause with the insurgents when they took Gwálior, and thus the rebellion would have seriously affected Baroda and all Gujarát. Before the expiry of the ten years' term, Sindhiá in A. D. 1861 ceded the Panch Maháls in perpetuity to the British Government in exchange for territory equal in extent near Gwálior. The exchange has been of benefit to the Panch Maháls. Metalled roads have been constructed through the length and breadth of the district, regular revenue and judicial systems have been established, and schools and dispensaries have been opened. Railway communication has been established with Bombay and other places by a line from Godhrá to Dohad, and a further extension as far as Ratlam is in progress.

CHAPTER XIX.

The Share Mania. Riot at Surat in connexion with the introduction of the License Tax. The Taláviа riot at Broach. Bakri-Id disturbance at Dholká. Riots at Cambay. Management of that State undertaken by Government. Outlawries in Káthiáwár.

From 1866 TO 1892 A. D.

The period of eight years subsequent to the mutiny was of great prosperity to the country. The breaking out of the American War in 1863, with the consequent demand for Indian cotton, and the opening of the Bombay, Baroda and Central India Railway between 1860 and 1864 contributed to this result. The cultivating classes, especially in the cotton growing districts, had perhaps never been so well off as they were during the decade beginning in 1856. The Share Mania, however, in 1866 ruined many of the respected families. Still on the whole, the country has been most prosperous, notwithstanding various natural calamitous occurrences such as storms, fires, floods &c., a detailed mention of which would unduly swell this volume. Those mentioned below are, however, too important to be entirely omitted :—

In A. D. 1868 there was heavy rain at Ahmadábád between the 11th and 15th of August, the quantity registered in these four days being twenty-seven inches. This, together with the wind which blew very violently, destroyed no fewer than nine thousand five hundred houses of the computed value of upwards of nine lacs, and fifty thousand rupees. Much loss was also caused in the district.

The flood of 23rd September 1875 is fresh in the memory of the people of Ahmadábád as the highest on record, by which a great part of the city was under water. Upwards of three

38

thousand eight hundred houses fell, causing a computed loss of five lacs and eighty-two thousand rupees, besides injury to other property calculated at one lac and sixty-four thousand, and the loss of twelve lives. Outside the city walls about one hundred villages suffered more or less. Also the railway bridge over the Sábarmati, constructed at a cost of more than three lacs of rupees, and the Ellis Bridge over the same river, which only five years before had cost Government five lacs cf rupees were swept away.*

On both these occasions strenuous efforts were made by Government and by the liberal public of Bombay, Surat, Ahmad ábád and other cities to alleviate the distress.

Surat suffered from a very severe flood on the 3rd of July 1883, and also from a great fire in 1889.

In Broach there was very heavy rain at the end of July 1891, about twenty-four inches falling in one night and day, and causing the destruction of a number of houses in low lands and the loss of two or three lives.

As regards local disturbances, a riot broke out in the city of Surat in A. D. 1878 to oppose the introduction of the License Tax (subsequently converted into an Income Tax), when the traders of that city combined to close their shops from 1st to 5th April. On this occasion the mob had the audacity to go to the railway

---

* While this book was passing through the press, the city of Ahmadábád narrowly escaped a similar calamity on the 15th of September 1893, when, in consequence of heavy rain towards the north, the water in the Sábarmati rose about 32 feet high between 11 P. M. and 3 A. M. Indeed some of the lower portions of the city were flooded, but fortunately the water abated from 3 A. M. on the 16th. There was also much destruction of house-property at Disá, Pálanpur, and other towns, the quantity of rain registered in the former town alone on the day in question being no less then 14 Inches.

station, and demand the stoppage of trains, in order to make the strike more effective. On their refusal to disperse, three of the rioters were shot dead and two wounded. Several were put on their trial, and were sentenced, some to transportation and others to long terms of imprisonment. A punitive post was also kept up for some five years at the cost of the inhabitants*

Another serious disturbance was created by certain Taláviás, a low class of aborigines kindred to the Bhils. 'Of late years Government had made several efforts to induce the Taláviás to become peaceful cultivators in the Panch Mahals, where there is much waste land, and with that object had incurred much expense, but owing to their want of thrift, all efforts failed. In the monsoon of 1885 a number of these Taláviás came to Broach under the leadership of two Bhagats of their own caste, who induced them to believe that their Mátá (goddess) had promised them a kingdom. At first they were treated with contempt, and so little notice appears to have been taken of them, that the headman was enabled to send circulars to people living in the district to gather round his banner at Broach on the day of the full moon, the 22nd of November 1885. About one hundred Taláviás arrived, armed some with bows and arrows, and others with swords or sticks. They went first to the Collector's bungalow, which was not far from the place where the Bhagat had put up under a tree near the Id-gáh. Learning from the peons that the Collector, Mr. William Allen, was not at home, the mob left the bungalow for the town. On the road they happened to meet Mr. W. B. Prescott, Superintendent B. B. & C. I. Railway Police, who was driving in his tonga. That gentleman was, of course, quite unarmed and unprepared for any hostile encounter. On shouting to the crowd to make room

* See Mr. Edalji Barjorji Patel's Gujaráti History of Surat, page 175.

for his carriage, they fell upon the unfortunate officer, and beat him so severely that he soon became unconcious, and died within three hours. Thinking him already dead, the mob left for the town, and on their way took from the first Police Choki on the road the swords of the policemen, who also were off their guard. They then marched on the Bombay Bank in the town, but were there opposed by the sentries. These discharged against them only unloaded muskets, whereupon the Taláviás exclaimed that their goddess had melted the bullets, so that nothing but smoke should come out from the guns. Finding that they could not enter the Bank, the Taláviás marched through the town. Outside the town, however, they were overtaken by the Hazur Deputy Collecter and Magistrate Mr. Bamanji Edalji Modi and the Police Inspector the late Mr. Krishna Ráo Gajánand, who, with a few men hastily picked up from the Police lines, had set off in pursuit. Near a culvert a slight engagement took place, in which four Policemen were wounded, one of them fatally. Mr. Modi is also said to have had a narrow escape from the arrows freely discharged by the Taláviás. The Police then fired on them, killing five and wounding the same number. After the second volley, the Taláviás fled, and in the immediate pursuit forty of them were captured, while many others, including Lákhá Bhagat, were subsequently arrested.* They were of course proceeded against and Lákhá, as well as two of his principal adherents, were hanged at the scene of the crime. Fifty-one were sentenced by the Sessions Judge to transportation for life, but the High Court remitted the sentences of seventeen of these. One of the ring-leaders, styled the Mátá, who had escaped, was afterwards captured and placed on

* That day was the day of the Sukaltirth fair, and, had the progress of the rioters not been arrested, they would in all probability have committed havoc among the pilgrims, and done very serious mischief.

his trial, but owing to his identity not being satisfactorily proved, this so called Máta was discharged.

Another, though a less important, disturbance occurred on the 30th of August 1887 at the town of Dholká, when the Musalmáns, in retribution for the Hindu traders having closed their shops on the Bakri-Id day, marched through the city in procession, taking with them a cow, which, in spite of the remonstrances of the Subordinate Magistrate and the principal Hindus, they killed in the middle of the market, close to a Hindu temple. They dressed the carcase there and then, and recklessly paraded it, much to the annoyance of the Hindus, who had assembled to prevent the slaughter. The local officers, only with the utmost difficulty, managed to preserve the peace and prevent immediate bloodshed. The writer of these pages, who was then District Deputy Collector and Magistrate at Ahmadábád, on hearing of the disturbance, lost no time in proceeding to Dholká with the Police Inspector, Mr. A. F. Grey, who brought with him a few Policemen, both horse and foot, from the head quarters. Mr. G. B. Reid, then Collector and District Magistrate also came up, and a most searching enquiry was instituted, in which fourteen of the persons arraigned for the disturbance were convicted and sentenced to various terms of imprisonment, and ordered to furnish security for their good conduct for one year.

The year 1890 was an important one in the administration of Cambay. The people of that state had long been expecting the introduction of the British Survey rates in their villages, and were grievously disappointed on learning that not only was the former system to be retained, but the rates of assessments were to be enhanced. The opposition of the villagers in the month of September took the form of open resistance, when they held Cambay in a state of siege*. Accordingly the Political

* See Bombay Administration Report for 1890-91, pages 9 and 10.

Agent, the late Mr. H. R. Cooke thought it necessary to obtain military assistance from Ahmadábád, and the riot was not quelled until the insurgents were fired upon and some had fallen.

In October 1890 a Special Political officer was appointed by Government, to whom His Highness the Nawab has delegated his authority, and the administration is conducted by that officer with the assistance of a Diwán, also nominated by Government. It is satisfactory to remark that the new administration has succeeded in liquidating a great portion of the State debts, in introducing the Survey rates, and in effecting other much needed reforms.

It must also be recorded that in portions of Káthiáwár there has been, during the last few years, considerable lawlessness, and Bahárvatiás (outlaws) have committed serious robberies and dacoities. According to the General Administration Report of the Presidency for 1885-86 there occurred, in that year, no less than one hundred and twelve robberies, and ninety-nine dacoities. It would appear that most of the dacoits were Makránis, who had gone into open rebellion against the Junághad Darbár. Nineteen persons are reported to have been killed by these outlaws, while ninety-three were wounded, and eighteen carried off as hostages. A distinguished Police officer, Colonel J. Humfrey, who was well acquainted with the country, and whose tact and ability eminently fitted him for the work, was appointed for the apprehension of the dacoits. With that officer's strenuous exertious outlawry was for the time effectually checked. It is, however, to be regretted that in 1891-92, the spirit of outlawry again broke out on the part of a daring band of Miánás, subjects of the Thakor of Máliá. Beginning the year in Kachh, where they carried off the Dák horses laid for His Excellency the Governor for his journey to Junághad, they crossed to Káthiáwád, where they committed several dacoities, and some encounters took place between them and the Police of Dhrángadhrá, Morvi, Návánagar and other States. The Agency and State Police having failed to terminate the career of the new gangs, special measures for their arrest were taken by Government. These comprised the appointment of several additional European Police officers, and the re-inforcement of the local Police by detachments of regular troops, both cavalry and infantry. On Monday the 29th of December 1892, Lieutenant H. L. Gordon, who had only lately been appointed Assistant Superintendent of the Agency Police, received information that certain Miáná dacoits were in the vicinity. That officer, with seventeen or eighteen sowárs, at once marched against them, and turning them to the Ran of Khodiár, fell upon them, and destroyed the entire band of about a dozen. Lieutenant Gordon, while rushing bravely forward, was killed, receiving no less than nine bullet wounds. A Dafedár and a Náik of the Agency Police also fell, and three sowárs were wounded. It being evident that the chief of Máliá was unable to control his more refractory subjects, that State has, since September 1892, been placed under the direct management of the Agency.

Another event worth recording was the breaking out into open fight of the longstanding animosities between the Hindus and Musalmáns of Prabhás Pátan in Junághad, which resulted in serious loss of life and destruction of property. The agitation caused by the sympathizers of the two parties in Bombay was so great that the contagion spread to that town, where also serious riots took place in August 1893 between the lower classes of Hindus and Muhammadans, and resulted not only in the destruction of temples and mosques, but in loss of life on both sides. The riots grew to such proportions that it became necessary to obtain the assistance of the military to put them down.

Chapter XX.

Brief notice of the arrangements made for the Civil Administration of the Province from the time that Gujarát came into the possession of the British Government Conclusion.

From 1800 to 1892 A. D.

Having, in the preceding three chapters, narrated the chief political and other occurrences subsequent to the period when it pleased the Almighty to place Gujarát under the benign rule of the British Government, it is now our pleasing duty to indicate briefly the features of the arrangements introduced by the East India Company for the internal administration of the country. To do this in detail would require a minute study of the records of Government and other authorities, and would moreover fill a separate volume. It is therefore proposed briefly to notice only the most important of the changes introduced. In A. D. 1800 an Act was passed for regulating the administration of the then newly acquired district of Surat. In 1802, a Collector of Land Revenue was appointed for that district, his duties being defined by Regulation 13 passed in the same year. A Revenue Commission was also instituted to inquire into the several tenures then existing. On the recommendation of that Commission, a detailed and scientific survey of the Broach district was commenced as early as 1811, and in little more than two years this work was completed. The benefits to be derived therefrom being obvious, the Survey was extended to other districts of Gujarát. This was called the "Máji Jarif" or old survey, which has been superseded since 1853 by a regular system of Revenue Survey and classification of Assessment*. These are,

* A detailed account of the Revenue Administration is given in Vol. I of Mr. Rogers' recently published History of the Revenue Administration of the Bombay Presidency.

in the interest of the ryots, guaranteed for the long period of thirty years, and have contributed greatly to their convenience.

In the Kairá Collectorate, large tracts were flooded every year causing thereby great loss in cultivation and a high death rate. The Government accordingly undertook extensive drainage works, which in course of time have proved very successful in remedying the evil. Stipendiary Accountants, called Talátis, were appointed in A. D. 1814–15 to realise the revenue direct from the ryots, instead of through farmers who were often oppressive to cultivators, and to keep correct statistical and financial registers. In 1827 elaborate regulations were judiciously framed for the constitution of the district and village Police, and for the conduct of the Civil, Revenue and Criminal jurisdiction, as well as on a variety of other subjects. In 1829 the horrible crime of Sati (self immolation of women after the death of their husbands), for the suppression of which Government had long made strenuous exertions, was prohibited by law, and abettors were made criminally responsible.

As regards the city of Ahmadábád, it has already been mentioned that the town duties had been reduced, after which its commerce rapidly revived. The city-wall had fallen to ruins, and as a consequence thefts and robberies had become frequent. It was, therefore, in the year 1832 thoroughly repaired out of the proceeds of a special voluntary cess, called the Kot-fee (town-wall fee). The balance remaining over became the nucleus of a Municipal fund, which has since proved of much benefit to the city. Many useful public schemes have been completed, prominent amongst which, in recent times, is the water supply for the city. This was carried out mainly through the advocacy of the energetic President of the Municipality, the Honourable Ráo Bahádur Ranchhodlál Chhotálál, C.I.E., at a cost of about eight lacs of rupees. The works were formally opened by Lord Harris, Governor of Bombay, on the 11th of June 1891. Drainage works on an extensive scale have also been started.

Municipalities have been created at Surat, Broach, Kairá, Nadiád and other towns of importance, and have proved very useful in providing for the sanitation and conservancy of these towns, as well as for the construction and repair of several useful works. To these as well as to Local Boards,* established for the provision of roads, water supply, rest-houses and other works in the districts, the franchise of Local Self Government has been given in accordance with Bombay Acts I and II of 1884 under the initiative proposed by the late Lord Mayo, and carried out by Lord Ripon.

Education, the great pioneer of all reforms and of the social advancement of the people, has made rapid strides. Numerous schools have been opened all over the province. In the British districts of Gujarát alone, there are, besides an Arts College, with a Law Class attached, 4 high schools, 52 middle schools, 5 special schools and 1339 primary schools.†

---

* Local Boards have the control of a fund created by imposing an additional cess of one anna on every rupee of assessment of Land Revenue payable to Government. Two-thirds of this levy are set apart for the providing and maintenance of roads, wells, tanks and other useful objects, and one third for education.

† As regards education in English, it would be ingratitude to omit mention of the fact that the country is much indebted to the endeavours of the missionaries, sent out by several Societies in Great Britain, Ireland and America. Long before the establishment of Government English Schools, these charitable associations had founded their schools in the cities of Surat and Ahmadábád. It is true their object was primarily the propagation of the Christian religion, but it should cordially be acknowledged that the Mission Schools were for years the only institutions where a knowledge of English was imparted to the people of Gujarát. Large Mission High Schools still exist at Ahmadábád and Surat.

In the native states too, educational progress has been almost equally rapid and diffused. The educational work in Baroda has already been alluded to. Bhávnagar has an Arts College of its own, and it is pleasing to mention that that state, and also many others, have liberally provided for the education of their subjects. Before the country came into the possession of the East India Company, the only schools which are known to have existed for the education of the masses were those maintained by private school masters, mostly Bráhmans, and the standard of education may be judged from the fact that boys who had learnt merely to read and write, and to keep a few simple accounts were regarded as having "finished their education". None the less, in spite of difficulties, several men of literary reputation flourished in the province. Names of some of these are given below :—

1. Bhálan Poet, born at Pátan in or about Samvat 1495, (A. D. 1439).
2. Bhálan's son Bhim.
3. Bhim's contemporary, Narsi Mehta.
4. Sámalbhat, born at the village of Sihuj, Taluká Mahmudábád.
5. Sámal's contemporay, Premánand, born at Baroda in or about Samvat 1488 (A. D. 1432).
6. Premánand's son Vallabh.
7. Dayárám Kavi of Chándod.
8. Dalpatrám Dáyábhái, C. I. E.
9. Narbadáshakar Lálshankar.

The under-mentioned are the chief Musalmán historians of Gujarát:—

1. Ali Muhammad Khán, author of the Mirát-i-Ahmadi.
2. Sikandar bin Muhammad, or, Manjáh, author of the Mirát-i-Sikandari.

3. Halvai Shirázi, author of the Tawárikh-i-Ahmadi.

4. Abu Turáb, author of Tawárikh-i-Gujarát.

5. Háji Khán, Poet, who flourished in the time of Sultán Mahmud Begadá.

Last to be mentioned, but not the least, are the means of communication so very necessary for the development of trade and commerce. It may safely be said that, before the country came into British possession, there was not a metalled or made road in the province. Shortly after the East India Company assumed the Government of Gujarát, a good road was constructed from the port of Goghá, *via* Dhandhuká and Bávlá, to Ahmadábád and thence to Harsol, a length of one hundred and sixty-two miles. After this a branch from Sarkhej to Viramgám, a distance of thirty miles, was constructed at a cost of upwards of two hundred twenty-six thousand rupees. Since then numerous roads and bridges have been constructed throughout the province at an enormous cost, to the great development of trade. Since 1860 still greater benefits have been conferred on the country by the B. B. & C. I. Railway, also by the Rájputáná Málwá Railway opened in 1877, and by the several Káthiáwár railways constructed since 1880 by the chiefs of Bhávanagar, Gondal, Junágadh, Porbandar and Morvi.

These facilities have greatly improved the conditition of the people, both traders and agriculturists, whose produce now finds its way to the remotest parts of the country and to foreign lands, whereas formerly the demand was for the most part confined to the province itself, and prices were consequently low.

With all these advantages, the facilities afforded by postal and telegraphic communication must not be lost sight of. These are not confined to cities and towns alone, but arrangements for receipt and delivery of letters have been extended to those villages where there are schools, and letter boxes are placed at most of the smaller villages even. Thus for the trifling cost of a quarter or half an anna, all persons are enabled to communicate with the most distant parts of India.

As education, and with it the condition and status of the people increased, Government created new posts such as those of Deputy Collectors and Magistrates, Judges of Small Cause Courts and other appointments. Government have also raised the pay and grades of Subordinate Judges and Mámlatdárs (Reveme officers with magisterial powers), and have opened to natives, on their passing a certain standard of exanimation in England, appointments in the Civil Service, with the result that now native gentlemen are holding some of the most responsible appointments in the Revenue, Judicial, Educational, Postal and other departments, appointments formerly reserved for European officers alone. It is to the credit of the natives also that they have generally discharged faithfully and efficiently the high trusts reposed in them. Each of the High Courts has a native judge on its Bench, and natives have seats in the Legislative Councils, which have very lately been enlarged in order to provide for the better representation of the people. The right of interpellation has also been granted under certain conditions and restrictions.

Peace abroad and tranquillity at home are the mottoes of the British Government in India. By the feuds of neighbours, the quarrels of chiefs, and the strife of nations, the inhabitants of Gujarát were, for hundreds of years, exposed to all the losses and horrors which civil war and foreign invasion can bring upon a people. Irregular and arbitrary taxation, forced labour, uncertainty of possession, religious persecution, plundering, extortion, torture and murder, these were too frequently the characteristics of the rule of the Muhamnadans and the Maráthás. In their place the British Government raises its revenue by regular and comprehensible assessments, and with that revenue provides for the even administration of justice between man and man, gives perfect religious freedom and equality, and secures the life of the individual from private attack, and the safety of the province from foreign invasion.

And with peace have come the blessings of peace, the increase of trade, the increase of intercourse, the increase in facilities of communication, and the increase of civilization. No Government can be accounted perfect, and the criticisms of a press, freer through the magnanimity of the ruling power than that of the continental nations of Europe, may indicate with no uncertain voice the deficiencies of the British rule; but the thoughtful man, who compares the history of India and of Gujarát in the 17th and 18th centuries with that of the 19th century, and who reads his history in a manly and truth-seeking spirit, will acknowledge that the principles under which he is now ruled are principles based on a high morality, a strict adherence to justice, and an honourable endeavour to promote the happiness and prosperity of the people. Nor will he escape the conviction that any change in the conditions of rule in India will assuredly restore the anarchy, the ruin and the desolation from which the country has been delivered by the British rule; and in this conviction the author, in now laying aside his pen, humbly prays that God, of His infinite grace and goodness, will establish for ever the throne of Her Gracious Majesty the Queen-Empress, and grant unto her and her heirs to reign in peace and prosperity over the many millions of her loyal and devoted Indian subjects.

Appendices.

APPENDIX A.

List of the Kshatrapa Kings, who held sway in Western India, comprising Gujarát Proper, Sauráshtra (Káthiáwár), Kachh, Sindh, Málwá and the Northern Konkan, from the last quarter of the first century till the end of the fourth century A. D., extracted from an article by Pandit Bhagvánlál Indraji, Ph. D., M.R.A.S., published in the Journal of the Royal Asiatic Society, July 1890, pages 639 to 662.

No.	NAME.	Earliest and latest dates of coin or inscription yet discovered. A. D.	REMARKS.
1	Nahapána.	78—110	This name is mentioned on an inscription in the cave at Násik, mentioned on page 52. See also Indian Antiquary, vol. X, pp. 213-227.
2	Chashtana, son of Zamotika.	111—136	Chashtana was not of the same dynasty as Nahapána.
3	Jayadáman.	136—141	The names of Nos. 2 to 6 correspond with

4	Rudradáman.*	141—165	those given in an inscription at Jasdan in Káthiáwár, mentioned in the Indian Antiquary, vol. X, page 227 ; also with an inscription on a well at Gundá in Navánagar mentioned in the Bhávnagar Práchin Shodh Sangrah, No. 178. Chashtana appears to have conquerred Western Rajputáná and Málwá.
5	Dámazada.	165—172	
6	Jivadáman.	178	
7	Rudra Simha.	181—196	
8	Rudra Sena.	200—218	
9	Sanghadáman.	222	
10	Prithivi Sena...	222	
11	Dama Sena.	226—235	
12	Dámajada Sri...		
13	Vira Dama.	236—254	
14	Yaso Dáman...	238—239	
15	Vijaya Sena.	241—248	
16	Isvara Datta.		Isvara Datta appears to have belonged to a separate family. Coins are dated in the 2nd year of his reign.
17	Damajada Sri...	254	
18	Rudra Sena.	258—268	
19	Bhartridáman.	278—292	
20	Visva Simha.	276—292	
21	Simha Sena.		No dated coin.
22	Visva Sena.	294—301	
23	Rudra Simha...	309—318	

40

24	Yaso Dáman...	318	No dated coin.
25	Simha Sena		
26	Rudra Sena.	348—376	
27	Rudra Simha.	388	

* There is a bridge near Girnár known as the Rudradáman bridge which had been constructed by Pushyá Gupta about 300 B. C., the inscription on which (full translation given in Dr. Bháu Dáji's Literary Remains) shows that in Saka 72, there was very heavy rain (so heavy that it has been compared in the inscription with the Deluge) during the dark half of the moon in the month of Mágshir, November–December, which swept away the bridge, and that it was reconstructed in the time of King Rudra Dáman by his Governor of Sauráshtra, Subvisakha, which name Dr. Bháu Dáji considers as a Sanskrit adaptation of the Persian Siávakshâh. This suggests the early connexion between Persia and the peninsula of Sauráshtra.

APPENDIX B.

Chronological Tree of the Sena or Valabhi Kings.

1. BHATÁRKA SENA.

(160 Gupta Samvat, A. D. 479).

- 2. Dhara Sena.
- 3. Dhron Simha.
- 4. Dhruva Sena. (207, 210, 216).
- 5. Dharapata.
  - 6. Guhá Sena. (240,246,247,248,250,256,258).
    - 7. Dhara Sena II. (272, 277).
      - 8. Siláditya I, or Dharmáditya. (286, 290).
        - Derábhata.
      - 9. Kharagraha I.
        - 10. Dhara Sena III.
        - 11. Dhruva Sena II.

Siláditya. | 13. Dhruva Sena III. | 14. Kharagraha II. | 12. Dhara Sena IV. or Baláditya. (326, 329).

15. Siláditya II.

16. Siláditya III. (356, 358).

17. Siláditya IV. (403).

18. Siláditya V.

19. Siláditya VI.

Note I. The figures placed *after* some of the names denote the years (Gupta era) of coins or inscriptions of the respective kings which have hitherto been discovered and published in the Journals of the Royal Asiatic Society and Indian Antiquary. The Gupta era is placed by different writers in different years as under, but the year 319 is generally admitted to be correct. (See Indian Antiquary Vol. XV, page 338).

By General Cunningham, in 167 A. D.
By Sir E. C. Bayley ... ... 190 A. D.
By Biruni ... ... 319 A. D.

II. The figures placed *before* some of the names denote the order of succession to the throne.

APPENDIX C.

List of Kings of the Chávadá dynasty.

		From A. D.	To A. D.	Period of Reign.
1.	Van Ráj ...	746	806	60 years.
2.	Yog Ráj ...	806	841	35 „
3.	Kshem Ráj...	841	866	25 „
4.	Bhuvad ...	866	895	29 „
5.	Vir Sinh ...	895	920	25 „
6.	Ratna Ditya.	920	935	15 „
7.	Sámant Sinh.	935	942	7 „
				Total......196 years.

APPENDIX D.

List of Solanki Kings of Gujarát.

Consecutive No.	NAME.	Reign. Commenc-ed A. D.	Reign. Ended A. D.	Period. Years.	Period. Months.	Remarks.
1	Mul Ráj...	942	997	55	...	Names 1, 2 and 4 to 11 are mentioned in a copper plate inscription, dated Samvat 1266, A. D. 1210, found in a Treasure room at Ahmadábád and sent by the author of the Rás Málá to the Bombay Branch of the Royal Asiatic Society (vide page 49 of the Rás Málá, 2nd Edition). The name of Valabh Sen, No. 3, does not appear in this inscription. But this is probably owing to his reign having been very short. It is also reasonable to suppose that Valabh's father being alive, and having proceeded on only a short pilgrimage,
2	Chámund.	997	1010	13	...	
3	Valabh Sen.	1010	1010	...	8	
4	Durlabh Sen... ...	1010	1022	12	...	
5	Bhim Dev I.... ...	1022	1072	50	...	
6	Karan.	1072	1094	22	...	
7	Siddhráj Jaysinh...	1094	1143	49	...	
8	Kumárpál.	1143	1174	31	...	
9	Ajaypál...	1174	1177	3	...	
10	Mul Ráj II, or Bál Mul Ráj. ...	1177	1179	2	...	

						Valabh may have been considered by the writer of the inscription as merely regent for the short period of eight months here mentioned, and hence the omission of his name. In the annals of Jesalmir, where reference is made to the marriage of Valabh Sen's daughter to the king of that district, Valabh Sen is expressly mentioned as "Solanki Rájá of Pattan" (vide Tod's Rájasthán, quoted at page 52 of the Rás Málá, 2nd Edition). His name has accordingly been inserted in this list. Valabh Sen's name is also mentioned in an inscription, dated Vikram Samvat 1273 (A. D. 1217), on one of the gates of Prabhás Pátan (see No. 97 of the List published in the Bhávnagar Shodh Sangrah).
11	Bhim Dev II, or Bhim Bholo. ...	1179	1242	63	...	
12	Tribhovanpál. ...	1242	1244	2	...	

NOTE. Dr. Bháu Dáji mentions, on the authority of the Patávali, one Páduká Rájá as successor of Bhim Dev and gives the period of his rule as six days. He mentions Tribhovanpál as Páduká's successor, and the period of his reign as two months and twelve days.

APPENDIX E.

Kings of the Vághelá dynasty in Gujarát, and the approximate period of their reigns:—

No.	NAMES.	Period of Reign.		REMARKS.
		From A. D.	To A. D.	
1	Visal Dev.	1244	1262	An account published in the Indian Antiquary for April 1882, pages 98 to 108, shows that Visal Dev succeeded his father at Dholká in V. S. 1298, which corresponds with A. D. 1242. He seems to have been regarded as king from the time he took possession of Pátan. The same account gives V. S. 1318, A. D. 1262, as the year of his death. The document published in the Indian Antiquary for September 1891, vol. XXI., pages 276 and 277, also confirms this information.
2	Arjun Dev	1262	1275	See Indian Antiquary vol. XXI, pages 276-277 above quoted. Also in an inscription of V.S. 1320,

				A. D. 1264, on a reservoir at the village of Kantelá, in which the founder of the reservoir, Sámat Singh, has been mentioned as Arjun Dev's Kárbhári (minister).
3	Sárang Dev....	1275	1296	The inscription in volume XXI of the Indian Antiquary, above mentioned, appears to have been written in this king's time.
4	Karan Dev.	1296	1297	

NOTE. The period during which each of the kings above named ruled, has been written as correctly as possible from Inscriptions &c. In a valuable contribution by Dr. Bühler, based on a manuscript found by Dr. Bhandárkar and Professor Abáji Vishnu Káthavate of the Gujarát College, published in the Indian Antiquary, Vol. XVIII, page 184, the period of reign of each king of the Vághelá dynasty has beeen given as under:—

Visal Dev.	years 18, months 7, days 11.
Arjun Dev.	years 13 months 7, days 26.
Sárang Dev.	years 21, months 8, days 8.

APPENDIX F.

List of the Muhammadan Sulta'ns of Gujara't:—

No.	Name	Year of accession.
1.	Sultán Muzaffar I.	1407 A. D.
2.	„ Ahmad I.	1410 „
3.	„ Muhammad I...	1442 „
4.	„ Kutb-ud-din.	1451 „
5.	„ Dáud (reigned only one week).	1459 „
6.	„ Mahmud Begadá.	1459 „
7.	„ Muzaffar II.	1511 „
8.	„ Sikandar (reigned two months and sixteen days)....	1526 „
9.	„ Mahmud II.	1526 „
10.	„ Bahádur.	1526 „
11.	„ Muhammad Fáruki.... ...	1537 „
12.	„ Muhammad III.	1537 „
13.	„ Ahmad II.	1554 „
14.	„ Muzaffar III.	1561 to 1572.

APPENDIX G.

List of Sirkárs, or districts in Gujarát in the time of the Muhammadan Sultáns.

I. Central plain of Gujarát.

1. Pátan.
2. Ahmadábád.
3. Godhrá.
4. Chámpáner.
5. Baroda.
6. Broach.
7. Nándod.
8. Surat.

II. In the North.

1. Jodhpur.
2. Jhálor.
3. Nágor.
4. Sirohi.

III. In the North-East.

1. Dungarpur.
2. Bánswádá (now in Málwá).

IV. In the East and South-East.

1. Nandurbár (now in Khándesh).
2. Mulher (Baglána), now in Násik.
3. Rámnagar (Dharampur), now in Surat.

V. In the South.

1. Dándá Rájpur (Janjirá).
2. Bombay. } now in the Konkan.
3. Bassein. }
4. Daman (now held by the Portuguese).

VI. In the West.

1. Somnáth. }
2. Sorath. } now in Káthiáwár.
3. Navánagar. }

VII. In the North-West,

1. Kachh.

Total 25.

	Rupees.
1. The territorial revenue of the above 25 districts yielded	584,00,000.
2. Tribute from the rulers of Ahmadnagar, Bijápur, Berár, Golkondá and Burhánpur. ...	112,00,000.
3. Custom dues from 25 ports on the western coast of India and 26 foreign ports, some of them in India and others in the Persian Gulf and along the Arabian Coast.	450,00,000.
Total...	11,46,00,000.

NOTE. The amount of revenue mentioned in item 1 appears to be that recovered in A. D. 1571.

That in item 2 shows the revenue prior to Sultán Bahádur's death, inasmuch as the tribute from ports held by the Portuguese and the Deccan kings ceased after that Sultán's death.

Item 3 gives the amount realized prior to 1560 A. D.

APPENDIX H.

List of Sirkárs (districts) during the Mughal Rule.

Of the 25 districts mentioned in Appendix G. the following were reannexed to their original provinces by the Emperor Akbar's order in or about A. D. 1578.

1.	Jodhpur.	Transferred to Rájputáná.
2.	Jhálor.	
3.	Nágor.	Transferred to Ajmer.
4.	Mulher.	Transferred to Khándesh.
5.	Nandurbár. ...	
6.	Bassein	Remained in the possession of the Portuguese.
7.	Bombay,(Mumbai).	
8.	Daman.	
9.	Dándá Rájpur, (Janjirá). ...	Given to one of the rulers of Ahmadnagar as dowry on the occasion of his marriage with Bahádur Sháh's daughter.

There remained sixteen Sirkárs, of which six were held by Zamindárs, or feudal chiefs, paying tribute to Government.

1.	Kachh.	4.	Rámnagar (Dharampur).
2.	Sirohi.	5.	Dungarpur.
3.	Somnáth.	6.	Bánswádá.

The remaining ten districts were administered by Imperial officers.

			No. of subdivisions.
1.	Ahmadábád	...	33
2.	Broach	...	14
3.	Pátan	...	17

4.	Baroda	...	4
5.	Nándod	...	12
6.	Chámpáner	...	12
7.	Godhrá	...	11
8.	Sorath	...	63
9.	Navánagar	...	17
		Total...	184

The revenue of the Surat district was separately assigned to its manager, who was styled Mutsadi. That district is therefore not included in this list.

The revenue of the 10 districts, including Surat, and the tribute from the six tributary chiefs, amounted in Akbar's time to Rupees 1,99,91,130. This revenue continued, according to the Mirát-i-Ahmadi, up to the time of the Emperor Muhammad Sháh, A. D. 1719-1748, but before 1762 it fell to 1,23,50,000 rupees.

APPENDIX I.

Showing the area, population and revenue of the five districts now comprising the Province of Gujara't.

Nos. Consecutive.	Names of Districts.	No. of sub-divisions.	Names of Parganás or sub-divisions in each district.	Year in which each sub-division was acquired by the British.	No. of towns according to Census of 1891.	No. of villages according to Census of 1891.	Area in square miles according to Census of 1891.	Population according to Census of 1891.	Net land revenue exclusive of alienations etc. as per Col. 21 of Administration Report for 1891-92.	Remarks.
				A. D.						
1	Ahmadábád.	1	Daskrohi.	1817	18	839	3949	9,21,712	16,58,713	The population of the chief city, Ahmadábád is 1,48,412. Thefirstterritorialconnexion of the British with the Ahmadábád district commenced in A. D. 1802, when the Garásias of Dholerá, to save themselves from the encroachments of the Bhávnagar Chief, made it over to the
		2	Dholká.	1802–3						
		3	Viramgám.	1817						
		4	Dhandhuká.	1802–3						
		5	Sánand.	1817						
		6	Parántij, including Petá Mahál of Modásá.	1817						
		7	Goghá, lately converted into a Petá Mahál.	1802–3						

										British Government on condition of receiving half its revenue.
2	Kaira.	1 2 3 4 5 6 7	Nadiád. Borsad. Anand. Mahmudábád. Mátar. Thásrá. Kapadvanj.	1803 1816-17 1817 1817 1803 1817 1816-17	10	573	1609	8,71,589	20,25,871	The population of the chief city, Nadiád, is 29,048, that of the head-quarter town, Kaira is 10,101.
3	Panch Maháls.	1 2 3	Godhrá. Dohad, including the Petá Mahál of Jhálod. Kalol including the Petá Mahál of Hálol.	1861	4	652	1613	3,13,417	3,08,710	The population of the chief city, Godhrá, is 14,691. This district was exchanged by Sindhia for territory near Jhánsi in A. D. 1861.

4	Broach ...	1 Broach. ... 2 Ankleshvar including Petá Mahál of Hánsote... 3 Jambusar. ... 4 Wághrá. ... 5 Amode. ...	See col. of remarks.	5	400	1463	3,41,490	22,90,520	The population of the chief city, Broach, is 40,168. This district came under British rule in A. D. 1772. It was ceded to Sindhiá in 1783, and retaken in 1802.
5	Surat ...	1 Olpád. ... 2 Chorási. ... 3 Bardoli including Petá Mahál of Válod. ... 4 Balsár. ... 5 Chikhli. ... 6 Mándvi. ... 7 Párdi. ...	1817 1800 1817 1802-3 1802-3 1839 1817	9	788	1662	6,49,989	23,58,556	The population of the chief city, Surat, is 109,229.

APPENDIX J.

Showing area, population and estimated revenue of tributary states in Gujarát.

Name of State.	Name of ruler or chief, with title, if any.	Area in square miles.	Population according to Census of 1891.	Gross estimated revenue.	REMARKS.
	GROUP I. North Gujarát.				
Baroda. ...	His Highness Mahárájá Sir Sayáji Ráo Gáekwád, Sená Khás Khel Samsher Bahádur, G. C. S. I.	8570	24,15,396	1,43,82,129	
Kachh. ...	His Highness Mahá Ráo Shri Mirzá Rájá Savai Sir Khengárji Bahádur G. C. I. E.	6500	5,58,415	17,85,043	
Cambay. ...	His Highness Nawáb Jáfar Ali Khán Sáheb Bahádur.	350	89,722	6,30,192	The Nawáb has delegated his authority to the special Political Agent since 11th October 1890.

	Káthiáwár consisting of the undermentioned states.	20880	27,52,404	1,47,88,146	
	CLASS I.				
Junágadh. ...	His Highness Rasul Khánji Mohbat Khánji Nawáb.				
Navánagar...	His Highness Jám Shri Sir Vibháji Ranmalji K. C. S. I.				
Bhávnagar....	His Highness Mahárájá Sir Takhtsinghji G. C. S. I.				
Porbandar ...	His Highness Ráná Shri Vikramatji Khimáji.				This state is at present under British administration.
Dhránga-dhrá. ...	His Highness Ráj Sáheb. Sir Mánsinghji Ranmalsinghji K. C. S. I.				
Morvi. ...	His Highness Thákor Sáheb Sir Vághji K. C. I. E.				
Gondal. ...	His Highness Thákor Sáheb Sir Bhagvatsinghji Sagrámji K. C. I. E.				
	CLASS II				
Vánkáner. ...	Ráj Shri Amarsinghji alias Gagubhá.				This state is at present under British Administration.
Pálitáná. ...	Thákor Sáheb Mánsinghji.				

Dhrol	Thákor Sáheb Harisinghji Jaisinghji.				
Limbdi. ...	Sir Jasvantsinghji Fatehsinghji K. C. I. E., Thákor Sáheb.				
Rájkot. ...	Thákor Sáheb Lákháji Bávàji.				This state is at present under British administration.
Vadhván. ...	Thákor Sáheb Bálsinghji.				
Jáfarábád. ...	Sidhi Ahmad Khánji Nawáb of Janjirá.				
174 states belonging to Classes III to VII.					
	Mahi Kánthá.				
	CLASS I.				
Idar.	His Highness Mahárájá Shri Sir Kesrisinghji Javánsinghji K. C. S. I.	9300	5,81,662	11,47,005	
62 minor states.					
	Rewá Kánthá.				
	CLASS I.				

Rájpiplá ...	His Highness Maháráná Shri Gambhirsinghji.	4980	7,32,831	21,73,368	Deprived of share in the state administration since October 1887.
	CLASS II.				
Chhotá Udaipur. ...	Mahá Rával Shri Motisinghji.				
Báryá.... ...	Mahá Rával Shri Mánsinghji.				
Lunáváḍá. ...	Maháráná Shri Sir Wakhatsinghji K. C. I. E.				
Bálásinor. ...	Nawáb Munawar Khánji Bábi.				
Sunth.... ...	Maháráná Shri Partábsinghji.				
4 minor states. 51 petty Mehwás states.					
	Pa'lanpur and Radhanpur group.				
Pálanpur. ...	His Highness Shri Sir Sher Mahmad Khánji Lohání K. C. I. E.	7775	6,45,526	14,57,753	Was invested with the insignia of K. C. I. E. at Ahmadábád by His Excellency the Governor on the 28th of November 1893.
Rádhanpur...	His Highness Nawáb Mahmad Bismillá Khán Bahádur Bábi.				
9 other Táluká's.					

	GROUP II. *South Gujara't.*			
Dharampur.	Mahárání Shri Mohandevji Nárandevji.	**794**	**1,20,498**	**2,82,898**
Vánsdá. ...	Mahá Rával Shri Partábsinghji Gulábsinghji.	**215**	**41,373**	**2,55,154**
Sachin. ...	Nawáb Sidhi Najaf Ali Khán valadé Sidhi Abdul Kádar Khán.	**42**	**21,289**	**2,03,309**

INDEX.

A.

B.

C.

G.

H.

I.

J.

K.

N.

O.

P.

T.

CORRIGENDA.

Page	2	*Line*	14	*For*	Pándvs	*Read*	Pándavs.
„	19	„	10	„	returning	„	retiring.
„	26	„	18	„	approaohed	„	approached.
„	45	„	5	„	of	„	off.
„	46	„	10	„	prabably	„	probably.
„	56	„	5	„	effict	„	effect.
„	65	„	14	„	Ahmadábád	„	Ashával.
„	70	„	2	*after*	hit	*add*	upon the.
„	„	„	18	*for*	ofcers	*read*	officers.
„	114	„	16	„	Jin	„	Jin.
„	128	„	16	„	destestation	„	detestation.
„	135	„	25	„	where	„	were
„	164	„	1	„	son	„	nephew.
„	170	„	12	„	pludered	„	plundered.
„	177	„	19	„	Sirohi	„	Sihor.
„	„	„	27	„	Sirohi	„	Sihor.
„	214	„	27	„	Peshwá	„	Peshwá's minister.
„	223	„	5	„	thei	„	the
„	236	„	19	„	cesion	„	cession.
„	238	„	29	„	vengence	„	vengeance.
„	242	„	18	„	assasinate	„	assassinate.
„	257	„	13	„	prohibting	„	prohibiting.
„	276	„	18	„	repitition	„	repetition.
„	280	„	7	„	abitity	„	ability.
„	282	„	1	„	effectully	„	effectually.
„	289	„	21	„	misguide	„	misguided.
„	„	„	23	*after*	defeat	*omit*	on.